BATH SPA UNIVERSITY
LIBRARY

D1356251

B.S.U.C. - LIBRARY

00220741

Secrets of Customer Relationship Management

Secrets of Customer Relationship Management

It's All About How You Make Them Feel

James G. Barnes

McGraw-Hill

New York   San Francisco   Washington, D.C.   Auckland   Bogotá
Caracas   Lisbon   London   Madrid   Mexico City   Milan
Montreal   New Delhi   San Juan   Singapore
Sydney   Tokyo   Toronto

Library of Congress Cataloging-in-Publication Data

Barnes, James G.
    Secrets of customer relationship management : it's all about how you make them feel
/ by James G. Barnes.
        p.   cm.
    ISBN 0-07-136253-3
    1. Customer relations.   I. Title.

HF5415.5.B3683 2000
658.8'12—dc21

BATH SPA UNIVERSITY COLLEGE NEWTON PARK LIBRARY	
Class No. 658.812 BAR	
Phil Dutch 20. DEC. 2001	55435

McGraw-Hill

A Division of The McGraw-Hill Companies

Copyright © 2001 by McGraw-Hill. All rights reserved. Printed in the United
States of America. Except as permitted under the United States Copyright Act of
1976, no part of this publication may be reproduced or distributed in any form
or by any means, or stored in a data base or retrieval system, without the prior
written permission of the publisher.

    3 4 5 6 7 8 9 0   MMN/MMN   6 5 4 3 2 1

0-07-136253-3

*The sponsoring editor for this book was Kelli Christiansen and the production
supervisor was Tina Cameron. It was set in Times Roman by ProImage.*

Printed and bound by Maple-Vail.

This publication is designed to provide accurate and authoritative information in
regard to the subject matter covered. It is sold with the understanding that neither
the author nor the publisher is engaged in rendering legal, accounting, or other
professional service. If legal advice or other expert assistance is required, the
services of a competent professional person should be sought.

*—From a Declaration of Principles jointly adopted
by a Committee of the American Bar
Association and a Committee of Publishers*

McGraw-Hill books are available at special quantity discounts to use as premiums
and sales promotions, or for use in corporate training programs. For more information, please write to the Director of Special Sales, Professional Publishing,
McGraw-Hill, Two Penn Plaza, New York, NY 10121-2298. Or contact your local
bookstore.

This book is printed on recycled, acid-free paper containing a minimum of 50%
recycled de-inked fiber.

For

LIAM GLYNN

my friend and colleague
who touched the lives of so many
and for whom relationships were special

and for

DIANE, JENNIFER,
STEPHANIE AND KAREN

Contents

3. Customer Satisfaction: Necessary Precursor to Customer Relationships — 51

4. The Customer's Definition of Value — 81

5. The Nature of Relationships   111

6. Building Long-Term Relationships   137

yey

7. What Small Firms Can Teach Us about Relationships   161

8. Measuring the Equity in Customer Relationships   183

9. Identifying Relationships at Risk   211

Preface

**"They may forget
what you said,
but they will never forget
how you made them feel"**
— Carl W. Buechner

This book is about relationships—genuine relationships between businesses and the customers they serve. It is based on my view of how customers approach their decisions to do business with certain firms and not with others, and to continue doing business with some firms over many years. That view has been formed through research and consulting projects with many companies, during which I have interviewed and obtained information from thousands of customers. I am indebted to them, for they have provided me with the insight I needed to write this book. I often observe that much of what I know about marketing I have learned from customers.

This book is not a marketing book in the sense of addressing the topics that most would associate with marketing. On the other hand, if you subscribe as I do to the view that the goal of marketing is to achieve long-term customer satisfaction, then we are dealing with a broadened view of marketing. This book is certainly not about how marketing has been traditionally practiced. Rather, it addresses and endorses the view that is increasingly being adopted by progressive companies: that the long-term success of the organization and improved value for its shareholders lies to a very great extent in the company's ability to develop and sustain genuine relationships with its customers.

In many ways this is a commonsense notion of how organizations are supposed to operate. Aren't companies intended to satisfy their customers to the point where they will continue to do business with them well into the future, increasing the share of spending that they give to the firm, and bringing in their friends and family members to do business there as well? What is surprising, however, is that many companies with whom you and I come into contact every day simply do not behave that way. They do not send a consistent message to their customers that they want them to come back. Building long-term relationships seems to be the farthest thing from their collective minds.

I have long been intrigued by the apparent disinterest on the part of some companies in the creation of customer satisfaction and, by extension, of customer relationships. At the same time, I have also been impressed by those companies to whom the cultivation of genuine relationships comes naturally. They treat their customers well, not because some management consultant determined that this represents a solid strategy, but because that is simply how they do business. The result is the natural growth and development of relationships between customers and company, relationships that flourish for many years.

I make a clear and important distinction between what I consider to be genuine customer relationships and those that are maintained artificially, through the use of some form of incentive program or by locking in the customer so he or she can't go elsewhere. I firmly believe that so-called loyalty programs have little to do with the creation of genuine loyalty, that is, loyalty that is grounded in positive emotions.

A relationship-based approach to marketing, on the other hand, expands our view of marketing to include virtually anything that has the potential to influence how a customer feels about doing business with a company. In this sense, responsibility for long-term customer satisfaction, and by extension, for customer relationships, must be shared across the company, and not delegated solely to the marketing department.

Throughout the chapters of this book, I make reference to what I have learned from having talked with thousands of customers in focus group sessions and one-on-one interviews over the years. Gradually, I have developed my own view of what drives customer satisfaction and what ultimately contributes to the development of an emotional connection between a company and its customers. Ultimately, what determines whether customers are satisfied and return to do business again depends largely on how they are treated and how they are made to feel by the company and its employees.

Subscribing to a customer-relationship-based approach to doing business often requires a change of corporate emphasis and culture in many firms. I prefer to deal with business people who have an *investment* rather than an *expense* view of the world. Cultivating genuine customer relationships requires a long-term strategy and an investment in people and processes that will create enduring customer satisfaction, not because costs and prices are lower, but because the customer simply feels better about his or her dealings with the firm. The most successful relationship-focused companies are those that are led by visionary CEO's who simply believe in this approach.

My objective in writing this book has been to share with the reader my understanding of customer behavior and the factors that contribute to the development of genuine customer relationships. In some ways, I am acting as an intermediary, one who is trying to interpret for managers the perspective of the customers with whom they deal. I have attempted to capture the essence of genuine relationships as perceived by the customer, so that managers may develop better approaches to dealing with their customers, and form mutually rewarding relationships in the future.

I am fortunate to have had a dual career for many years, one that has allowed me to combine the rewarding life of a university professor with the equally satisfying and mutually supportive role of marketing researcher and consultant. I have learned much from my students as we have encouraged each other to enquire why things are as they seem in the fascinating and dynamic world of marketing. I am equally fortunate to have had colleagues at Memorial University and elsewhere with whom I have collaborated on research projects that have enhanced our understanding of customers and why they behave as they do.

Over the years I have worked with many clients who share my view that to be effective marketers they must *truly* understand their customers. They have afforded me the opportunity to apply much that I have learned in my research. These clients have provided me both the challenge to make a difference in how they approach their customers and the opportunity to learn even more about the complex and fascinating mind of the customer. They too have provided the inspiration for me to attempt to bring together in this book my views of how customers develop lasting, solid relationships with companies.

Although this book emerged from detailed proposal to final manuscript in just over a year, it has been several years in the making. Since the mid-1990's, I have been fascinated by the concept of customer relationships and the attention that the topic has been receiving in academic and trade publications. I have tried to present my own view of what such relationships really mean *from the customer's perspective*. I have been assisted in that process by many people.

I have benefited immensely from discussions with graduate students in courses that I have taught at Memorial University, University College Dublin, and Macquarie University. Their feedback and input to the discussion has been invaluable.

I am indebted to my most consistent co-author, Judy Cumby of Memorial University, who served as a sounding board for many of my very early ramblings on the subject and who then joined forces with me to explore the nature of customer relationships. Judy, who is an accomplished researcher in her own field of accounting, brought an insight to complex aspects of relationships that contributed to my evolving understanding of the subject. Her particular contribution to issues relating to the measurement and the valuation of obviously intangible customer relationships was especially valuable.

My interest in the subject of relationships, and in understanding customer relationships in particular, owes much to the writings of many learned scholars, whose work is cited in the footnotes of this book. I would single out three individuals who I believe have contributed a great deal to my perspective and to my understanding of the field. Steve Duck of the University of Iowa must be placed among the leading social psychologists in the field of human relationships. As I began my quest to understand customer relationships with a study of social psychology, I was fortunate to have found Steve Duck's work. I quickly learned that much of what Duck had written about interpersonal relationships could be applied to customer-firm relationships. The principles are essentially the same.

Many marketing authors have written about customer relationships, none with more impact than Len Berry of Texas A&M University. His coining of the term *relationship marketing* more than 15 years ago led the way for my thinking on the subject. His writing has always acknowledged the essential emotional content of the concept. Equally impressive has been the more recent writing of Susan Fournier of the Harvard Business School who has, I believe, a most comprehensive understanding of the factors that contribute to genuine customer relationships.

I am, of course, grateful for the supportive climate that is provided me by Memorial University, my academic home for the past 32 years. I am particularly indebted to Dean Bill Blake, who has been a constant source of support and who has allowed me the flexibility to balance many activities and eventually to produce this book.

Within the university community, I have been fortunate to have worked with a series of graduate students who have become research assistants and, in some cases, co-authors. Much of my very early research on customer relationships benefited from the input of Daphne Sheaves, who carried out early field research and co-authored one of the early papers. Jan Dicks brought her usual insight into another project and continues to engage in stimulating discussion on the subject from time to time. Shirley Noseworthy made an important contribution to the compilation of material and the preparation of early drafts of some of the chapters. Finally, Peter Dunne has contributed in many ways to this book, through his insights in the classroom and through collaboration on recent papers.

At Bristol Group, I have been fortunate to have worked for many years with my friend and colleague, Rick Emberley, who has always seen the value in fusing the academic with the pragmatic. He and my other colleagues at Bristol, particularly Brian Cull, Bob Carter, Meg Vis, and Noel Sampson, have been most supportive in encouraging a view that is not always popular or even accepted in mainstream marketing circles. I must single out for special mention the team at Bristol with whom I work most closely on "relationships" projects. Don Barnes brings a fundamental understanding to this field and shares my enthusiasm for it. He has been a constant source of support and a valued colleague. David Ryan is responsible for data analysis and has an innate ability to spot things in the numbers that is truly impressive. Chantelle MacDonald has a true feel for this field and has been a valuable recent addition to the team. Finally, I owe a special debt to Darin Steeves, who played an important role in preparing portions of the manuscript and in generally identifying sources of content. He assisted immeasurably in allowing me to make deadlines.

Over the years, I have been fortunate to have worked with clients who have seen the value in exploring concepts like service quality, customer value and customer relationships. They have provided a receptive and encouraging environment in which to carry out the work that is summarized in this book.

NewTel Communications has been a wonderful client over many years and has enabled me to try many new ideas. Vince Withers has always been supportive of customer research and created the climate that allowed us to explore first service quality and later customer relationships within NewTel. I am fortunate to have worked with very enlightened senior managers at NewTel who were genuinely interested in knowing their customers. These include Frank Fagan, Keith Collins, Heather Tulk, Leigh Puddester, and Harry Connors. I must single out for special thanks Bob Newell, who approved the early projects designed to explore customer relationships. Now that NewTel forms part of Aliant, under Stephen Wetmore's leadership we continue to participate in exciting projects that further extend our mutual understanding of customer relationships.

In the early days at Telecom Eireann in Dublin, I was fortunate to have had the opportunity to work closely with Alan Corbett and Michael Ryan, who were instrumental in creating a more customer-focused company. Over the years, I have worked with Noel Donnelly and Andrew Conlan, both of whom contributed to a better understanding of how the company serves its customers. Now that Telecom Eireann is *eircom*, I continue to be fortunate to be working with Fergus Synnott, Greg O'Brien, and Gerry O'Sullivan in furthering the emotional connection between the *eircom* brand and the Irish people.

Others who have enabled me to examine customer relationships in different contexts include Bruce Hunter of Kraft Foods Canada, Bill Cameron of CIBC, Petra Cooper of McGraw-Hill Ryerson, and Martin Colthorpe and Stuart Anderton of Tesco.

A number of people have assisted in bringing this book to print. I appreciate the encouragement and support received from John Dill and Julia Woods of McGraw-Hill Ryerson. At McGraw-Hill, I thank Jeffrey Krames, Ruth Mannino, Tina Cameron, and especially Kelli Christiansen who has been a constant source of assistance and advice throughout the publishing process. Thanks also to Lucy Luckenbaugh of Pro-Image for facilitating the copy editing process.

Finally, I must single out for special mention others who have had a significant effect on my work and on the publication of this book.

Monty Sommers has been an important part of my life for almost 30 years. As my doctoral supervisor at the University of Toronto, he allowed me the flexibility I needed. He introduced me to publishing in 1973 and we have been publishing together ever since. He is my co-author, mentor and friend.

Finally, I come to Liam Glynn. I first met Liam only ten years ago and he immediately injected himself into my life as he did so many others, with his infectious personality and boundless enthusiasm. He introduced me to his friends and colleagues at UCD and at Telecom Eireann, and Ireland and the Glynn family became central to my life and to the lives of my family. We became collaborators and close friends, and together we explored the psyche of customers on both sides of the Atlantic. We worked on many projects that took us through an exploration of service quality and ultimately to customer relationships. In that sense, Liam represents a catalyst for the early work that culminated in this book. I owe him a great deal. Sadly and tragically, Liam passed away on July 25, 2000. I and many others will miss him greatly.

James G. Barnes
St. John's
August 15, 2000

1

The Changing Nature of Marketing and Customer Service

I have long been intrigued by the fact that some customers are able to establish very close, long-lasting relationships with businesses. I have learned from more than 30 years of talking with customers in many different industries that genuine customer relationships do exist and that many companies are very successful at managing them. I have also learned that there are numerous factors that contribute to the establishment and maintenance of such relationships. Several years ago, I was fortunate to be involved in a research project on behalf of a local firm of funeral directors. That project turned out to be one of the most interesting on which I have worked, simply because I learned so much about customer relationships.

I was fascinated by the fact that many of the people we interviewed were not only familiar with the various funeral homes in the city, but knew precisely which one they would call in the event of a death in the family. This was the case *even though they may never have been involved in arranging a funeral before* or had not set foot in the funeral home in ten years or more. As many as 60 or 70% of those interviewed had a very definite sense of loyalty or attachment to a particular funeral home.

This may seem an unusual example with which to begin a book on customer relationships, but I have never forgotten this evidence of such deep relationships, even in a situation where contact with the service provider is very infrequent. I am convinced that the formation of customer relationships in this case has a great deal to do, not only with the level of service provided by the various firms, but also with the high level of emotion associated with the situation that occasions the need for funeral services. Imagine my interest, therefore, when I recently discovered Thomas Lynch's book *The Undertaking: Life Studies from the Dismal Trade,* a delightful account of the author's career as the local funeral director in a small town in Michigan. Not only does Lynch provide a fascinating

1

account of the relationship between an undertaker and the townspeople he serves, but he comments as well on customer relationships generally in a small-town setting.

Consider for a moment Lynch's description of Wilbur Johnson, a long-time employee of the local supermarket.

> Wilbur Johnson knew everyone in town. It was his style. For seventy years he'd worked in the produce section of the local market, proffering welcome to newcomers and old timers over heads of lettuce and ears of sweet corn. The market first owned by his father and then by his brother had changed hands a couple more times since Wilbur's youth. But Wilbur always went with the deal—an emblem of those times when people came away from the market with more than what they'd bought. Once known by Wilbur, you were known. Unafraid of growth and change, he thrived on the lives of those around him from children in shopping carts, their young mothers, husbands sent to market with a list, bag boys, and cashiers. His own life, perfectly settled—he never changed jobs or wives or churches or houses—gave him an appetite for changes in the lives of others. He kept an open ear for the names of newborns and newlyweds, news of setbacks and convalescences, the woeful monologues of the jilted, the divorced, the bereaved. He remembered the names of children, visiting in-laws, friends of friends. He had a good word for everyone and everyone knew him. Nowadays we call this "networking" and the store of information Wilbur kept on the lives of others, a "data base." But Wilbur called it "neighborly"—the attention we pay to others and each other's lives.[1]

Lynch is describing a relationship between a service provider and his customers, who are in fact more than customers. We all know of such individuals and companies—Maureen at the neighborhood deli who knows exactly how thick you want the Jarlsberg cheese sliced; the owner of the video shop around the corner who holds a new movie for you because she "thinks you might enjoy it"; Brian at the menswear store downtown who knows exactly what tie will go with the suit he sold you last fall.

There is no doubt in my mind that many firms *are* able to develop longstanding, genuine relationships with their customers. We see it all the time. There are many examples in our lives where we keep going back to the same companies; not only because they offer us great products at great prices, but more likely because we feel welcome when we enter the store, or because we feel comfortable dealing with the staff. This is what makes relationship-based marketing different. It means that the people in charge not only accept the unassailable logic for developing long-term customer relationships, but that they also under-

---

[1] Thomas Lynch, *The Undertaking: Life Studies from the Dismal Trade* (New York: Penguin 1997), 113–14.

stand *why* it is a good idea, and what it means to customers to have a relationship with a firm. As we will see, the payback from such an approach is potentially enormous.

This book is not about marketing; or, better said, is not *only* about marketing. I have resisted the temptation to select the title *Relationship Marketing*. Since the focus of the book is on the customer, many who believe as I do in customer-focused marketing will believe that this *is* a "marketing" book. I prefer to view it as an exploration of customer relationships. Before an organization can practice a relationship-based approach to marketing, its owners and managers must understand and accept what it means from the customer's viewpoint to have a relationship with a firm. Some may even doubt that it is possible to have a genuine relationship with a retailer, an insurance company, or a brand of soft drink. I believe it is possible, and I will endeavor in the chapters that follow to offer you my view of how customers form relationships with firms and other organizations and why they are important in ensuring long-term business success.

Nothing New Here

Relationship marketing is not new. The principles that underlie it represent the essence of marketing, with its focus on concepts like trust and commitment. It predates the mid-20th century view of marketing as a set of tools pertaining to product, price, distribution, and promotion. If we accept that the ultimate goal of marketing activities is customer satisfaction, and that this satisfaction is achieved through the creation of value for the customer, then many small firms have been practicing "relationship marketing" for centuries without realizing that was what they were doing.

Although I didn't appreciate it at the time (and he likely did not either), my father was the consummate relationship marketer. He operated his own business for more than 40 years, never having more than two or three employees. He would not give a second thought to being called from his bed because one of his customers was having a problem with equipment that he had sold them. He would travel great distances and work through the night and the weekend to install new equipment that a customer needed. He considered himself a salesman, but his business was much more than that. His customers were also his friends, and he earned their respect. He was completely responsive to their needs, and they responded with their loyalty.

Most of us are familiar with small businesses that operate as if their customers are really important to them. We develop an attachment to such firms. We reward them with our continued patronage and recommend them to our friends. By treating us as they do and by making us feel as if they genuinely appreciate our business, these small firms have succeeded in accomplishing what surely must be the objective of marketing—a level of customer satisfaction that will see customers coming back again and again, and will cause them to recommend us to their friends, relatives and associates.

As we will see later, the way that some small firms treat their customers seems to come quite naturally to them. They will tell you that "it's nothing special"; "that's just how we do things around here." But it *is* special! Customers encounter such special treatment all too infrequently. When they do, they are prepared to give these firms all of their business and to become their biggest boosters.

Getting to "My"

I have always thought that when a customer refers to a business as "*my* hairdresser," "*my* mechanic," or "*my* broker," this represents solid evidence that a genuine relationship exists. The challenge that we will explore in this book is whether we can extend the concept of customer relationships from the largely interpersonal realm of small business to the generally more impersonal context of large firms. Can Blockbuster be more like Churchill Square Video? Can Hilton be more like the B&B you stayed in last summer? Can Safeway or A&P be more like Belbin's Grocery? Can we take the things that make for genuine relationship-building in a small-firm context and translate them so that they are relevant and appropriate in the context of the large business? I think we can. I think there is tremendous potential for larger companies to really get closer to their customers. But to do so, they must first accept throughout their entire organization that building relationships is important. They must also have an appreciation for the difference between *genuine* customer relationships and those that are sustained through artificial means. *Then* they must gain a complete understanding of what a relationship means *from the customer's perspective.* Only then will the concept have any relevance, and only then will there be a likelihood of successful implementation of a relationship-based marketing strategy.

Through Customers' Eyes

This latter point is an important one. We must understand relationships as the customer sees and defines them. It is dangerous for a company to implement a relationship-based marketing program by relying on management's own definition and interpretation of what constitutes a relationship. Many firms, for example, obviously feel that a frequency marketing program that rewards loyal customers with "points" constitutes a relationship or that, because a customer has been doing business with them for many years, a relationship exists. Such is not necessarily the case. Repeat buying does not constitute a relationship.

From the production orientation of business at the start of the 20th century to relationship building 100 years later, marketing has become focused on customer satisfaction, customer service, and value for the long-term benefit of the company and the customer. The concept of relationship-based marketing has evolved in recent years as a result of increased competition and consumer demand for better service and greater attention to individual customer needs. But it has also been the result of many *marketers* having come to appreciate the shortcomings of an approach to doing business that tended to rely on a view of the customer as a passive target. Many companies have launched programs and initiatives to build relationships with customers. Some of these programs have been successful; many have not. Those that have failed have generally not viewed the relationship from the customer's perspective.

Driven by a desire to secure customer patronage rather than a genuine desire to better understand and serve the customer, many relationship-building initiatives have done little to gain consumer loyalty or deliver value. Companies have rushed to establish frequent-shopper or other "club-card" programs that have as their goal the encouragement of repeat buying behavior. The result is that a large percentage of consumers now carry around in their wallets and handbags several cards that are testimony to their "membership" in various "clubs." Supermarkets, department stores, airlines, hotel chains, and many others have jumped on the bandwagon, so that the customer often feels "clubbed" to death. Do such "relationship marketing" techniques work? Yes, they do, in that they do lead to repeat buying and to increased "share of wallet." Do they contribute to genuine customer relationships? That is another issue.

In fact, if implemented incorrectly, some frequency marketing or club-card programs do little to cement genuine customer relationships. They may actually have the opposite effect. Consider, for example, the TAB frequent-flyer program of Aer Lingus, the Irish airline. It is one of the few that I have encountered which actually deducts points if the "valued" customer does not redeem them within a certain time period—in this case if the points have not been used within 36 months of the customer's earning them. Think of how the club member feels, having been loyal to Aer Lingus for several years and being only a few hundred points away from a flight for two to New York, to find that points that he or she has been accumulating are now being deducted.

Other airlines, such as United Airlines, American Airlines, and Air Canada, have similar terms and conditions in their frequent flyer programs, albeit not to the same extent as Aer Lingus. In most cases, if there is no account activity for a 12-month period, the club member will stop receiving contact from the airline in the form of periodic newsletters and account updates. Should the member not fly with the airline for 36 months, the account will be automatically closed and all unused points forfeited. Clearly, the message being sent is that you are a valuable customer, but only if you keep doing business with us.

Rather than penalizing customers for not using airline services for a period of time, airlines should be more proactive in identifying the reasons for the lack of activity. Is it because of a bad experience during a recent trip? If so, then the company needs to know this and make an attempt at recovery.

Building solid, long-term relationships with customers requires a concentrated effort on the part of all employees and management to get to know what satisfies the customer and what the customer values, for what is valued by the customer is more broad than many managers seem to realize. To build genuine, close, long-lasting relationships with customers requires more than a frequent-shopper program; more than a database that allows us to send regular mail shots that are targeted to the customer's interests as reflected in his or her most recent purchases; more than locking the customer in with a service agreement that gives him or her no choice but to come back to us. None of these approaches to building customer "relationships" is sufficient, as none addresses the fundamental question of what constitutes a relationship in the customer's mind. What is missing is the emotional content that one normally associates with a relationship, and that is what we will explore in the chapters of this book.

The Evolution of "Marketing"

Understanding the customer and identifying his or her needs was unheard of in many businesses in the early 20th century, when marketing was production oriented. Business generally knew that whatever could be produced would be sold. Little attention was paid to what consumers wanted; in an era when ready-made goods were scarce, people were willing to buy almost anything for a reasonable price, regardless of a product's attributes or quality.

This *production orientation* continued into the 1920s, when manufacturers faced increased competition and, as a result, began to emphasize selling as the foundation of their marketing initiatives. This *sales orientation* focused on finding customers to buy the products manufactured by a company. Still, there was little attention paid to individual customer needs or trying to understand the customer.

Unfortunately, there are still many companies who practice the selling approach to marketing. The stereotype of the salesman, as epitomized by Willy Loman and by Herb Tarlek of WKRP, unfortunately lives on. Many businesses still seem to subscribe to the Barnumesque view of marketing: that there is a sucker born every minute and the role of the marketer is to separate him or her from his or her money. This fundamental emphasis on *sales* stresses the movement of inventory—"get it out the door." It seems not to pay a great deal of attention to quality, either of product or service, and certainly not to encouraging the customer to come back to do business with us again. It is an outgrowth of a production or manufacturing mentality in which the goal was to sell *things*. Today, many companies perpetuate this emphasis on sales by compensating and rewarding senior executives on the basis of how much *stuff* they sell, rather than on how successful they have been in cultivating customer loyalty—not the same thing at all.

Although some companies today still cling to a sales orientation in carrying out their business, by the middle of the 20th century, many companies began to take a more customer-oriented view of marketing. Many awoke to the realization that maybe they should produce what customers want and need. This orientation became known as the *marketing concept*. It is based on three objectives: a customer orientation, the coordination and integration of all marketing activities, and a focus on the long-term profitability of the organization. (Today we would characterize this as an emphasis on creating shareholder value, a concept to which we will return in Chapter 8.)

While the *new* view of marketing which began to emerge in the 1950s, fuelled largely by the packaged goods or fast-moving consumer goods industries, represented something of a breakthrough in management thinking, today some may consider it quite restrictive. While the focus was ostensibly on the consumer and his or her needs, those needs were generally interpreted as a good product at a good price, and marketing was (and still is today in many organizations) viewed as "something we do to people"—we market *at* them. During the next 40 years, the concept of marketing came to be very closely aligned with McCarthy's "four P's"—product, price, promotion, and place. The implication behind this view of marketing is that if we can get these four elements of the marketing mix right, then we will enjoy marketing success.

This "toolkit" view of marketing was reflected in trite sayings and icons that came to be closely aligned with marketing in the 1950s and 1960s: "Build a better mousetrap and the world will beat a path to your door;" "The three most important principles of retailing are location, location, and location." The used-car salesman, Madison Avenue, fancy packaging, and gasoline price wars came to be associated with marketing; contributing to a somewhat superficial image for the profession.

The value of the marketing concept as it was originally practiced lay in the fact that it *did* at least begin to draw attention to the customer. The objective was on what a firm could do to attract the customer, even if it was merely to *sell* him something. This was fuelled by the increasingly competitive postwar marketplace and by a realization that maybe the customer had to be persuaded to buy our wares. What was unfortunate, but not surprising, was that the view of what would satisfy a customer was rather narrow in scope. The assumption was that if you could make a better product, price it low enough, and advertise it widely, you had a success on your hands. Customers were seen to be passive; if bombarded with advertising, they would respond.

As the field of marketing matured, managers and academics began to realize that maybe the customer was not as passive as had been thought. Customers did know value when they saw it. They didn't buy shoddy merchandise a second time. They didn't necessarily believe advertising. Not only that, but all customers are not alike. What one will find attractive, another will find repulsive. By the late 1960s, marketers began to pay a lot more attention to taking a much more strategic approach to marketing. Some began to realize that "running it up the flag pole to see who salutes" was an unfocused, wasteful approach that demeaned customers. The result was a new era of marketing, one dominated by great progress in a strategic approach toward market segmentation, product and brand positioning, differentiation of the product offering, and *really* understanding what customers want and need.

Emerging Focus on Relationships

The marketing concept as reflected in the four P's of the marketing mix was prominent in marketing practice and thinking until the mid-1980s, when reference to customer relationships and relationship building began to appear in the literature and became the focus of much research. The marketing concept, although still relevant, was expanded to include the dimension of relationships. Why did marketing scholars and practicing managers in larger firms begin less than 20 years ago to start paying attention to building long-term relationships with customers, something that small businesses had been doing quite naturally for generations?

I believe a number of factors together served to increase the awareness of marketers of the benefits of a relationship focus. First, information systems in many firms were being refined to the point that managers, many for the first time, were able to calculate at least a rough estimate of the value of a customer and therefore of the cost of losing that customer. Suddenly, the economics of customer "churn" became obvious. The revolving-door view of customers, which saw a firm working very hard and spending lots of money to attract new customers who were merely replacing those who were leaving, became very unattractive. The cost of replacing defecting customers became obvious. As a result, many firms began to focus for the first time on strategies to satisfy and retain existing customers, as well on trying to attract new ones. For many of them, it was the first time they had been able to treat the customer as an asset or an investment to be managed.

Secondly, with the growing emphasis on the rapidly expanding service sector and on services in business in general, marketers began to pay a great deal more attention to the "softer" side of their interaction with customers. Many came to realize that having a great product and a great price may not be enough; that maybe a large part of a customer's decision to continue to deal with a firm is related to how he or she is treated or even to how he or she is made to feel in dealing with that business. With advances in services marketing thinking came a realization that many factors contribute to whether or not a customer comes back. A much more holistic view developed of what marketing is all about and of the factors that contribute to customer satisfaction.

Thirdly, the nature of competition has changed so much in most industries that firms simply need to be able to compete at a completely different level than they did in the past. Not only has competition become global, it has been raised to a new plane. Some years ago, those firms that were able to deliver products of high quality gained an advantage over their competitors. Today, in most manufacturing industries production standards and advances in technology mean that products rarely fail. Similarly, in many service industries the delegation of service provision to technology and generally increased service standards mean that service provision is often accomplished without error or disruption. Most companies are able to "get it right" when it comes to the provision of their core products and services. Companies that now compete by trying to develop genuine relationships with their customers realize that *getting it right is no longer enough.*

Long-term customer satisfaction should be the goal of all marketing activities, indeed of all organizations. The focus of a relationship-based approach to doing business is an understanding of what the customer wants and needs and a view of the customer as a long-term asset who will provide a stream of earnings as long as his or her needs are satisfied. The view that successful marketing meant having a great product and a great price was no longer seen to be sufficient. That is not to say that product and price are not important—they are—but rather that having them is not sufficient to guarantee marketing success in the form of customer loyalty and a long-term mutually beneficial relationship.

From Transactions to Relationships—Making the Sale Is Not Enough

Marketers in the early years of the 21st century must accept the principle that customers are long-term assets of a company. It is necessary to invest in them and to manage that investment to ensure their repeat business. Getting customers to come back again and again is a challenge for businesses that operate in a competitive environment. Consumers exercise their freedom to do business with whomever they want. In an age when many products and services can easily be duplicated by competitors, companies must find ways to differentiate themselves from the competition so that customers will choose them over and over.

Customer turnover is expensive because of the costs associated with the attraction of new customers and the employee time spent setting up new customer accounts and files and in getting to know them. It is also costly in a different way if dissatisfied customers leave and tell their friends and family members. More and more companies are placing an emphasis on customer retention through superior service and increased knowledge about individual consumers, with the view that this will lead to more satisfied customers. The Ritz-Carlton hotel chain has gained a well-deserved reputation for the way in which it uses a combination of employee attention to detail and technology to build relationships with its guests. The hotel chain uses its database as a foundation to more completely satisfy its guests. When a guest at any Ritz-Carlton hotel requests a late-night hot chocolate, chilled white wine, extra pillows, or any other item or service, staff note the request on a "guest preference pad." At the end of each day, all preferences are entered into the company-wide database. When guests check into any one of the chain's hotels worldwide, they will find the room and the service customized for personal comfort. Guests are likely to return, not because the Ritz-Carlton's rooms are any better appointed than those of other high-end hotels (although they may be), but because of how they are treated at the Ritz and because someone takes the time to remember their needs.

Technology is everywhere. We read about it and see its impact on our lives every day. If used properly, technology can have a very positive impact on the relationships companies have with their customers. However, in all too many cases the technology is implemented to minimize costs rather than to add value and ultimately to enhance customer satisfaction. Many companies, however, have successfully used technology to strengthen their relationship with their clients.

One such example is Federal Express, which describes itself as the "world's largest express transportation provider." Since its inception in 1973, FedEx has prided itself on its ability to challenge the business model upon which its industry is based. The company has put enormous effort and resources into the development of technology-based systems to simplify the interaction customers have with FedEx, as well as to add value for the customer in terms of convenience and accessibility. FedEx customers are able to track their parcels throughout the entire delivery cycle and to know in real-time exactly where a parcel is and when they can expect delivery. FedEx also offers customers options on how to track parcels, including by telephone, through FedEx's website, and by using specially designed FedEx software. Customers are also able to place shipping orders online, schedule pickup requests, and increase the speed of invoice processing by using FedEx software.

The automation of services has many positive benefits for FedEx, including an obvious reduction in cost to handle customer inquiries. However, from its customers' perspective, benefits include reduced anxiety levels because customers can feel confident that the parcel will arrive on time at its intended destination. Indeed, FedEx has taken a relatively mundane but critical business process—logistics and distribution—and humanized it. FedEx's service delivery systems get the parcel to its intended destination on time to ensure high-quality performance, but ultimately it is the employees—the couriers and customer service representatives—that make the key difference. Thus, FedEx has combined leading-edge technology with human interaction to produce a company that delivers exceptional service to its customers.

Let's Close the Marketing Department

Moving from transaction-based to relationship-based marketing does not come easily to some companies. It requires a different view of the customer and of what will create long-term success for the organization. To some extent, it takes us from a "toolkit" view of marketing to one that suggests that marketing is really a way of thinking about how we deal with customers. For many people a redefinition of the concept of marketing may be involved. Historically (and to this day in many organizations), marketing has been seen as a distinct function or department within the company with responsibility for the things that marketing traditionally has done—product development, advertising and promotion, pricing, retail channels, and so on.

When I deliver management seminars on customer relationships or address conferences on the subject, I often try to stimulate managers to think about a broadened view of marketing by suggesting that we close down the marketing department. This usually sends a shiver up the spines of the marketing vice-

Table 1-1 Stages of Marketing Evolution

Stage	Marketing as Toolkit	Marketing as Strategy	Marketing as Service	Marketing as Culture
Emphasis	Marketing mix	Understand the customer	Service industries and service delivery	Customer relationships
Elements	Product Advertising Promotion Distribution Price	Segmentation Differentiation Competitive advantage Positioning	Customer interaction Service encounter Service quality	Customer retention Customer value Referrals Shareholder value

presidents seated in the audience. What I really mean, of course, is not that we dispense with the marketing function, but that we think more broadly about what marketing is. Marketing today is all about increasing customer satisfaction through creating value for the customer. This is far too important and complex a job to be done by the marketing department alone. If this is the modern view of marketing, then marketing is the job of everyone in the organization, in that every employee has the potential to influence customer satisfaction directly or indirectly.

All employees must realize the benefits to the firm of long-term customer retention and recognize ways to improve their relationships with customers as they serve them. This becomes difficult in situations where there is high employee turnover or little opportunity to get to know the customer, as in convenience stores, movie theaters, and fast-food restaurants, where customers can be "anonymous." Such situations represent a challenge to relationship building and may suggest that developing a customer relationship is not always possible. What it should suggest instead is that different forms of relationships are appropriate in different settings. As many very successful fast food chains, such as McDonald's, Burger King, and Baskin-Robbins, have proven, it is indeed possible to create customer loyalty, principally through the establishment of brand relationships. We will return to this concept in Chapter 11.

Marketing, therefore, is not a department; it is a state of mind. It is a way of looking at a business. It is a culture that permeates a successful organization. Customers will tell you that they can *feel* when a company is marketing oriented. Thus, they can recognize those companies that are genuinely interested in creating satisfied customers. Marketing today means that firms must really understand what it takes to create satisfied customers. It also means that management in marketing-oriented organizations must get their employees on-side to present a consistent face to the customer, one that says, "we really care about you and about meeting your needs." We have to demonstrate to the telephone operator and the billing clerk, the baggage handler, the repair technician, and the housekeeping staff, that they are all in marketing. Whether or not they meet the end customers or even interact with them by telephone, they can positively or negatively influence the end customers' satisfaction.

Keep Them Coming Back

Many companies have come a long way in recent years toward the realization that it makes considerable economic sense to concentrate on bringing customers back again and again—to focus on customer *retention*. This requires that management and employees in these firms recognize that making a sale is not the ultimate objective of customer interaction. In fact, there are situations where *not* making an immediate sale may constitute a successful outcome of a customer interaction. This makes little sense to an individual who believes that selling is everything.

The shift from transactional to relationship-based marketing has many implications for business. Marketing can no longer be viewed as a separate function to which we can assign responsibility for the customer while the rest of the firm gets on with their jobs. Rather, the relationship-based view of marketing places the responsibility for marketing (as defined very broadly) on everyone in the firm; that is, it is everyone's job to satisfy customers. I don't really recommend closing the marketing department. There will always be a need to manage the nuts and bolts of marketing—someone has to ensure that new products and services are brought to market; someone has to get the ads out and run the promotions; someone has to decide what prices to charge and what discounts to offer. We still have to get the four P's right. Someone in the firm will also have to be given responsibility for the development of a coordinated strategy to achieve customer satisfaction. In that sense, there will always be a need for a formalized marketing function, *regardless of what we call it*. But, more importantly, there is an abiding need in many companies to ensure that the marketing view of the world permeates the entire organization, from the CEO to the billing clerk.

However, there is that issue of getting the four P's right. In fact, the marketing activities of a firm have never been so widespread and diverse as they are in firms that are concentrating on building genuine customer relationships. The focus of marketing has shifted to include both customer acquisition and customer retention. This retention is achieved through long-term customer satisfaction, based on the creation of value for customers. When customers feel they have received value, they will reward the company with loyalty. The model really is very simple. The customer won't come back to deal with us again unless he or she is satisfied. To create customer satisfaction, we must offer something of value. Value creation for the customer is an important focus of this book, but it is essential to make the point early that value can be created in many different ways.

So, why do customers come back? If product and price are perceived by the customer to be virtually the same everywhere, what will be the differentiating factor? Customers will return to businesses where they feel good, where they are treated well. When all else is perceived to be equal (price, product, warranties, delivery, etc.), how the customer is treated and made to feel before, during, and after the transaction will be the deciding factor in whether the customer returns. *Whether a customer comes back to deal with a company again often has absolutely nothing to do with what we sell or even what we charge for the product or service*. The customer's decision has everything to do with how he or she is treated and is made to feel when dealing with us. For example, very few people select a service station because of the quality of its gasoline. One of the least important things in the product and service mix that a company like Shell, Amoco, or Exxon offers its customers may be the gasoline sold at the pumps.

This latter point was made abundantly clear to me several years ago when we were conducting a project on behalf of a bakery client. The objective was to determine what supermarket managers look for when dealing with suppliers; or, stated a little differently, to identify what factors contributes to satisfaction and solid relationships between suppliers and supermarket managers. We conducted a series of depth interviews with supermarket managers and grocery managers, asking them to tell us about their dealings with suppliers of fast-turnover products such as soft drinks and dairy and bakery products. Most explained that they like to deal with suppliers' representatives who make sure that the product arrives in the store early in the morning, who clean up after themselves, and who call them from time to time, not to sell them things, but to enquire whether everything is okay and ask whether there is anything they need.

When we zeroed in on the bakery category and asked the managers what they look for in a bakery supplier, the responses were essentially the same, prompting the conclusion that the qualities of a good supplier transcend grocery categories. One surprising thing, however, was that throughout the interviews very few managers mentioned bread! When this was brought to their attention, the managers explained that having good, fresh bread is a given in the bakery business. If you can't supply fresh bread, there's no point calling yourself a bakery. Bread, I observed, may be a relatively unimportant competitive tool in the bakery business.

A Different Four P's

Figure 1-1 shows another view of marketing, based on a different set of "four P's." If we view the core *product* or service as the essence of what the company offers its customers, then we can also consider a set of *processes* and systems that are essential to the effective provision of that core product or service. The core product is the telephone call (in the case of AT&T), the room at the Four Seasons hotel, the flight from Chicago to Los Angeles (in the case of United Airlines). This represents the essence of what the company delivers. In order to be in the hotel business, we must have rooms, but then so too do all other hotels. The core product gets us to the starting line, but it rarely gives us a competitive edge. The processes that support the provision of the core product or service include scheduling, staffing, billing, delivery, reservations systems, and so on. Again, most companies provide these so that they can deliver the core product efficiently and conveniently.

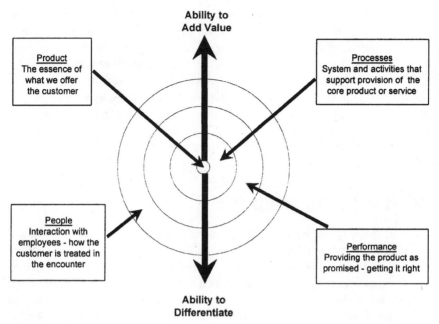

Figure 1-1 The Four P's—a Different View

The third P in this alternate view of what we offer the customer refers to *performance*—essentially, do we get it right? It is what Christian Grönroos refers to as living up to our promises.[2] If Sears tells us that the new refrigerator will be delivered at 4 o'clock this afternoon, do they deliver? If that United Airlines flight is scheduled to arrive in Los Angeles at 7:35 PM, is it on time? Is the bill correct? Is the room clean? Many companies have incurred customer dissatisfaction because of their inability to deliver, even though the core product may have been quite acceptable or even superior. Although they may have put in place the systems, procedures, and processes to deliver the core product or service, they just don't get it right.

Finally, we have to consider the *people* who work for us. Customers encounter our employees on our premises, in their own homes and offices, over the telephone, and increasingly through the Internet. How is that interaction carried out? How do the customers view our employees? Are our people helpful, competent, understanding, caring, polite? The interaction with employees can make or break a customer service situation. Many customers go back to a company time and time again *because* of how they are treated by employees.

---

[2]Christian Grönroos, *Service Management and Marketing* (Lexington, Mass: Lexington, 1990), 137–38.

We will return to this view of what we offer the customer in a slightly different format in Chapter 3. At this point we can make two important points which relate to marketing strategy. It is my view that a company's ability to set itself apart from its competitors increases as we move away from focusing on the core product (which in many industries today is virtually nondifferentiable) and pay greater attention to the effect on the customer of the interaction with employees. Also, a concentration on service performance and interaction with the customer enables a firm to add more value for the customer; or more correctly, a different form of value.

What a Relationship Is NOT

Most of us today are members of a "points" program of some kind, whether it's a department store's frequent-buyer club, an airline's frequent-flyer program, or a video store's "Rent 10, get 1 free" club. These clubs are often referred to as loyalty programs because they are aimed at getting consumers to spend more of their money with one service provider and, be rewarded for doing so. In a survey by the Retail Advertising and Marketing Association International, 42.7% of consumers in the United States said that since joining a frequent-buyer reward program they had spent more at that retailer. And 16.4% said that the reward program got them to purchase more *and* deal exclusively with that retailer.[3]

With 83% of all shoppers participating, the United Kingdom has the highest number of customers involved in frequent-shopper loyalty programs; 52% are involved in two or three points-based programs. Interestingly, the United Kingdom rated lowest in all of Europe in store loyalty, with 24% of shoppers switching stores every year. When surveyed, 40% of consumers in the United Kingdom said that they did not consider these loyalty programs worthwhile. Meanwhile, Switzerland had the lowest participation in frequent-buyer loyalty schemes and the lowest percentage of customers switching stores—only 7%.[4]

What do these numbers tell us about points programs? Basically, that it takes more than the promise of a discount or free merchandise to gain a customer's loyalty. Loyalty programs do work, in that they can increase the "share of wallet" enjoyed by the firm. But can these buyer clubs be considered genuine relationships? The answer is almost certainly NO! Customers who buy from a department store or fly with an airline to collect points have a form of relationship with the company, but as soon as the competition comes out with a better scheme, customers will sign up for that as well.

---

[3] Frederick Newell, *The New Rules of Marketing* (New York: McGraw-Hill, 1997).
[4] Ibid.

In reality, frequency marketing and loyalty programs represent a form of discount scheme. They bring customers in by offering rewards or discounts (every 10th purchase free) in return for a larger portion of their total category spend. Can a frequent-shopper connection evolve into something approximating a genuine relationship? I think it can, but only if the company understands what makes such a relationship.

One inevitable outcome of operating a frequent-buyer program or some other form of customer "club" is the creation of a database, which is a repository for volumes of data on the customer, his or her purchases, and any other information that the company can collect. This database represents an extremely valuable resource for the firm, in that not only does it allow the firm to know its customers better and to learn a great deal that will drive the marketing program, but it allows for the creation of a direct marketing operation. With such a database, it is possible (as it always has been in many firms that maintained "customer accounts") to select certain customers for particular marketing attention, based upon their characteristics and purchasing patterns. A catalog company such as Lands' End can thus select from its database all customers who have spent more than $500 in the past year on camping equipment and send them a special promotion on camping gear, or a cross-promotion with a travel company featuring camping vacations in the Rockies.

Does the existence of the database which results from frequency marketing programs create an opportunity for more efficient, targeted marketing efforts? Absolutely! Does it lead to close, long-lasting relationships? Possibly. Is having a frequent-shopper program and customer databases necessary to creating strong, long-lasting customer relationships? Absolutely not! Some of the strongest, longest-lasting customer relationships are found in very local, low-tech companies, where the employees have gotten to know customers extremely well and where the interaction is customized and personalized.

In addition to frequent-shopper programs, there are many other ways to restrict a customer's ability to take his or her business to the competition, but these also cannot be considered genuine relationships. One example is locking the customer into an agreement that is costly to get out of. Financial institutions do this when they impose penalties for switching mortgages and other products to another bank. Keeping a family locked in this way for five years is detrimental to relationship building since no one wants to be "trapped" in such a situation.

Managers in financial services organizations have on occasion indicated to me that they feel they have a relationship with a customer if that customer "has four or more products with me." What an interesting view of a relationship! It suggests that we can define a relationship on the basis of volume of purchasing or number of products bought. The fact that it says nothing about other indicators of the strength or health of the relationship tells me that proponents of such a view know little about what motivates a customer. It may be that the customer who "has four products with us" has more than four products with the bank down the street, or has just bought mutual funds on the Internet, or can't wait for the mortgage to come up for renewal so he or she can shop around.

Increasing Relationship Content: Much More Than a Catalog

Lands' End is a good example of how a direct marketing company can evolve from a conventional catalog operation to something more closely approximating a customer relationship. Lands' End now uses their Web presence to replicate the shopping experience that customers would find in a traditional retail setting. For example, while on the Lands' End website, shoppers have the option of talking to a customer service representative online or over a separate telephone line. Lands' End has also implemented an online service called "Shop with a Friend" that enables a shopper to interact with another person while shopping online at the Lands' End website. One customer begins the shopping experience by selecting the "Shop with a Friend" service from the menu of services on the Lands' End site, at which point he or she is prompted to enter a password. A friend or family member is able to join in on the shopping experience by following the same procedure as the first shopper and entering the same password. Throughout the shopping "trip," either shopper is able to make recommendations on clothing size or color and actually add items to the shopping cart.

This service can have enormous positive implications. Consider the situation where a child is away at university or lives some distance from home. For a birthday gift, the parent and child are able to make a purchase together to ensure the proper item is chosen and that it is the correct color, style, and size. But the benefits do not stop there. The shopping experience has not just solved the problem of getting the gift right, it has helped to bridge the distance between child and parent. Customers may be left with an emotional tie and feel closer to Lands' End because the company has made an otherwise difficult situation easy and convenient. Part of the enjoyment of the shopping experience for many people is doing it with someone else. Lands' End has added some of the emotional content of the traditional shopping experience to the potentially sterile environment of Internet shopping.

Genuine Customer Relationships

One fundamental element of customer relationships is a focus on customer retention. Another is an appreciation for the value of the customer. The objective of a *genuine* customer relationship is long-term customer satisfaction that goes beyond individual transactions. For businesses to establish meaningful customer relationships, they must have a genuine understanding of what constitutes a relationship. It does not consist of getting the customer in a database, locking in the customer, or setting up barriers to exiting. Nor does it come from raising the switching costs so that customers have no choice but to stay. Although the terms *database marketing* and *direct marketing* are often used synonymously with *relationship marketing,* they are not in and of themselves sufficient vehicles for the creation of meaningful relationships with customers. While a good database can help in the building of relationships by storing important customer information, it cannot be a substitute for genuine customer relationships.

By the same token, while frequent-buyer clubs may sometimes attract a customer to a vendor, they may actually be counterproductive in that they represent for some customers an uninvited intrusion into their lives. This possibility will be explored in greater detail in Chapter 3.

The "BIG" Picture

The establishment of a relationship-based view of marketing within a company requires that all employees be focused on much more than getting the marketing details right. I do not mean to imply that the traditional focus of marketing is not important. It is, in fact, essential that the core product be of acceptable quality because it is extremely difficult, if not impossible, to get customers to come back to buy an inferior product. The price has to be acceptable and, in combination with the core product, must represent good value for money. Advertising must be effective at creating interest in and getting out the right messages about the company and its products, and distribution must be efficient and convenient. But focusing on these things alone, and assuming that this is what marketing is about, misses some fundamental points.

In a relationship-based marketing environment, a company must be focused beyond transactions, beyond making the sale. There must be acceptance within the firm that every customer represents a potential stream of revenue and long term earnings for a company. Customers who continue to do business with a firm over the long-term are more profitable for many reasons. First, new customers cost money to recruit and serve because of the start-up expenses associated with attracting them in the first place; advertising, credit searches, application processing, and other initial expenses. Secondly, as customers become more comfortable with a company, they are likely to spend more money on additional products or services. They tend to give that company a greater share of their total spending in the product or service category. This is the phenomenon now widely referred to as increased "share of wallet." Long-term customers are

also more likely to refer friends and family to a business where they have been
satisfied with the service and value received. This referral business represents a
potential new stream of revenue for the company.

Companies who consider the long-term value of a loyal customer, including
the potential for referral business, are those who understand that shareholder
value is maximized by building a loyal client base over an extended period of
time. Those who concentrate on maximizing the number of transactions will be
locked into a continuous customer "churn" or turnover that is costly and inef-
ficient. A loyal customer base is established by creating many different ways to
satisfy the customer.

Is There Value?

Step into the customer's shoes for a moment. This shouldn't be difficult, as we
are all customers of many different product and service providers. What satisfies
you? What keeps you going back again and again to firms that you have dealt

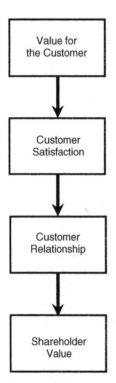

Figure 1-2 Payback from Customer Value Creation

with before? There are clearly occasions when, regardless of service quality, the customer must return to the same supplier. Electrical utilities that operate in a monopoly environment represent one example where the customer has little choice—unless he or she chooses to live without electricity, or to try to generate his or her own; not a prospect that most of us would entertain! In the case of monopolies (and there are still some operating today), customer satisfaction may not be a concern for the company. Small attempts may be made occasionally to improve service quality, but these rarely change consumer perception of the supplier or do anything to forge strong relationships.

We encounter monopoly or near-monopoly situations more often than we might think. True monopolies still exist in regulated industries and in situations where the service is provided by a government or publicly licensed authority. But consumers also encounter what they consider to be monopoly situations where they perceive that they really have no choice or where the prospect of switching suppliers is not realistic. We see such situations in conventional utilities such as electricity and natural gas, and also in former public utilities where competition is now available. Most consumers would consider cable television and local telephone service to be monopolies, even though technically there may be alternatives in some markets. Many consumers also consider banks to be near-monopolies because of the effort that they perceive to be involved in switching accounts to a new bank, and also because many subscribe to the view that "they are all alike anyway." Retaining a customer when that customer perceives that he or she has no alternative cannot be considered a relationship.

Do customers feel they receive value from such monopoly-like organizations? Probably not. Having very little contact with the employees of the organization and no input into the delivery process is not conducive to the creation of value. If we agree that achieving customer satisfaction over the long term will involve an ongoing process of delivering value, then we have to ask what value the customer derives from his or her interaction with a company. Certainly, when asked in a focus group session to describe their relationship with their local electrical utility, many customers will look quizzically at the moderator and are likely to respond, "That's not a relationship; to me they're just a bill."

A good product at a fair or competitive price does not always translate into value for consumers. Value is created when customers receive more than "the advertised special"; when they receive more than what *had* to be given. This doesn't always mean product upgrades or add-ons; actually, consumers rarely rate value based on these things. Rather, value creation often occurs when customers receive something more from the person serving them, when they are made to feel important, respected, and appreciated. Employees can create value with simple gestures and by doing a little more than the basic requirements. When a salesperson offers to wrap a gift or carry a customer's packages to the car (even if the packages are from other stores), the customer feels like more than a transaction. When a salesperson follows up with a customer to ensure that he or she is satisfied with a purchase, the customer feels important.

The Four R's of Marketing

The "four P's" or "marketing mix" view of marketing does not encompass everything that marketing should be, nor does it equip managers with the insight needed to achieve long-term customer satisfaction. Of course, it is of critical importance that a firm do a good job of product development, setting attractive prices, developing good advertising, and making its products and services available conveniently—without the right mix of these four elements, there is little on which to base a relationship and the firm is unlikely to succeed. However, these four elements are only a basis for serving the customer. To borrow a phrase from our research colleagues, the traditional view of the marketing mix represents a necessary but insufficient condition for success.

There are four other concepts that must be taken just as seriously in order to achieve long-term success. These represent a more current view of what is involved in achieving marketing success. The four R's of marketing—*retention, relationships, referrals* and *recovery*—are of critical importance in the establishment of a successful marketing program. Rather than focusing management's attention on the tools of marketing, this view requires that management understand what will lead to long-term success and increased shareholder value.

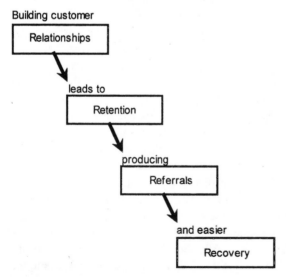

Figure 1-3 The Four R's of the New View of Marketing

Retention involves keeping those customers we want by meeting and exceeding their needs. Customer retention is far less costly than customer acquisition. The focus must be on the *voluntary* retention of customers. Retention of customers because they have no alternative or by locking them into a reward program does little to foster long-term relationships. In fact, it does the opposite. Quite often, as soon as they can break free from a situation in which they feel trapped, these customers will take their business elsewhere.

Relationships are likely to exist when customers voluntarily or even enthusiastically do business with a firm for extended periods of time. Relationship building means getting close to customers in an attempt to understand and serve them better. Relationships, by their very nature, require trust, commitment, communication, and understanding. In the everyday mayhem of business life, it is easy to put off calling a long-time client or making relationship building a priority. However, it is necessary to place as much importance on relationships with customers as we do on any other aspect of the business.

Referrals address the word-of-mouth effect that results from customer satisfaction—the powerful message that satisfied customers will convey to others. When customers are completely satisfied with a service or product, they are more likely to spread the word. People are more likely to try something new if it is highly recommended by a trusted colleague, friend, or family member. Not only will they come back to buy from us again, but they will bring their friends and family members.

Recovery from poor customer service must also be an important component of managing customer relationships. Mistakes happen. That is a fact of life and business. The unpredictable will undo the best-laid plans and leave customers and employees feeling frustrated. However, mistakes can be turned into opportunities to impress customers and win their loyalty. Recovering from a mistake can reaffirm a loyal customer's commitment as well as demonstrate to a new customer your pledge to customer service and satisfaction. In order to do this, employees must be empowered to deal with gaps in service and product quality when they occur. Customers become frustrated when they have to go through several layers of management and wait for replies to trickle back through the system before problems are corrected.

Creating a Relationship Culture

We see many examples of companies not paying sufficient attention to the relationship implications of their marketing decisions. Two examples will illustrate.

Several years ago, I was contacted by a major oil company to do some research into a recent loss of home heating oil business in a large metropolitan market. The company had recently implemented a price decrease in response to aggressive competition from a large independent. The independent had launched its service in the market with a price that was four cents a liter lower than that charged by my client, the market leader. When existing customers called the client's sales office to say that they had been contacted by the new competitor and offered a lower price, the client immediately matched it by dropping its price by four cents a liter. We decided to do a series of focus group interviews to talk with customers who had left to go to the competition and others who had stayed despite the lower prices. Loyal customers who had stayed with the client were angry when they learned that others had been offered a price reduction of four cents a liter, just because they had called. They said that they had been loyal to the company, some of them for as long as 30 years, and were *hurt* and *betrayed* that they had not been informed of the lower price that was available. They felt that they had been treated badly.

A similar situation has existed in the long-distance telephone business in recent years as price competition has followed deregulation. As low-price competitors have entered the deregulated market, the original suppliers have found themselves competing, not only to retain customers, but to win back those who have defected to the competition. Inevitably, this win-back strategy has involved price discounts and offers of one or more months of free service. Such strategies have left loyal customers, those who have never left, feeling *dismayed* and *offended* by disloyalty seemingly being rewarded with lower prices. The loyal customer is left wondering why he is paying a higher price while the customer who has openly demonstrated his willingness to defect is rewarded with incentives to come back.

In both of these situations, when discussing their treatment at the hands of companies to which they had demonstrated loyalty—companies with which they felt they had a relationship—customers used very emotional language: *hurt; betrayed; dismayed; offended.* Surely they could have expected to be treated better!

Managers in most organizations need to think about the relationship impact of their marketing decisions. While competing to gain new customers and to keep customers who are in danger of going over to the other side is undeniably good business, we can see from these examples that there are risks associated with certain responses. One of the issues here is fairness. Customers like to be treated fairly. Those who have been customers for a long time feel that they have invested a great deal in the relationship and that the company should reciprocate. There is no doubt that they feel the relationship must be a two-way street.

Getting managers and others in the organization to think in relationship terms is not an easy task. They must consider the implications of their actions and programs for already-existing relationships with customers and ask, how will what we are planning make the customers feel?

There must be a realization within the organization at all levels that retaining customers through cultivating customer loyalty is what will ensure the long-term success of the firm and the now-popular focus on increased shareholder value. Relationships are built and sustained through a concentration on achieving customer satisfaction, and that satisfaction is ensured only when the firm is creating value for its customers—value that extends well beyond value for money.

We will explore the nature of customer loyalty and the economic importance of retention in Chapter 2. The factors that are critical in driving customer satisfaction will be discussed in Chapter 3, and the creation of customer value in Chapter 4.

2

The Economics of Customer Relationship Building

Customer Retention and Loyalty

Most business people will agree that achieving loyalty among one's customers is a good thing. Loyal customers are better than less loyal ones. And having loyal customers will generally pay dividends down the road. But despite this general acceptance of the value of a loyal customer, I'm not sure that many business people have a very good idea of what loyalty really means. If a customer has been dining regularly at a certain restaurant for 12 years, is he loyal? What if he only comes in twice a year? If a family buys 90% of its groceries from a particular supermarket, is that family loyal? What if they buy only 65% percent of their groceries there?

Loyalty, like so many other concepts that we encounter when discussing consumer psychology and marketing, is a state of mind. As is implied in the questions above, loyalty is a subjective concept, one that is best defined by customers themselves. There are, of course, *degrees of loyalty*. Some customers are more loyal than others, and customers are very loyal to some companies and less loyal to others. Some customers may be loyal to more than one company or brand within a product or service category. This is particularly so where to give one company all of one's business simply doesn't make sense, as in the case of restaurants. Very few people will be completely loyal to one restaurant to the point where it is the only restaurant they would ever patronize. But it is possible to be loyal to a restaurant, or even to have a relationship with it, and yet visit it very infrequently.

Most of us have favorite restaurants in a number of different categories. We may consider ourselves loyal to a particular Mexican restaurant because we have been going there for years and would never consider going to another Mexican restaurant. But eating at Mexican restaurants may constitute only 10% or less of our eating-out occasions. We will also eat at many other types of restaurants, possibly in several cities, but still may consider ourselves loyal to Casa Grande. Not only are there degrees of loyalty, but there is also *shared loyalty*.

One Manhattan restaurant decided to take advantage of its customer loyalty and its relationship with its regular patrons to enlist their help in attracting prospective employees. Faced with a very thin labor pool and about to open two new restaurants, Danny Meyer of Union Square Café decided to ask his regular customers to recommend individuals who might work in his new establishments. He put a notice in the newsletter that he sends twice annually to his core patrons, inviting recommendations for "caring and knowledgeable individuals" by whom they would like to be served. Two hundred of his customers responded, and Meyer hired 25 new waiters and maître d's. Meyer clearly demonstrated the existence and the two-way value of customer relationships. Regular diners demonstrated their personal investment in the restaurant. Meyer said that some of his customers were like proud parents when he told them that someone they had recommended had been hired or promoted.[1]

Why Retention Is Not Loyalty

Consumers and businesses will define loyalty in many different ways. Often longevity of customer patronage and repeat buying are used by businesses as proxies for loyalty. In other cases, loyalty is equated with or even defined as the percentage of total spending in the product or service category. However, none of these in and of itself captures the essence of customer loyalty. It is, for example, quite possible for customers to appear to be loyal and yet be poised to leave as soon as circumstances change.

What are the main components of loyalty? Time, continuity, and duration of the connection are indicators of loyalty, but, these alone cannot lead us to conclude that a customer is loyal. A customer may patronize a business for many years without really being loyal to that business. Some bank customers, for instance, may deal with a bank for many years; however, if we look more closely at their financial services buying behavior, we may find that they have recently purchased products from other financial institutions. Many may, in fact, be reluctant customers, feeling themselves locked into a relationship that they would really like to change.

Keeping some products at one main bank while going elsewhere for other products may be related to the customer's desire for convenience; that is, he or she maintains the accounts that are used most often at one location for ease of access. The customer may be reluctant to move these core, established accounts because he or she feels that the service will be no better elsewhere. However,

---

[1] Rebecca Mead, "Customer Service Department," *New Yorker,* 12 April 1999, 26.

as the need for new products arises and the customer becomes more comfortable dealing with financial institutions, he or she will often begin to shop around for the products and services that best satisfy changing needs. This is, of course, becoming easier all the time as most consumers today have very easy access to a wide variety of financial products through the Internet.

The Reluctant Customer

This example suggests the existence of artificial or *spurious loyalty*. It illustrates a situation where customers *appear* to be loyal because they continue to do business with the firm, but these patterns of buying behavior mask the reality. That reality is often defined by negative attitudes and feelings of frustration because customers, despite the fact that they continue to buy, wish they could move their business elsewhere. Such customers are not loyal; they are trapped, can't wait to get out, for the mortgage to come up for renewal, or the service contract to expire. In fact, if that feeling of entrapment or of being a "hostage" is strongly felt, the apparently loyal customer could become a "terrorist," one who is openly and publicly critical of the company.[2]

Share of Wallet

This brings us to another aspect of loyalty that demands attention: *share of wallet*. When we assess a customer's loyalty, it is imperative that we consider the share of the customer's overall business for our products and services we have secured. If we go back to the example of the bank customer, we can see that although there may be a long relationship between the customer and the bank, the bank should not assume that it has all of the customer's business or even a large portion of it. The customer may not be as loyal to the bank as the length of the relationship suggests. If we think of our own dealings with businesses, not only with banks, but with hotels, airlines, and retailers, it is obvious that we spread business around, often within a set of alternatives. This gives rise to *situational loyalty*, a sense of loyalty within bounds. We may be loyal to a certain restaurant in one market or for one occasion and another restaurant at a different time or place.

The "share of wallet" measure of customer loyalty is valid only in situations where spreading business around is feasible. Obviously, if one gives all one's electricity business to the local power company, to say that this company has

[2] Thomas O Jones and W. Earl Sasser, Jr., "Why Satisfied Customers Defect," *Harvard Business Review* 73 (November–December 1995): 88–99.

100% of the business is meaningless. Where a competitive marketplace operates, and products and services are bought regularly and frequently, the customer's share of wallet represents a reasonable indicator of loyalty. This is so in financial services, the retail food industry, and in telecommunications, where we can calculate the percentage of the customer's total expenditure on local telephone service and related communications services such as cellular phone, Internet, and long distance. In other cases, where the range of products and services is much less homogeneous or comparable, the calculation of share of wallet as an indicator of loyalty is much less useful. This is the case in retail clothing, restaurants, and situations where products and services are bought very infrequently.

The Partially Loyal

Loyalty may be eroded over time. What starts out as a completely loyal situation may gradually become a situation where the company has only a portion of the customer's business. This situation is again reflected in the example of the bank customer who gives his or her main bank all of his or her business for a few years but over time begins to spread that business around. That customer has engaged in *partial defection*. In the absence of good customer information, the problem for banks or retailers is that they do not know the total spend of the customer and therefore do not know what share of business they are getting. It is entirely possible that a customer may be spreading his or her business around a number of companies, while the initial supplier remains under the erroneous belief that the customer is loyal.

Many companies are not in a position to make even rough estimates of the share of a customer's wallet that they enjoy. They don't know what total amount the customer spends with their firm and have no way of knowing what he or she is spending elsewhere. We see this with telephone companies who have a customer's local telephone service business but have no idea whether or not the customer has Internet service or a cellular telephone or pager.

Another aspect of customer loyalty that is indicative of the existence of a customer relationship is the willingness of the customer to recommend the company to friends, family members, and associates. Customers who are satisfied to the point of being prepared to refer others to the company are demonstrating their loyalty. Satisfied customers will be more likely to tell others about their experiences and to recommend the business. Loyal customers want to see the business thrive to the point where they feel a sense of *ownership* toward the company. They feel comfortable making a recommendation because they know that a friend or family member will not be disappointed.

The Emotional Connection

To this point, our discussion of customer loyalty has for the most part concentrated on a behavioral view of the concept. Loyalty is, for many people, operationalized largely or even exclusively in behavioral terms—longevity of the relationship, purchase patterns, frequency, share of spend, share of wallet, word of mouth, and so on.

A critically important aspect of customer loyalty that is often overlooked and seldom measured is the emotional connection between a loyal customer and the business. Customers who are genuinely loyal feel an emotional bond to the business. When interviewed in focus groups, customers will often say that it how the business makes them feel that keeps them going back, or that they feel a closeness to the staff that makes them feel good about doing business there. This emotional bond is what keeps customers genuinely loyal and encourages them to continue to patronize the firm and to make referrals. For this reason, it is important for businesses to focus on how they treat their customers and how they make them feel. Creating the right emotions and feelings is a critical element in the building of relationships. The absence of those emotions reduces repeat buying behavior to a mechanical, behavioral process, devoid of substantive reasons for a customer to stay.

Genuine customer loyalty cannot exist in the absence of an emotional connection. It is this evidence of emotion that transforms repeat buying behavior into a relationship. Until the customer feels some sense of attachment or closeness to a service provider or other organization, then the connection between the customer and the company is not taking on the characteristics of a relationship. Customers themselves know, and are quite able to say, when there are stirrings of emotions between them and a company or between them and an individual service provider.

At what point would they describe it as a relationship? Possibly never. They may reserve that word for close family and other personal ties. However, they will admit to feeling a certain *closeness* or *attachment* to a company, that they have a certain *comfort level* in dealing with them. They may even begin referring to the store as, for example, "my supermarket." At some point they will offer the observation that they *trust* the company; that they *rely* on them. Eventually, if the company is very good at cultivating customer relationships, they may reach the enviable position enjoyed by the member companies of Aliant, a Canadian telecommunications company, where over 75% of residential customers agree that they are *proud* to be customers of the company. The key to success for most firms lies in transforming a behavioral connection into one characterized by such emotion. Only then is a company on the road to establishing genuine relationships with its customers.

Longevity Is a Clue

Customers demonstrate their loyalty to a firm or a brand by making repeat purchases, buying additional products from the company, and recommending the firm to others. Longevity cannot be misconstrued as loyalty. There are many companies that customers have dealt with for many years, not because of an emotional connection or sense of loyalty, but because of convenience, price, or inertia. By definition, these customers are not genuinely loyal. Their business is, in fact, vulnerable because their continued patronage is predicated not on any emotional connection that would bond the customer with the company in a meaningful sense, but on negative incentives or barriers to exiting, or on the absence of a viable or attractive alternative. It may simply be too much trouble to switch!

That is not to say, however, that longevity is a bad thing. If asked to choose between customers who stay with a firm (even under negative circumstances) and those who are constantly switching or moving from one company to another, most companies would be wise to choose the long-staying customers. In most companies, those who remain customers for a long time are much more satisfied—if they were not, they likely would have left long ago—and give the company more of their business. In our Canadian research, customers who have been with their local telecommunications supplier for more than 15 years score an average of 8.1 on a 10-point satisfaction scale, while those who have been customers for 5 years or less score only 7.3—this in an industry where there has been no option with respect to local service carrier. Almost 94% of those who have been customers for 15 years or more have both their local and long-distance service with the company, as compared to only 75% of those who have been customers for 5 years or less. This latter group is much more willing to spread their telecommunications business around.

In the financial services sector, almost 90% of customers who have been with their main bank for 15 years or more say that they are very likely to still be customers 2 years from now, as compared with only 68% of those who have been customers for 5 years or less. Again, in telecommunications, 75% of those who have been customers for 15 years or more are very likely to recommend the company to others, as compared with only 45% of those who have been customers for 5 years or less.

Satisfaction and Loyalty

The length of time a customer has been doing business with a firm is only one indicator of loyalty. Loyalty is, after all, very closely related to the concept of

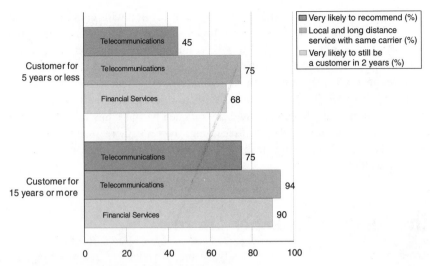

Figure 2-1 Keeping Them for the Long Term

a relationship. Those individuals to whom we feel the closest are also those to whom we are the most loyal and who are likely most loyal to us. Genuine loyalty stems not from some artificial bond that makes it difficult for one of the parties to the relationship to leave. The foundation of loyalty is in sustained customer satisfaction; it is an emotional, attitudinal connection, not simply a behavioral one.

To increase loyalty, we must increase each customer's level of satisfaction and sustain that level of satisfaction over time. To raise satisfaction, we need to add value to what we offer the customer. Adding value leaves customers feeling that they got more than they paid for or even expected. It does not necessarily mean lowering prices or providing more tangible product for the money. In fact, as we will explore in greater detail in Chapter 4, value often has absolutely nothing to do with the price being paid!

Satisfaction is tied to what the customer gets from dealing with a company as compared with what he or she has to commit to those dealings or interactions. It is useful to think laterally about what it is that your customers get from your firm and what it is that they must "spend" to get it. You will soon conclude that customers give much more than money and in return get much more than a product or service. These are the core elements of a transaction-based view of the exchange principles inherent in marketing, but they are not the essence of marketing itself. We have to get well beyond viewing customers as people to whom we "sell" things and beyond defining value as a function of product and price alone.

Adding value can be as simple as improving service with convenience and access. It can also include employee training so staff members are better able to answer customer questions and make recommendations for products and services that will satisfy the customer. By increasing the value that the customer perceives in each interaction with the company (even if it does not end in a sale), we are more likely to increase satisfaction levels, leading to higher customer retention rates. When customers are retained because they feel good about the value and the service they are receiving, they are more likely to become loyal customers. This loyalty leads to repeat buying, referrals, and increased share of wallet.

The Curse of Customer Churn

Acquiring new customers can be costly. In many businesses and other organizations, advertising, promotions, discounts, checking credit histories, and processing applications are one-time costs associated with recruiting new customers. If customers stay with a business only for a short time, or if they buy once and never come back, these costs are not recovered by the company and must be spent again to recruit more new customers. As a result, the business does not realize the potential profits from a customer if he or she leaves after a year or two. This is the curse of customer "churn," to which many businesses are exposed. It is best exemplified in cable television and cellular telephone companies, which are often plagued with high levels of customer churn.

This revolving-door phenomenon is endemic in highly competitive industries where there is little product differentiation and competition is based largely on price. In these situations, customer turnover and short-term customer attraction

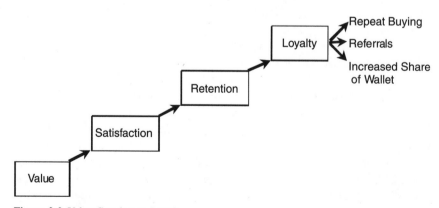

Figure 2-2 Value Creation to Loyalty

is encouraged through cutthroat price competition. A certain segment of customers—the switchers—do very well for themselves by constantly switching companies to take advantage of the best price incentives. Most managers realize that these are not the most valuable customers because they do not stay around long enough to become profitable. A major problem in some companies that do not have good customer records and databases is that it is extremely difficult to identify those customers who are leaving. In any case, the challenge is to give them a reason to stay, which means having to overcome the attraction of price incentives by adding a form of value that transcends price appeal.

In addition to the one-time costs associated with recruiting new customers, some additional factors contribute to a customer's profit-making potential over time:[3]

They spend more. Customers tend to spend more money with a business the longer they deal with it. This is the so-called share of wallet phenomenon. One example of this can be found in the insurance industry. Many people, when they first choose an insurance agency for auto or homeowner's coverage, will base their decision largely on price. The challenge for the insurance company is to attract them through price and then encourage them to stay for other reasons. As additional needs for insurance arise when major purchases are made, policies expire, or family circumstances change, customers will often take more of their business to the same insurance company if given a reason to do so. In addition, people tend to acquire more valuable assets over time. Acquisitions such as cottages, recreational vehicles, jewelry, and art increase the need for insurance and the money spent to acquire coverage. As customers mature and become more confident that their needs are being met, they have an incentive to deal only with one company and to give that firm all of their business.

They get comfortable. When genuinely loyal customers are asked why they go back to a company over and over again for many years, they often say they feel "comfortable" dealing with the firm. They have come to know the staff and have a sense of routine and even habit. They have no incentive to leave. They have developed a feeling of trust that comes with familiarity and will go back because "they know me there." When customers stay with an insurance company for several years, they are less likely to shop around for

---

[3] See, e.g., Frederick F. Reichheld, and W. Earl Jr., Sasser, "Zero Defections: Quality Comes to Services," *Harvard Business Review* (September–October 1990): 105–11; and Evert, Gummesson "Return on Relationships: Building the Future with Intellectual Capital," *European Journal of Marketing,* Second WWW Conference on Relationship Marketing, 15 November 1999–15 February 2000 (http://www.mcb.co.uk/services/conferen/nov99/rm/paper5.html).

small price breaks if they are satisfied with the coverage and service they are receiving.

They spread positive word of mouth. Long-time, loyal customers are a source of free advertising. They become ambassadors for the company, or what some authors refer to as "part-time marketers." Referrals from friends and family are powerful endorsements for a company's products and services and are often taken more seriously and given greater credibility than paid communications from the firm. As loyal customers refer others to a business, the business realizes new earnings potential and opportunities to build even more customer relationships.

They cost less to serve. New customers are costly to attract. As well, employees spend time getting to know new customers and recovering from mistakes because they are not familiar with their wants and needs. Loyal customers, on the other hand, are already established in the database (whether actual or virtual), and employees are familiar with them, so that they are easier to serve. Because they are well known to the company, their needs are also known and can be more easily met; needs can even be anticipated if the customer is especially well known to the company. Customers who come back again and again can be served more easily, to the point where dealing with them becomes routine. This is, of course, a potentially dangerous situation if the customer begins to feel as if he or she is being taken for granted.

They are less price sensitive. Loyal customers are much less likely to quibble over prices and may even reach the stage in their relationship where they *may not even ask the price.* This is not an open invitation for less than scrupulous marketers to take advantage; rather it is evidence that customers place more *value* on other things. In many situations where genuine relationships exist, the price charged for the product or service may be among the least important determinants of customer satisfaction.

They are more forgiving. The relationship that has been built with genuinely loyal customers represents an insurance policy for the firm. It's like money in the bank when things do go wrong. Genuinely loyal customers are more likely to give a firm a second chance or to overlook mistakes, within reason. Whereas a first-time customer who has not built up a relationship will be more wary of errors and may even be on the lookout for mistakes, the long-term loyal customer is likely to forgive and give the firm a second chance.

They make us more efficient. A company has an opportunity to get to know its customers and their needs really well when it has a solid base of loyal customers. This makes the company much more efficient than when its marketing efforts are dedicated to bringing in a crop of new customers and its marketing activities are spread over a variety of programs designed to appeal to a wide audience. The company can target its marketing activities much more effectively.

They have greater profit potential. Whereas new customers have to be attracted with price deals or other incentives or discounts, loyal customers have much greater profit potential because they are much more likely to pay full price. They don't wait for the sales to buy. They don't stock up on product when it is discounted. They help a company maximize the percentage of their products and services that are sold at full price, thereby increasing profitability. As a vice-president of marketing for a major grocery products company explained to me a couple of years ago, his company was striving to build relationships with customers that would lead to "increasing the percentage of the company's products that would sell through at full price."

Frederick Reichheld and Earl Sasser indicate that an increase of 5% in customer loyalty can double a firm's profitability. Much of this is because 70% of sales come from loyal customers.[4] These authors define loyalty rather simplistically as the length of time a customer stays with a business. They say that loyal customers give increasing amounts of business to a company over time as their satisfaction and comfort levels increase. It has been noted that 80% of profits are generated by 20% of a company's customers—some firms will actually argue that 20% of their customers generate 120% of profits! This 20% is the loyal customers who give the firm the lion's share of their business. Customer loyalty is achieved by providing the highest-quality service and ensuring that the customer is completely satisfied. This cannot occur unless everyone in the firm is committed to internal and external service quality and to retaining customers.

---

1. Recruiting new customers costs money.
2. Customers spend more with us: increased "share of wallet."
3. They get comfortable dealng with us.
4. They spread positive word of mouth.
5. They cost less to serve.
6. They are less price sensitive.
7. They are more forgiving when something goes wrong.
8. They make our marketing program more efficient.
9. They have greater profit potential.

Figure 2-3 Customer Retention Pays Off

[4] *Ibid.*

What Is a Loyal Customer *Really* Worth?

Here we take a different view of "value," by focusing on the value to the firm of a loyal customer. This is not unrelated to the concept of value that we offer to the customer as an incentive to continue as a customer. Quite simply, by offering increased value to customers—better value than they can get elsewhere—we contribute to a decision by those customers to stay with us, thereby turning them into more *valuable* customers. If we do this long enough and with enough customers, we will gradually make a sustained contribution to increased *shareholder value*—a concept to which we will turn our attention in Chapter 8.

When customers defect to the competition, they take their profit-making potential with them. Although this "stream of earnings" represents the future of the company, it is not accounted for in the company's financial statements, and customer loyalty never shows up on the balance sheet. If a company could see the real cost of losing a customer, it would be more likely to make greater investments in time and money to retain as many customers as possible. Few companies measure the cost of losing a customer, despite the fact that it is obvious that a customer's value to the firm increases over time.

What is at risk to the firm if a customer decides to leave and take his or her business elsewhere? A simple, financially focused view would lead us to conclude that we lose that customer's stream of business. Take our average revenue from that customer, multiply it by an estimate of the future active life of the customer, and discount it by some appropriate discount rate, and we have the net present value of that customer's business. If we are really sophisticated, we can even compute profitability estimates. From that, we may conclude erroneously that the customer is not really worth all that much and that we should really discourage his or her business, send him or her to the competition. This may, in fact, contribute to a simplistic, narrow view of the customer on the part of employees—one that prevents them from seeing the true value of a customer and of the company's relationship with that customer.

Let's contrast that view with the termination of a customer relationship with a bank, as related to me by a friend. Although not particularly impressed with the attention being paid to them by the bank with whom they had been banking for more than 30 years, the family had nevertheless maintained their entire banking business with the bank, as had their three grown children. Two of the children had graduated from university and were employed in professional positions with major corporations, while the third was about to complete a master's degree.

As my friend explained, his relationship with the bank was not a particularly negative one; it was more like a nonrelationship. He heard from them rarely, and then usually to try to sell him some investment product. This was even though he and his wife were at the stage in their lives where they would have much more money available to invest and some retirement planning to do. Nevertheless, he was not provoked to alter the situation until two events happened within a few weeks of each other. On the first occasion, a fairly senior employee of the bank made a rather rude and flippant remark to his daughter in front of other customers in the bank branch where the family did its banking business. The daughter was left speechless and made to feel extremely unimportant. She vowed to close her account and never to do business with that bank again.

The second event happened only two or three weeks later when the same employee of the bank made an error in quoting a foreign exchange rate on a rather large transaction that my friend was doing. If he had not checked the rate himself and found the error, the incorrect rate would have cost him more than $3000. To his surprise, when he brought the mistake to the attention of the employee, he was met with an argument, as the employee proceeded to explain the mistake away by placing blame on the bank's computer system. I think what most angered my friend was that the employee did not even offer an apology for the mistake.

The family was so upset that within a couple of months all three of my friend's adult children closed their accounts with the bank, and my friend and his wife systematically placed their investments and their business accounts with another major bank. They paid off their home mortgage, opened personal lines of credit, and took out a major business loan with their new bank, where, understandably, they were treated very well.

The old saying is that we often don't miss things until they are gone. Think about what my friends' bank of more than 30 years lost, and why. The bank lost much more than the stream of earnings associated with my friends' accounts. It lost the right to participate in that growing stream of earnings going forward. But, maybe even more importantly, the bank lost the ability to grow and sustain the business of the three adult children and their spouses and partners, none of whom now deals with that bank and all of whom are young professionals employed in high-paying jobs, with many years of considerable earning power ahead of them. It is important to consider the referral and influencing power of customers. If we view their value narrowly, we miss the point. The customer controls or influences much more than his or her own business.

Why Profitability Grows

But why did the bank lose this very attractive piece of business? The important lesson is that the reason for losing the business had nothing at all to do with bank products or services, with the rates being charged or paid, or with what is generally considered marketing. The vast volume of current and future business was lost because of a thoughtless comment and a failure to apologize for an error. The sad thing is that the bank made no attempt to recover or retain the business.

The increase in a customer's profitability over time is evident in many industries. Credit cards, laundries, auto servicing, and retail banking all show evidence of huge profit increases over time. Reichheld and Sasser in 1990 showed that in as little as five years, a credit card customer goes from being a $50 loss in the first year to being a $55 profit in the fifth year. In auto servicing, the customer generates a profit of $25 in the first year, which grows to an $88 profit in the fourth and fifth years.[5]

Several elements of the relationship contribute to this increase in profitability. First, customers who stay with a business for an extended period of time are likely to increase the share of their overall category spending that they give to that business. Customers who stay are satisfied and feel that they are getting value. As a result, they tend to increase their spending as they experience consistently good service and extremely high levels of satisfaction. As well, customers who remain with a business because they receive superior service and experience satisfaction will be less price sensitive than customers who are shopping around. As a result, a company that delivers on its promises and satisfies its customers may decide not to charge higher prices than the competition; however, there will be less need for sales and promotions that emphasize price reductions in order to retain customers.

Customer defections are considered part of doing business, and since many customers are anonymous, they can leave without being noticed. For example, a person who eats at the same fast-food restaurant for years can take his business elsewhere without it being noticed. Unfortunately, each customer who silently defects takes away a potential stream of earnings, referral business, and the opportunity to build a lasting relationship. Certain retail businesses are most vulnerable in this regard, as are other businesses that operate principally on a cash basis, such as movie theaters and public transit systems.

This points to the need for more information about customers. More companies are now using technology to compile information about their customers, identifying the customer and tracking purchase behavior electronically. These companies can track customer behavior over time and recognize changes in spending and frequency of contact. Because most customers will not move all of their business at once, it is important that businesses use the information they have in order to recognize customers whose patterns of behavior are changing. When companies recognize these *relationships at risk*, they can take steps to

---

[5] *Ibid.*

attract the customer back to the business by finding out what the source of dissatisfaction is.

Satisfied Employees Produce Satisfied Customers

The concept of service as a component of the offer to the customer may be viewed from a number of different perspectives. The essence of what is offered may itself be a service, in that it is an intangible. Air travel is a service, as are hotel accommodation and a haircut. Service may also be defined very formally as the elements of the "package" of goods and services that a company includes with the purchase of a tangible product or a core service that enhances the total offering. These elements of the offer include repairs, delivery, installation, and warranty, and represent aspects of service that are quite inseparable from the core product or service itself.

But these are not the aspects of service that a customer refers to when he or she states that he or she is no longer going to deal with a company because its "service" is poor. The customer here is usually referring to the level of service that he or she experiences dealing with the company and its personnel, either face to face or on the telephone. This deals with how the customer is handled and treated, how he or she interacts with staff, and what his or her experience with service provision has been. The customer is talking about the speed of service, the responsiveness and attentiveness of employees, and the convenience experienced.

James Heskett and his colleagues at the Harvard Business School made an important contribution to the discussion on the effects of good customer service in their work on the service-profit chain.[6] In this representation, customer satisfaction is seen to be a function of the value created for the customer through the quality of service provided by a firm and its employees. That satisfaction is seen as a major contributor to customer retention and, by extension, profitability. Heskett's model of the service-profit chain is particularly important because of its acknowledgement that the quality of service provided to customers is a function of the satisfaction levels of the employees who are responsible for service provision.

The model depicts a series of effects within the employee group which parallels similar effects among customers. Satisfied employees are more likely to

---

[6] James L. Heskett et al., "Putting the Service-Profit Chain to Work," *Harvard Business Review* (March–April 1994): 164–174.

provide superior levels of service; they stay longer with the firm and have a greater sense of commitment to the company and its customers. The concept of employee retention is as important, therefore, as customer retention and is a major contributor to it. Employee churn is as much to be avoided as customer churn. Just as treating customers well leads to customer satisfaction, treating employees well leads to employee satisfaction. Thus, marketing and human resources meet.

When a firm provides value for its employees, it improves the value that will ultimately be delivered to its customers. Employees want many of the same things from their jobs that customers want from businesses. Satisfaction, respect, quality, and value are all important in the workplace. Employees who feel satisfied with their jobs and with their employer are more likely to want that employer to succeed and will work harder to ensure success. This often translates into better relations among employees and between employees and management. It is no secret that satisfied employees are more likely to deliver higher-quality service both within the company and to external customers than those who are not satisfied in their jobs.

For this reason, companies who wish to deliver superior service and increased satisfaction among customers must first focus on the quality of service being delivered within the organization. This quality of service determines the satisfaction and loyalty of the employee. To improve satisfaction among employees, companies must improve the value the employee receives by working for the company.[7] This does not automatically translate into higher wages or better benefits packages, although these cannot be ignored in the overall value proposition to the employee. Improving internal service quality, communications, and the treatment of individual employees will add value. As the anxiety and stress associated with miscommunication, inadequate resources, and poor internal service are decreased, value is added for the employee in that the psychological costs of having to perform certain tasks or achieve set objectives have been decreased. This parallels the way that increased value is delivered to customers through reductions in nonmonetary costs.

In companies and organizations where service to the customer is important (and where is it not important?), *the most important marketing decision made by management is the decision to hire.* Not only those who work with customers or develop the marketing programs and advertising campaigns, but all of the employees in a company, are responsible in some way for the marketing of that company. The way in which employees are treated and the level of employee

---

[7] Peter A. Dunne and James G. Barnes, "Internal Marketing: A Relationships, Value-Creation View," in *Internal Marketing: Directions for Management,* ed. Barbara R. Lewis and Richard J. Varey (London: Routledge, 2000).

satisfaction that results have an impact on customer satisfaction, retention, referral rates and overall profitability.

Not All Customers Are Valuable

Not all customers represent the same value to a firm. In fact, companies serve a wide range of customers, from those who produce very little revenue to those who produce a great deal. But many companies have no idea who their customers are or how valuable they are to the business. The prevailing wisdom today in business is that greater attention should be paid to satisfying the most valuable customers. If we are going to protect customer relationships, then we should start with protecting those that have the greatest potential value. But many firms do not know where to begin in assessing customer value.

That is why some companies are spending time and money to determine which customers are costing more than they are worth. Technology today allows many companies to track sales and gain an improved understanding of their customers.[8] Making the effort to assess the value of individual customers will pay off if the company uses the information to determine how much to invest in building a relationship with a customer or customer segment. The logical outcome of making such an assessment is that there will be some customers on whom the company will lavish attention and whose relationship will be protected almost at all cost, and other customers whose connection to the firm is deemed much less valuable and who may even be encouraged to end their relationship.

At first glance, the idea of helping or encouraging customers to defect seems a rather harsh step to take, one that may even prove detrimental to a company; however, it can be a means to improved profitability for the company and higher-quality service for the best customers. Shedding those customers who are genuinely not paying their way makes considerable business sense. One critical problem, however, is that most businesses are ill-equipped to identify such customers. And even if they could identify these customers, the concern remains that these customers may spread negative word of mouth after they have been "dropped" by the company.

Most companies have customers who spend little but cost as much to serve as those who bring in greater revenues. For example, in our research with financial institutions, the customers who represent the lowest value to a bank in terms of their deposits and other fee-generating products are generally also the

---

[8] William Band, "Not All Customers Are Worthy," *Globe and Mail* (Toronto), 1 January 1998, B6.

most costly to serve. They may also be the type of customers who will continue to use the bank's branch network, rather than ATMs and other technology, and be most demanding of the time of employees.

Credit card holders also vary greatly in the extent to which they use their cards and how they choose to pay their balances. Some customers use their cards minimally each month and pay their balance as soon as they receive the monthly statement. These customers represent a small source of revenue for the credit card company since they are light users and pay no interest. The administrative costs associated with these clients are the same as the costs to serve clients who are heavy users and carry over balances, thereby earning interest for the bank. The profits realized from each of these two groups are different because of their usage rates and payment patterns. What can the credit card company do? There are several alternatives, including increasing usage rates among light users and minimizing spending on these customers. As well, it may be possible to increase usage further among heavier users, which will offset the costs associated with light users. Cards issued with a fixed annual fee deter light users, who will not benefit by having the card because of their low spending levels.

Consciously encouraging the defection of unprofitable customers unprofitable is a decision that requires information about customers and their spending patterns over time. It also requires a better understanding of the customer's spending potential. Many businesses will serve young clients for many years without realizing substantial revenues. However, these companies often attempt to retain those clients because of their potential as long-term, profitable customers as they mature and their earnings increase. An example is the bank that carries a student's small balances for years in anticipation of the individual's greater needs when he graduates and is employed. Because of this potential, businesses cannot make broad-based decisions to "lose" the bottom x% of their customers. Rather, they must make that decision based on knowledge about the customer's past and present spending as well as his or her future spending potential.

Attempting to deliver an appropriate level of customer service to a customer's estimated value to the company is a risky strategy. In the first place, unless the company has very good information on the true value of the customer, the risk is very real that it could be wrong in labelling a customer "low value." In such a situation, the strategy adopted to "serve" the low-value customer may involve reducing service levels to the point where the customer may decide to take his or her business elsewhere, or charging fees or higher prices to such customers so that they either become profitable or are encouraged to leave. The danger, of course, is that the firm may offend customers who are in fact more valuable than available data may indicate, or create a public relations problem because customers voice publicly their views on how they are being treated.

Tailoring levels of customer service to some estimate of customer value is a challenge for a business and a dangerous strategy to implement. Clearly, a company really does not want to maintain close relationships with all of its customers, but deciding which ones to maintain and encourage and which ones to cut loose or ignore is not an easy task. Such a decision may be made for the wrong reasons and in the absence of full information. The concept of customer value— that is, the value OF a customer, as opposed to creating value FOR a customer— is very important as companies consider how to implement a customer relationship strategy. It's worth our while to spend some time examining it in detail.

Monetary and Nonmonetary Value of the Customer Relationship

In the past, and simplistically, most companies have regarded customer value, if they have done so at all, in historic monetary terms. That is, they have based their estimates of the value of a customer on how much that customer has spent with the firm in recent years. Thus, a customer who has spent $10,000 over the past 12 months is deemed to be more "valuable" than one who has spent only $6,000.

What the customer has spent in the past and is currently spending with the company represents direct revenues in that they can be tracked directly to the specific customer and monitored. This is the case, of course, only in those situations where the customer is identifiable and where information is collected continuously at each interaction or sale. For many companies, customers are anonymous and tracking revenues by customer is impossible.

However, another aspect of the monetary value of a customer involves projecting forward the potential business that the customer can produce for the company. Some companies that are targeting a youth or student market have taken this model to heart. Financial institutions that compete for the student business on campus fully realize that serving these young people while they are students is likely a losing proposition. It's difficult to make profits on minimal balances and $10 ATM transactions. The bank is making an investment in the future, realizing that these students will become much more profitable customers over time.

Estimating the future value of a customer is difficult. Some companies are reluctant to spend money on attracting new customers who *might* turn into valuable customers at some time in the future. But a relationship approach to doing business is very much oriented to such thinking. This is an area where companies that treat such expenditures as an *investment* can be separated from those that look upon them as *expenses*.

Focusing on historic and current sales, or even on future revenue projections, does not provide a sufficient measure of true customer value. If we really want to know what a customer is worth to us, in strictly monetary terms that can be related to current profitability, then we need to know something about what it is costing us to serve that customer. Research that I conducted a few years ago led me to conclude that very few firms are in a position to collect such information.[9] Only those companies with sophisticated information systems that can capture data about customer purchases and purchasing behavior are in a position even to get close to an estimate of current customer contribution to profits.

Retailers with scanner systems are in the best position to make such estimates. These companies have data systems that allow them to capture data on a customer's purchase whenever the customer uses his or her frequent-shopper card in making a purchase. Such systems can compute the retailer's margin on each item purchased, allowing the retailer to conclude, for example, that a customer who buys primarily full-price items is more "valuable" than one who buy mostly specials. The system may even have built-in measures that can compute the cost of completing a transaction. Thus, a customer who uses a debit card to pay for his or her purchases may be contributing more to the firm's profitability than one who pays by check.

Those companies that can capture such information on the transactions being completed by their customers may also be able to track other data, such as number of returned items. Thus, they can get fairly close to an estimate of the current monetary "value" of a customer. But something very important is missing from this picture. Not only do many firms pay little attention to the future value of the customer, fewer still ever attempt to take into consideration the *nonmonetary value* of a customer.

Loyal customers who have established relationships with a firm bring that company far more than the direct monetary benefits that are generally accounted for in the form of sales revenues. This may, in some cases, represent the tip of the benefits iceberg. Small firms who really know their customers well—that is, know much more about them than what they buy and how often they use their frequent-shopper cards—are in a position to gain an appreciation for the ability of loyal customers to influence other business through word of mouth and referrals.

Relationships as Assets

What is the value of a solid customer relationship? How can employee satisfaction provide insight into future financial performance? More and more firms are

[9] Judith A. Cumby and James G. Barnes, "Strategic Investment in Service Quality: Protecting Profitable Customer Relationships," in *Advances in Services Marketing and Management,* vol. 4, ed. Teresa A. Swartz, David E. Bowen, and Stephen W. Brown (Greenwich, Conn.: JAI Press, 1995), 228–48.

The current approach tends to be . . .
Internal—based on easily captured internal data
Historic—looks at what the customer has spent in the past
Monetary—looks at value in strictly monetary terms
Revenue focused—based on easily measured sales revenues
Direct—looks only at what sales the customer brings us directly

In the future, companies should consider measures that . . .
External—get beyond the informaiton that is automatically captured
Future-looking—consider the customer's future potential for growth
Nonmonetary—consider other forms of payback, like referrals
Cost-based—take into consideration what it costs to serve the customer
Indirect—take into account business that the customer can influence

Figure 2-4 Understanding Long-Term Customer Value

asking these questions as they attempt to measure nonfinancial or soft assets and attribute economic value to them. This is happening at a time when intellectual capital, human resources, and training are more important to some companies than the value of their tangible assets.[10] For example, a small IT firm made up of capable, hardworking, creative people will want to evaluate the company based on its potential to deliver quality services and solutions to their clients rather than on the value of the hardware and software used to create the solutions. The services provided by the company will be valued by its clients as well as the relationships forged through the interaction and quality work done. For the most part, these solutions are the result of the people who work on the problems rather than to the equipment and facilities used to produce them. In other words, it is the abilities and quality of the people to produce results as well as their willingness to provide high-quality service and form relationships that will differentiate these companies. To be fair to these types of businesses, more attention should be paid to the measurement of intangible assets when valuing the firm.

When a company is sold or when it issues an IPO, the marketplace and investors apparently have little difficulty placing a value on the firm's intellectual capital and its potential for future profits. What is required to provide a better understanding of the true value of the future potential of a company is more than financial measures. In this context, a traditional accounting approach is inadequate because it fails to take into account the kinds of measures that are of critical importance to those who are involved in marketing and who are focused on the long-term value of the customer relationships that the company

[10] Michael Baltes, "Measuring Non-Financial Assets," *Wharton Alumni Magazine* (Winter 1997): 7–12.

has built. It is the customer who is responsible for the future earnings of the company. It is essential, therefore, that the company place a value on the long-term stream of earnings produced as a result of customer relationships.

Evert Gummesson, Professor of Marketing at Stockholm University, speaks of intellectual capital being divided into two components—*human capital* (the value of the employees who work for the firm and what they bring to the company, including their knowledge, motivation, and network of relationships) and *structural capital* (the embedded knowledge of the firm; the relationships the company has with its customers and others, its corporate culture, systems, contracts, and brands).[11] Human capital leaves the firm when an employee resigns or retires, structural capital goes on insofar as the company's relationships and brands have enduring value; a value, unfortunately, that has rarely been calculated.

The Payback from Solid Customer Relationships

When a company makes a commitment to retain its customers through superior customer service and the encouragement of genuine customer relationships, it incurs costs associated with employee attraction, retention, and training, as well as costs in providing the elements of the total offering that are valued by the customer. A decision to commit such time and resources is as much an investment decision as is the purchase of buildings or equipment. As a result, the business wants to realize a return on its investment in the creation of customer relationships. The payback from developing strong relationships with customers may be seen in many ways.

First is the retention of the customer. The customer becomes a stream of earnings rather than a transaction. The company that invests in satisfying its customers will realize gains through the long-term relationships that result. The customer is a source of repeat business that becomes easier to serve over time because employees recognize customers' needs and wants and are in a better position to satisfy them. For all of the reasons presented earlier in this chapter, cultivating genuine relationships with customers makes good economic sense.

Customers who have solid relationships with a business are more likely to make referrals. This is an invaluable source of advice that is taken more seriously by potential customers since the information is coming from a trusted source such as family and friends. This leads to another aspect of the payback: reaching the expanded customer unit. Many people will choose a product or service be-

[11] Gummesson, op. cit.

cause it is what their parents used, or because it comes highly recommended by close friends or associates. This is true for everything from airlines, automobiles, and banks to laundry detergents and toothpaste. People look to trusted sources for information when making purchase decisions and make choices based on experience.

It is important to realize that when a customer chooses a product or service, the potential for payback long into the future comes not only from the customer's wallet but also from the wallets and handbags of his or her family, friends, and colleagues. The relationship building that begins today represents a number of streams of future earnings. Over time, people increase the amount they spend with a business if they have a solid relationship. Increased share of wallet is an important source of revenue for a company since the new business is an extension of already existing business and costs nothing to attract.

Often a business doesn't realize exactly who it is impressing or offending or what volume of business it is placing at risk. The concept of sphere of influence or association is pertinent here. We established earlier that customers will leave a business or terminate a relationship for reasons that have absolutely nothing to do with marketing as we have known it. They may leave for reasons that have nothing to do with them personally, but rather because of how a friend, family member, or associate was treated. This ripple effect cannot be ignored. Developing a close, genuine relationship with customers is, therefore, something of an insurance policy. It protects not only the business that flows from that customer directly, but also the business that he or she may influence by association.

What's Important?

A number of lessons learned from this chapter merit emphasis at this point. Calculating or determining the long-term value of a customer is important for a firm. First, it demonstrates to employees that the firm is focused on cultivating customer relationships so as to maximize the long-term payback that flows from such relationships. It sends a very important message that, by engaging in behavior that in any way puts customer relationships at risk, the employee is jeopardizing a very important flow of revenue, not only from the customer directly but from any business that he or she might influence.

Secondly, determining the value of a customer relationship may influence a decision regarding those customers with whom the company wishes to establish and maintain relationships. It has the potential, once a concerted effort is made to place a value on a customer relationship, to identify those customers where long-term potential is very good and those where the most concerted efforts will not likely result in profitable relationships being formed. Thus, the firm can better target its resources toward establishing and maintaining those customer relationships that have the greatest potential for payback.

Calculating the value of a customer relationship or the payback to be obtained from that relationship is not easy. Many companies simply do not have the information available to do it properly, and most seem disinclined to embark upon the process, possibly because they do not appreciate the value of the results. Most companies, however, can develop an approach that would represent a good approximation, provided that it includes an attempt to calculate less obvious aspects of relationship value, including the future potential of the customer, the nonmonetary benefits to be gained through association with the customer, and the customer's potential to influence the business of others. Calculating long-term customer value, and in particular the cost of serving the customer and margins earned on what he or she purchases, is even more difficult in service industries where the product is intangible to begin with and the calculation of costs and margins is more problematic.

3

Customer Satisfaction: Necessary Precursor to Customer Relationships

What Is Customer Satisfaction?

Customers enter into purchase situations with certain expectations. Whether buying a car, a stereo, or a vacation, attending the symphony, or donating to a charity, customers have ideas about how they want to feel when they complete the interaction and while they are using or experiencing the product or service. They have expectations for the purchase situation and for the performance and consumption of the product or service. To be satisfied, the customer must have both sets of expectations met.

Achieving the highest possible level of customer satisfaction is the ultimate goal of marketing. In fact, much attention has been paid recently to the concept of "total" satisfaction, the implication being that achieving partial satisfaction is not sufficient to drive customer loyalty and retention. When customers are satisfied with how they have been handled during the purchase and how the product or service has performed, they are much more likely to come back to make additional purchases and to say good things to their friends and family members about the firm and its products. They are also less likely to defect to the competition. Sustained customer satisfaction over time leads to customer relationships that increase the long-term profitability of the firm. Marketing is not about single transactions and making the sale; it's about satisfying the customer over and over again. When customers are satisfied, additional sales will follow.

A word of caution may be appropriate here, however, lest we fall into the trap of believing that customers should be satisfied, regardless of the cost. As we discussed briefly in Chapter 2, not all customers have the same value to the firm. Some customers are deserving of greater attention and service than others, and some will never deliver a payback, no matter how much attention we lavish on them and no matter how satisfied they are. There comes a point in some customer relationships where trying to achieve total customer satisfaction is futile because the cost to get there is not warranted by the potential payback. Our enthusiasm for customer satisfaction must, therefore, be tempered with some hard-nosed analysis. If we are going to satisfy customers, then those we must strive hardest to satisfy are those who will be most valuable to us in the long run. The challenge is to discern which customers are likely to be most valuable in the long term.

A definition of "satisfaction" is not easy to formulate. Richard Oliver has proposed a formal definition:

> Satisfaction is the consumer's fulfillment response. It is a judgment that a product or service feature, or the product or service itself, provided (or is providing) a *pleasurable* level of consumption-related fulfillment, including levels of under- or over-fulfillment.[1]

This suggests that fulfillment creates pleasure and that pleasure is satisfaction. Unfortunately, the notion of fulfillment is no more straightforward than that of satisfaction. What satisfies one customer may not satisfy another; in fact, what satisfies a customer in one situation may not satisfy that same customer in a different situation. Think, for example, of eating in a restaurant. Say you and a colleague from your office decide to grab a quick lunch tomorrow at a nearby restaurant. You are probably on a fairly tight schedule—you want to get back to the office for that 2:00 PM meeting. You use the opportunity to discuss the proposal that has to be sent to the GlobalCom Corporation by end of day on Friday. It's a professional, businesslike lunch, and you want certain things from the restaurant and its staff. The most important factors that will influence your satisfaction with this dining experience are the speed and efficiency of the staff and the service. If things don't move quickly, you become frustrated and even angry. You are focused on having a *quick* lunch and getting back to the office.

Now think ahead to Saturday evening. You have booked a table at the same restaurant to celebrate your partner's birthday. What are your expectations and needs on this occasion? It's the same restaurant and the same you. But the circumstances are completely different. On this occasion, speed of service (within reasonable limits) is not that important. In fact, if you are hurried through the meal and are finished within an hour, you will feel rushed and disappointed. This is a much more relaxed atmosphere, and it takes quite different service and treatment to achieve customer satisfaction.

Customer satisfaction, therefore, is a moving target. To gain a better appreciation for this, we need to think about the *needs* that customers bring to each

[1] Richard Oliver, *Satisfaction* (New York: McGraw-Hill, 1997).

interaction with the firm. Each customer comes to the purchase situation with a series of needs that exist at a number of different levels.

Customer Needs

To satisfy our customers, it is essential that we understand what is important to them and then strive at least to meet, if not exceed, those expectations. These needs are not only product or service related. Many factors drive satisfaction beyond the core product. The food in the restaurant may be excellent, but the total experience may be so bad that you will never go back. We need only read some restaurant reviews by the food critics of major newspapers to have this point confirmed. One particularly acerbic review in *The Times* of London pointedly confirms the central role of service in restaurants. The reviewer rails on about everything from not being able to get through to the restaurant's switchboard to make a reservation, to not having the reservation honored, to being left alone with the menu for more than 20 minutes without a waiter in sight—a situation he likens to his recollection of his time at school when a schoolmaster "gave the class a poem to learn and left us in peace to commit it to memory."[2]

It is important for marketers and those responsible for customer service to have a solid appreciation for customer expectations and needs. It is through meeting and exceeding of expectations and addressing of customer needs that a firm produces customer satisfaction. As customers enter into interactions with businesses, they have expectations about several aspects of the interaction and about what is being exchanged.

It may be useful to spend some time considering just what is being exchanged when a customer deals with a business. The customer, when purchasing a product or service, is giving up certain things. The most obvious is usually the money being spent, but there are many others. The time and effort spent in shopping around, comparing alternatives, and making the purchase must be considered. In some exchanges, such as donating to a charity, a certain psychic cost is incurred. What it costs the customer to acquire the object of his or her attention is often oversimplified by a focus on the monetary cost.

What the customer gets in return is also extremely complex. It is far too simplistic to assume that the customer is interested only or even principally in the core product being offered. We need to consider all of the various components of the value proposition because certain customer needs are addressed by each component and customers bring certain expectations about each of them. It is also critically important to recognize that customer needs exist at several different levels and that, in order for customer satisfaction to result, attention

---

[2] Joe Joseph, "Look Back in Hunger," *Times* (London), 29 January 1997.

must be paid to addressing needs at all levels, from the basic product or service, through service delivery, to staff interaction with the customer, to engendering positive feelings. Later in this chapter we will examine what is being provided to the customer at these various levels.

To continue with our restaurant example, a couple out for a romantic dinner has expectations that extend far beyond the food being served. The food is important, but so are the level of service being provided by the staff, whether anything goes wrong, the way in which the customers are treated by employees with whom they interact, and generally the entire ambience of the restaurant. A lot is being written today about the overall customer *experience* dealing with the company and how many exchange situations may be enhanced by businesses paying greater attention to it.

We will return to this "give and get" model in Chapter 4 when we consider the concept of customer value. What the customer receives from the service provider or company with which he or she is dealing essentially represents that company's *value proposition*. The company can increase the value perceived by the customer either by minimizing what it costs the customer in both monetary and nonmonetary terms or by enhancing the value proposition in some way.

If customer expectations are met, they are generally satisfied. If they are exceeded, the customer is likely to express high levels of satisfaction. Customers have clearly developed top-of-mind expectations with regard to certain aspects of the interaction with a service provider. In the restaurant, patrons expect the food to be hot and delivered within a reasonable time. They expect staff to be friendly and knowledgeable. They expect the bill to be accurate. And they expect to be able to pay by a variety of means.

Implicit Expectations

Other expectations rise to the surface only when they are not met; they are either assumed or taken for granted. For example, we expect employees to conduct themselves with civility. It is only when we encounter a particularly offensive employee that we react negatively. Such expectations are subconscious in that they are important in influencing satisfaction only when the service that the customer experiences lies outside certain reasonable bounds.

Most interactions or encounters between a business and its customers take place within a set of boundaries that makes most of them routine. Nothing really stands out that would either satisfy or dissatisfy the customer. We don't give such encounters or interactions a second thought. For customers to be truly satisfied, to the point where they will definitely be back and will spread positive word of mouth about the firm, expectations have to be exceeded. The company has to do something that catches the customer's attention and causes him or her to respond with "Wow! I didn't expect that to happen!

One of my favorite "Wow!" experiences occurred many years ago. It was February and I had flown from Toronto to Halifax for a business meeting. Late in the afternoon, the cab deposited me at the door of the Delta Barrington hotel in downtown Halifax. It was dark and raining, but I decided that I had time before my dinner meeting to indulge my passion for running by donning my rain gear and going out for a run to Point Pleasant Park and back. An hour later, I was back at the hotel, drenched to the skin and trying to make my way inconspicuously to the elevator without disturbing other guests, who, I have come to realize over the years, for whatever reason, are somewhat ill at ease when they find themselves in an elevator with a sweating, dripping middle-aged runner.

As I was making my way across the lobby, a voice called out to me from behind the front desk: "Can we dry those things for you, sir?" I turned to look in the direction of this unexpected greeting and saw an enthusiastic bellman approaching me. In retrospect, I wish I had obtained his name. As he came up to me, he said, "You're not planning to pack those wet things in your suitcase are you, Mr. Barnes? Let us dry them for you." With an obvious expression of surprise, I thanked him, and we agreed that I would put my dripping wet running suit and other gear in a laundry bag and place it outside my door. I did as he suggested, showered, and went to my dinner meeting.

When I returned to my room at 9:30 or so, my running gear had not only been dried, it had been washed and ironed (!) and placed in a neat pile at the foot of my bed. It was almost certainly the first and only time that my running clothes had ever been ironed!

At the other end of the expectations spectrum, we have all had bad experiences where our hopes of a pleasant evening were dashed by a surly waiter or our expectations for a good night's sleep were ruined by the all-night party in the room next door. Most hotel stays, most airline flights, and most meals eaten in restaurants are routine events, with little happening—either positive or negative—to make them memorable. Most of us, as customers, don't set our standards or expectations unreasonably high, and they are usually met but not exceeded. As a result, most companies do not succeed in creating particularly satisfied customers. Most firms do what is expected of them. The problem is that *if you are doing everything that is expected of you, you are probably not doing enough.* Only by exceeding customer expectations—by creating a "Wow!" experience—can you stand out from the crowd.

Setting Yourself Apart with Surprising Service

To satisfy the customer and build a relationship, a company has to differentiate itself from the competition and add value every time a customer is served. The factors that drive satisfaction include value-added processes and services, technical performance of the product or service, and certain aspects of the business providing it. More important than these drivers of satisfaction is the treatment the customer receives while making a purchase or otherwise interacting with the business. The most intangible driver of satisfaction is often the most important in ensuring the complete satisfaction of the customer; that is, the *emotion* of the encounter—how the customer feels.

One of the ways in which emotions are stimulated during a service encounter is through the creation of surprise. Usually we associate the element of surprise with positive experiences, situations where the customer is *pleasantly* surprised with some component of the service encounter or interaction with the firm. Fortunately, such "Wow!" experiences do occur with surprising frequency. Most consumers, when asked to recall such a memorable encounter, will be able to recount some fairly recent event that left them feeling surprised and impressed with how they were treated.

Some companies have achieved a reputation for consistently meeting and exceeding the customers' expectations for service. One such company is Superquinn, an independent Irish supermarket chain which operates principally in the Dublin area but whose reputation for service extends through Ireland. Another of my favorite customer surprise stories was told to me by a focus group participant in Ireland who had recently moved to a new neighborhood in Dublin. During the turmoil of moving into her new home she realized that she needed to stock the new house with groceries. Leaving her husband and children to continue unpacking, she headed for the nearest supermarket, a Superquinn store less than a kilometer from her new home. She had never been in this supermarket before and was not a regular Superquinn shopper, but because it was close by and she was not inclined to shop around, she decided to stop there.

Having loaded her shopping trolley with food items and many other staples needed by a family just moving into a new home, she headed for the checkout. The grocery items were scanned and bagged, and the first-time visitor reached into her handbag to find the £90 or so to pay for what she had bought. To her horror, she realized that she had left her wallet at home. As she recounted to a sympathetic focus group, "I was mortified. I didn't know what to do." Realizing her predicament, the young lady at the checkout didn't miss a beat and simply said, "Don't worry, just settle up with us next time you're in."

The customer was understandably relieved, impressed, grateful, and otherwise filled with emotion. As she told her story, she observed, "She didn't have to do that. She didn't even ask me for identification or my phone number. She simply trusted me to come back. Do you think I will ever shop anywhere else?"

Unfortunately, however, surprises can be created in the opposite direction. How many shopping experiences can you recall where the experience was particularly negative, causing you never to go back? Most of us have such experiences even more frequently than we have positive ones. What continues to surprise me, even after more than 30 years of studying customer behavior and attitudes, is that many businesses seem not to realize the impact that surprisingly positive and negative experiences can have on the likelihood that customers will come back and establish a relationship with the firm. We can see the impact on the Dublin grocery shopper of that one very impressive experience at Superquinn. She not only continues to shop there, but she delights in telling anyone who cares to listen about her experience.

Emotional Tone

The research that I have conducted over the years reveals quite conclusively that the satisfaction a customer feels when dealing with any business is very much influenced by the *emotional tone* of the interaction.[3] This is a very useful concept borrowed from social psychology. It refers to the frequency with which customers are made to feel certain positive and negative emotions in their dealings with businesses. If we knew the extent to which the customer is made to feel relaxed, welcome, pleased, comfortable, and pleasantly surprised or, conversely, disappointed, let down, confused, neglected, and unimportant, we would know a great deal about the state of the relationship with that customer. Obviously, the tone of the emotional connection between the company and the customers is embodied in the difference between the aggregate positive emotions and the aggregate negative ones. This concept will be discussed in much greater detail in Chapter 5. Suffice it to say at this point that I have consistently found that *one of the best predictors of a customer's overall satisfaction in dealing with a business is the extent to which that company succeeds in creating positive as opposed to negative emotions in that customer.*

Zone of Tolerance

Real value for managers comes from determining how customers' satisfaction with their dealings with the firm is linked to subsequent behavior. When, and under what circumstances, will the performance by the company be deemed to be within a certain range relative to the customer's expectations and experi-

---

[3] James G. Barnes, "Closeness, Strength and Satisfaction: Examining the Nature of Relationships between Providers of Financial Services and Their Retail Customers," *Psychology and Marketing* 14 (1997): 765–90.

ences—the "zone of tolerance"[4]—such that neither a particularly positive nor negative response is initiated by the customer? Will this tolerance threshold change in different situations, in the context of various services, or over time? Will a customer's tolerance for performance during a service encounter depend on whether his or her feelings arise as a result of expected versus unexpected aspects of the service encounter? If the customer is provoked into action, what form is that action likely to take? Will the reaction be somewhat informal and immediate, as is the case when a customer delivers complaints or praise directly to the staff? Or will the voice of the customer be external and more far-reaching through word-of-mouth communication? If the customer actually decides to take his or her business elsewhere, will the exit be temporary or will there be a vow never to return?

The concept of a customer's zone of tolerance has been discussed by many authors in the services management and customer behavior literature in recent years.[5] Essentially, it proposes that customers bring to a service encounter a set of expectations that are related to *desired service*—the level of service that the customer hopes to receive—and *adequate service*—the level of service that the customer is prepared to accept. In between these two levels of service lies the zone of tolerance. If the experienced or perceived service lies within this zone, the customer will presumably be satisfied or the service will be deemed to be acceptable. If the service falls below the adequate service level, it will be deemed to be unacceptable and dissatisfaction will result. If the experienced service level exceeds the desired service level, the customer is likely to be quite satisfied or even delighted.

Robert Johnston,[6] proposing that there actually exist three interlinked zones of tolerance, defines an intermediary zone of performance lying between the expectations and outcome zones. In other words, customers enter a service encounter with a consciously or subconsciously held view of what constitutes an acceptable or unacceptable level of service. As we observed above, some of these expectations are not particularly well developed, because they pertain to

---

[4] See Leonard L. Barry and A. Parasuraman, *Marketing Services: Competing through Quality* (New York: Free Press, 1990), 58–60; Valarie Zeithaml, Leonard L. Berry, and A. Parasuraman. "The Nature and Determinants of Customer Expectations of Service," *Journal of the Academy of Marketing Science* 21(1) (1993): 1–12; Robert Johnston, "The Zone of Tolerance: Exploring the Relationship between Service Transactions and Satisfaction with the Overall Service," *International Journal of Service Industry Management* 5(2) (1995): 46–61; and Valarie A. Ziethaml and Mary Jo Bitner, *Services Marketing: Integrating Customer Focus Across the Firm,* 2d ed. (New York: Irwin/McGraw-Hill, 2000), 51–64.

[5] Leonard L. Berry, Valarie Zeithaml, and A. Parasuraman, *Marketing Services: Competing through Quality,* (New York: Free Press, 1991).

[6] Johnston, op. cit.

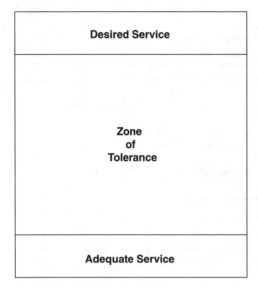

Figure 3-1 The Zone of Tolerance

unexpected aspects of the service encounter. As the customer proceeds through the service experience, those expectations are modified as a result of the customer's experience with individual components of the interaction. The end result of satisfaction or dissatisfaction is an aggregation process which results in the customer making an overall judgment, weighing the outcome of the individual components of the service.

Robert Johnston and others have also argued that the higher the emotional involvement and perceived risk on the part of the customer, the greater his or her sensitivity to satisfaction and dissatisfaction. They maintain that the boundaries of a customer's zone of tolerance are dynamic and may be adjusted during the service delivery. This supports the emphasis that we have placed in this book on the importance of effective human resource training. Employees should be prepared to identify potentially dissatisfying experiences and undertake effective recovery procedures to deal with the situation. This requires an understanding of the expectations that customers bring to service encounters. These expectations tend to relate to aspects of the encounter which are obvious or "visible" — possibly including such things as availability of the service, certain aspects of the delivery of service, and so on. These are "top-of-mind" in that the customer consciously considers them as he or she enters the service encounter. Other expectations are implicit; they are "subsurface" in that they become important and are acknowledged only when they are absent or are violated. The fact that a customer's prior expectations of service may exist at lower or subconscious

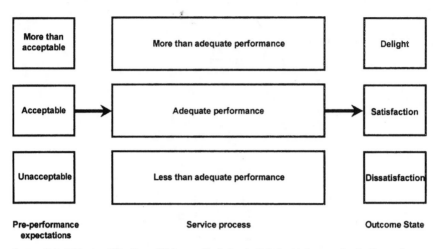

More than acceptable	More than adequate performance	Delight
Acceptable	Adequate performance	Satisfaction
Unacceptable	Less than adequate performance	Dissatisfaction

| Pre-performance expectations | Service process | Outcome State |

Source: Robert Johnston. "The Zone of Tolerance: Exploring the Relationship between Service Transactions and Satisfaction with the Overall Service," *International Journal of Service Industry Management* 5(2) (1995): 46–61, at 48.

Figure 3-2 Three Zones of Tolerance

levels does not diminish the importance that the feelings elicited may play in his or her overall evaluation of service. The customer's zone of tolerance is likely to be "tighter" for those types of service that may be considered to be high involvement or of higher importance to the customer.

It is important to note, therefore, that certain feelings elicited during a service encounter may be quite unanticipated by the customer. They may have little or nothing to do with the core service being provided or with the process of service delivery. They may relate to some little thing that is normally provided but in this instance is inexplicably absent. They may relate to the manner in which the customer is treated or to some comment made by an employee. Examples of such feelings include justice and civility, which enter the picture only when the service encounter involves events that are perceived by the customer to be unjust or when employees are uncivil.

The implications of the zone of tolerance are important to those companies who are trying to improve their service quality. When a customer's perception of service quality falls within the zone of tolerance, even if it is close to the desired level of service, mere satisfaction is the result. As well, customers may not be able to verbalize what they expect at service levels that lie above the desired level of service. In my experience, customers do not expect to be pleasantly surprised in service encounters. When such events do occur, all manner of positive emotions are elicited. Such softer feelings and emotions are difficult to express and to measure.

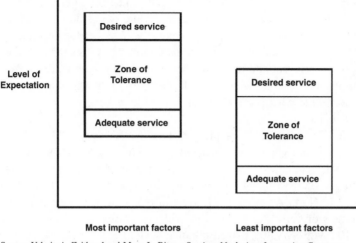

Source: Valarie A. Zeithaml and Mary Jo Bitner, *Services Marketing: Integrating Customer Focus across the Firm,* 2d ed. (New York: Irwin/McGraw-Hill, 2000), 54.

Figure 3-3 Zones of Tolerance for Different Service Elements

The Payback from Customer Satisfaction

Babin and Griffin refer to customer satisfaction as an *emotion* resulting from appraisals of a set of experiences. These appraisals consist of various categorizational processes that trigger *affective* responses.[7] What is important to recognize here is that the response is an emotional one, thereby contributing to the establishment of relationships, which are essentially emotional states. Customers appraise service and the company's offer at a series of levels because they experience the company and its offer at several different levels. They appraise not only the core product or service being offered, but all of the other components of what is generally termed the marketing mix or program of the company, including its prices, advertising, availability of product, accessibility, and location. But the appraisal certainly doesn't stop there. In fact, in many cases the offers of competing companies may be perceived by the consumer to be so similar, and therefore unimportant, that the appraisal does not even take place at these levels.

Overall customer satisfaction, then, is a composite variable consisting of a weighted compilation or assessment of the many different factors involved in a

[7] Barry J. Babin and Mitch Griffin, "The Nature of Satisfaction: An Updated Examination and Analysis," *Journal of Business Research* 41 (1998): 127–36.

company's interaction with its customers. Typically, some of the elements of a company's offer are perceived in a positive light, while others do not meet the customer's expectations and are perceived negatively. Whether the customer is pleased with the overall offer will depend on the importance weightings attached to each component or event and the company's perceived performance on each of them. The customer is able, without much effort, to do the necessary mental compilations to decide what score he or she would give the company on, say, a scale from 1 to 10.

Is it possible ever to achieve complete or total satisfaction with anything? Apparently it is: as a fairly large percentage of customers, when asked to indicate their level of satisfaction with their bank, their supermarket, or other service suppliers, will give them a rating of 10 out of 10. Typically, in research that I have conducted in North America and Europe in recent years, between 10 and 30% of customers of various organizations will give those companies a rating of 10 out of 10 on an overall satisfaction rating scale.

When customers experience "total" satisfaction, they feel that they have been involved in more than simply a business transaction; they are likely to feel that they have been treated differently than they usually are by other firms. Although the differences are subtle and may not be readily apparent to an observer, the customer feels different about his or her overall dealings with, and feelings about, the company. And that is what is important. Ongoing customer satisfaction leads to the creation of relationships. As a result of feeling good and being completely satisfied, as we will see later in this chapter, customers are much more likely to make repeat purchases and give a firm more of their business. Long-lasting and stronger relationships are likely to result. Customers who feel closer to the firm will generate positive word of mouth and will make referrals. What does this mean to business? It means that businesses are more likely to see improvements in their financial performance. These do not occur overnight, but for businesses that are willing to work at satisfying their customers, the payback in long-term financial growth and stability can be enormous.

A Reason to Come Back

One key factor in business strategy is to differentiate your firm from the competition. Often, businesses focus on differentiation of product features, product quality, price, and additional service benefits (warranties, service guarantees, etc.) and not on the other things that satisfy customers. Satisfying customers so that they do not want to go elsewhere is a successful differentiation strategy that is often overlooked. To keep customers coming back, we have to give them a reason to come back. One way to set a firm apart from the competition is through value creation. Value is not created merely by lowering the price of the core product or service. It is created at the higher levels of customer service, where customers feel differently when they are treated with respect and enjoy their interactions with the staff.

Businesses are usually so busy trying to get new customers in the door that they fail to focus on current customers and how to satisfy them more completely. Frederick F. Reichheld, author of *The Loyalty Effect*,[8] notes that, on average, U.S. corporations now lose half their customers in five years.[9] Changing suppliers because they are not satisfied is a daily occurrence in consumers' lives. Whether dealing with the company that cleans their offices or the garage where they get their car serviced, customers want to be satisfied. When they are not, they will take their business to someone who they think will do a better job.

Customers are prepared to go elsewhere and, unless they are locked in, will look for a new supplier even when they are satisfied. To ensure that they do not, we must try to satisfy them at all levels of the interaction and create situations where we can impress them with service beyond their expectations. This is where opportunities to differentiate a business or a brand beyond the core product become so important.

Such a strategy is also likely to create genuine long-term relationships because customers are attracted to the company by something they get that is not available elsewhere. This is a genuine strategic competitive advantage: strategic because it is tailored to the customer, and competitive because it is likely to be different from the approach taken by others, whose approach is usually based upon product improvements or price discounting. Competing on product improvements is a less successful strategy in a marketplace where most companies today can produce quite acceptable products or where the customer is hard-pressed to see any difference across competitive offers. Competing on price alone is, of course, a mug's game—nobody wins in the end, because customers who are attracted by lower prices will simply continue to follow them.

In the end, the competition for strategic competitive advantage is won by those companies that can give customers a good reason to deal with them or to buy their products rather than those of the competition. Where customers see no such reason, they will continue to shop around in search of the winner, and until that winner emerges, the marketplace is characterized by high rates of customer turnover.

What Will Satisfy the Customer?

Knowing what satisfies each and every customer can be an impossible task. After all, a large company may have thousands or even millions of customers.

---

[8] Frederick F. Reichheld, *The Loyalty Effect: The Hidden Force behind Growth, Profits, and Lasting Value* (Boston: Harvard Business School Press, 1996).

[9] Laura Hanson, "Keep the customer satisfied," *Marketing Tools* (1998). Accessed from www.demographics.com/publications, February 6, 2000.

The people who are closest to your customers often will know what satisfies them. And just as product modifications are made in order to meet the needs of different target markets, a company can make changes to service delivery and various other dimensions of customer interaction in order to increase satisfaction. Some of the factors that contribute to customer satisfaction are "no-brainers"; you have to get these right even to be considered part of the competitive market. In many industries, the core products now fall into that category. The bar has been raised so high in certain industries that customers expect a core product that rarely if ever fails. They now expect a very high level of quality of all competitors. Things that we considered really valuable additions to the core offer just a few years ago are now "standard equipment" and expected of everyone.

One example is the iron and ironing board in the hotel room. Ten years ago, if you wished to press your suit in your hotel room before a business meeting, you had to phone down to housekeeping to have the necessary equipment delivered to your room. Then some hotels started putting irons and ironing boards in rooms on their executive floors, and eventually in all rooms. Today they are standard equipment in almost all better hotels.

One extremely important point to remember is that customer satisfaction is a multidimensional concept, one dependent on a multitude of different factors. A company can get most things right in its dealings with customers, mess up on only one aspect of the interaction, and still lose that customer. This is an important lesson for employees and managers to learn: satisfaction depends on getting literally everything right. By doing so, the company will minimize the likelihood of the customer wanting to switch. Is it possible to achieve customer satisfaction in all aspects of how we treat them and what we offer them? Clearly, some companies have been able to achieve such total customer satisfaction. They leave nothing to chance. They know what will satisfy customers, and they deliver on that.

Customer Satisfaction—A Moving Target

Now, to complicate things a little, we must also remind ourselves that what will satisfy one customer will not necessarily satisfy another, and what will satisfy a customer in one situation may not satisfy that same customer in another situation. Unless a company and its employees have a good feel for what will drive customer satisfaction in various settings and for various customer segments, they are unlikely to get it right.

For instance, Mr. Lube, a chain of car service outlets, provides five-minute oil changes for $19.95. The staff at each outlet is trained to carry out the oil change and various other services. Speed of delivery is very important in this business. When my retired schoolteacher neighbor goes in every three months to have the oil changed on his car, he also has a chat with the mechanic about the weather, the hockey scores, and other current events. Although the chat is unrelated to the service being performed, the mechanic realizes that Ted can have his car serviced at any number of places within a few miles of his home. So why does Ted go back to Mr. Lube? Only part of the reason for his repeat business is the actual oil change—Ted feels good when he leaves. For him the conversation with the young guy who works on his car fulfills another need that is important to the customer and leaves him feeling completely satisfied. This pleasurable fulfillment goes back to the definition of satisfaction discussed at the beginning of the chapter. It also points out that what Mr. Lube offers the customer is much more complex than an oil change. In fact, this is a good example of an important point that we observed earlier. I would suggest that the oil put into Ted's car is one of the least important components of what he gets from Mr. Lube.

Are all customers satisfied with the same service? No. The customer who wants to chat with the mechanic after his car is serviced is looking for something different than the customer who wants to drive through, pay for the oil change from the car window, and be back on the road within five minutes. That customer's satisfaction derives from getting the service performed for a good price, quickly and conveniently. He or she may even be dissatisfied with a mechanic who took longer to service the car and tried to engage in conversation.

The employee who serves these customers must be able to make a judgment on whether to spend the extra time with a customer who wants to talk. Does the 15 minutes spent chatting with Ted represent three more 20-dollar oil changes, or does it represent a customer relationship that will retain this customer and lead to referral business? Those three oil changes may be forfeited for an additional share of Ted's business and more business from his family and friends in the future. Not to mention that the employee may enjoy his conversation with Ted and that it fulfills a certain need for the employee as well.

Virtually all core products and services—automobile maintenance, financial services, groceries, printing services—can be obtained at any number of places that have similar pricing structures, quality, guarantees, and distribution channels. Customers keep coming back because of the attention to needs that exist beyond the core product: the need to be treated with respect, the need for interaction with others, the need to be made to feel important.

Situational Factors and Satisfaction

Not only may what satisfies one customer not satisfy another, but what satisfies a customer in one situation may not satisfy him in another. Customer expectations and tolerance levels change with the situation. For example, a CEO will expect and demand professional service and attention to detail at a resort where the senior management team is spending three days to hammer out the strategic marketing plan for the coming year. The same executive will expect a more relaxed atmosphere when she takes the family to the same resort for a week of swimming, hiking, and golf before the kids return to school. The discrete, professional service at the business meeting satisfies the CEO because her needs and expectations are different than they are when she returns in the summer with her family.

What does this mean to the service encounter and to those who serve the customer? It is important for staff to be aware of the situational differences that exist and their importance in the delivery of quality service and creation of customer satisfaction. Customers approach every service situation with expectations for its outcome. Often these expectations are based on their own prior experience or that of trusted others, the promises made by the business through its communication efforts, and the situation at hand. Being able to identify the situation and respond to it in order to create a satisfied customer requires that employees be recruited and trained to do just that. It takes time and many encounters for employees to become well versed in reading the customer; however, there are many instances for which the employee can be prepared beforehand. Long-time staff can use their experience to prepare newer employees to respond to the situations.

The Drivers of Customer Satisfaction

As I have already noted, customer satisfaction often has little or nothing to do with product or price. The quality movement that emerged first in manufacturing and more recently in service industries has tended to address the quality issue. Today, customers are far more likely than in the past to experience acceptable or even superior quality in core products and services. Consequently, gaining a competitive advantage through improvements in core products is a far less likely strategy for success than it may have been 20 years ago.

We may view the factors that contribute to a customer's level of satisfaction with service provision or with his or her dealings with an organization at five levels. Each level generally involves progressively more interpersonal contact with employees of the service provider and consequently more of an affective or "feelings" dimension to the interaction with the supplying firm. Thus, the factors that influence customer satisfaction at each level are different. As we consider each stage of the *drivers of customer satisfaction* model, it is useful to think about what it is that the firm offers the customer. What can we do at each level that has the potential to influence customer satisfaction?

Each successive level in this model involves the satisfaction of progressively higher-order customer needs, and satisfaction of the customer at the lower levels of the model in no way guarantees satisfaction at higher levels. It is quite possible for a service provider to get things right on the first three or four levels and to fail to satisfy the customer because of something that is done at the fifth level. In this respect, the model borrows conceptually from Abraham Maslow, who is regarded by many as the father of humanistic psychology.[10] Maslow, writing in the 1950s and 1960s, developed his theory of a "hierarchy of needs," postulating that human beings proceed to satisfy progressively higher levels of needs, beginning with basic physiological needs such as hunger, shelter, and sex and progressing through safety, social, and self-esteem needs to self-actualization, the stage where an individual achieves inner peace and total satisfaction with his or her life.

Our model depicts five levels of what is provided to customers by an organization. This may be referred to as the "offer" or the "value proposition." Regardless of the type of company or organization, all offer their customers something at each of these five levels. In Chapter 4, we will talk about how each level of the offer creates a different form of value for customers. As is implied above, each level or component of the offer also addresses progressively higher levels of customer needs, corresponding roughly to Maslow's hierarchy. The five levels follow.

Level 1: Core Product or Service

This is the essence of the offer. It represents the basic product or service that is being provided by the company, whether the flight in the case of the airline, the book sold by the bookstore or publisher, the meal served by the restaurant, the bank account, the haircut, the telephone, fax, or Internet-access signal. This is the most basic of the things being offered to the customer and the one that affords the service provider the least opportunity to differentiate or add value. In a competitive marketplace, the firm must get the core right; if not, the customer relationship will never get started.

Increasingly, we find that the core product or service is not an issue. For many reasons, the customer often pays little or no attention to the core product. It is

The core product or service:
the essence of what we offer.

Figure 3-4 Drivers of Customer Satisfaction—Level 1

[10] Abraham H. Maslow, *Maslow on Management* (New York: John Wiley & Sons, 1998).

either so similar to the products and services of competitors that it offers nothing of value, or it is of such excellent quality that it rarely fails. In some industries, technology and other developments have created a situation where the core products and services offered by competing firms are virtually identical—a situation often referred to as *commoditization* (a topic to which we will return in Chapter 4). This is certainly the situation in public utilities and increasingly in financial services. Forty or more years ago, when consumers purchased many major appliances or automobiles, they *expected* to have to bring the item back to the shop to "get the bugs out." Today this is simply unheard of. Manufacturers, in particular, have embraced the quality ethos to such an extent that superior quality is the norm.

In situations such as these, where there are few differences in the core and where quality has been improved dramatically, customer needs are satisfied by the core product or service to the point where customers look to other components of the offer to add value or to give them a reason to deal with a specific firm. It is especially difficult in many industries today to demonstrate to the customer that value is being added at the level of the core or that one company's core product or service is particularly better than another's. Today, a good core product or service is absolutely essential to success. It represents the price of entry.

Level 2: Support Services and Systems

This includes the peripheral and support services that enhance the provision of the core product or service: delivery and billing systems, availability and access, hours of service, levels of staffing, communication of information, inventory systems, repair and technical support, help lines, and other programs that support the core. The main message here is that a customer may be dissatisfied with a service provider even though he or she receives an excellent core product. A

Delivery systems, billing, pricing policies, warranties, scheduling, complaint handling and other features that enhance and support the core.

Figure 3-5 Drivers of Customer Satisfaction—Level 2

customer may forgo purchasing precisely the car he or she wants if delivery will take eight weeks, or a customer may change Internet service providers because of inadequate help with access problems.

It may be argued that the three nonproduct components of the conventional marketing mix may be subsumed under this second level. If the core level represents the *product*, then pricing, communications, and distribution may be largely included under support systems. This is where decisions must be made concerning the "marketing" offer that is to be made to the customer: what price is to be charged, what discount structure is to be employed, what messages are to be communicated, how conveniently and through what channels we are to make our products and services available, what media we are going to use to reach target customers, and so on.

Some companies operate in industries where gaining a competitive advantage on the basis of a better core product or service is difficult, if not impossible. Such firms can begin to differentiate themselves and add value through the provision of support and ancillary services relating to distribution and information. They can make it easier for customers to deal with them. They can introduce no-hassle returns policies. They can provide customers with detailed information on the product. They can offer 24-hour service. They can arrange to provide routine service on a customer's car while she is out of town so that she won't be inconvenienced by not having it when she needs it. By taking steps to put such systems and policies in place, the company can begin to add value for the customer and to set itself apart from the competition.

Level 3: Technical Performance

There is little point in putting in place systems, policies, and procedures unless they are implemented as intended. This third level deals essentially with whether the service provider gets the core product and the support services right. The emphasis is on performing in the manner that was promised to the customer. Do we deliver the new dishwasher when we said we would? Does the flight arrive at 4:10 PM, as the schedule indicates it should? Do we make errors on the customer's bill? Is the hotel room cleaned and ready when the guest arrives?

In these examples, there may be nothing wrong with the core product. The company may even have the procedures and systems in place to deliver the core product, but they don't get it right; the processes and systems fail. Customer dissatisfaction and frustration will result from a failure to deliver on customer expectations that things will go smoothly and as promised.

Lots of business is lost at this level. Many restaurants which serve excellent food have driven customers away because of their failure to live up to customers' expectations with respect to explicit or implicit service delivery commitments.

Adherence to standards, delivering on time, living up to promises, lack of product and process failure.

Figure 3-6 Drivers of Customer Satisfaction—Level 3

This is why most of the world's airlines strive to meet tight arrival and departure standards; they know passengers don't like being late. Companies that do achieve high standards for meeting and exceeding customer expectations for service delivery achieve enviable competitive advantage. Customers know that they will be able to count on them. This is an extremely important component of relationships.

Level 4: Elements of Customer Interaction

This is where the company meets the customer in person. At this level, we address the way the service provider interacts with customers, through either a face-to-face service encounter or technology-based contact. Do we make it easy for customers to do business with us? Do our customers feel that they are being forced to use technology-based service options with which they are not comfortable? Are we so eager to trim operating costs that we overlook how the customer views our technological "improvements"? Do we treat customers with courtesy? Do we act as if they are important to us?

Understanding this level of customer satisfaction indicates that a firm has thought beyond the provision of core product and service and is focused on the delivery of service at the point where the company meets the customer. Traditionally, we would have focused at this level on the interpersonal interaction between customers and employees of the firm, either face to face or over the telephone. But companies are increasingly interacting with their customers and others via technology: through ATMs, interactive voice response (IVR) systems,

Level of personal service, attention, speed of service, general quality of the contact; how people are served and treated.

Figure 3-7 Drivers of Customer Satisfaction—Level 4

e-mail and the Internet. While it is easy to appreciate the importance of meeting and greeting customers positively in a face-to-face environment, it appears to be less easy for some firms to appreciate how badly they treat their customers when they deal with them through technology.

Increasingly, companies have to face up to the fact that much of their interaction with customers is already being handled through technology. Many customers are frustrated having to deal with companies through their technology-based systems. We will return to this subject in greater detail in Chapter 10, but suffice it to say at this point that so-called little things such as being put on hold can have a considerable impact on customer satisfaction.[11] One answer may be to ensure that companies put in place parallel or alternative systems to allow customers to deal with them in a more personal manner.[12]

---

[11] Deborah K. Unzicker, "The Psychology of Being Put on Hold: An Exploratory Study of Service Quality," *Psychology and Marketing,* 16 (July 1999): 327–50.

[12] James G. Barnes, Peter A. Dunne, and William J. Glynn, "Self-Service and Technology: Unanticipated and Unintended Effects on Customer Relationships," in *Handbook of Services Marketing and Management,* ed. Teresa A. Swartz and Dawn Iacobucci (Thousand Oaks, Calif. Sage: 2000), 89–102.

Most of us can recall examples of situations where we encountered employees who were surly or rude, or simply paid little attention to us, or even ignored us. In such situations, we often walk out and may never go back. This happens even though there was probably nothing wrong with the core products or services offered by the company or even with the support systems and procedures that it had in place to deliver technical service quality. One unfortunate outcome of such an encounter is that the customer feels extremely frustrated because he or she really wanted that jacket or to see that movie or to take that boat ride.

Level 5: Emotional Elements—the Affective Dimensions of Service

Finally, managers in service companies must think beyond the basic elements of the interaction with customers to consider the sometimes subtle messages that firms send to customers, messages that may leave them with either positive or negative feelings toward the company. Essentially, this means *how we make the customer feel*. Much evidence exists from research with customers that a considerable amount of customer dissatisfaction has nothing to do with the quality of the core product or service or with how that core is delivered or provided to the customer. Indeed, the customer may even be satisfied with most aspects of his or her interaction with the service provider and its employees. But the customer's business may be lost because of some comment from a staff member or because of some other little thing that goes wrong that may not even be noticed by staff members.

Customers regularly make reference, during the course of focus group interviews and service quality surveys, to how they are made to feel by service providers. I would suggest that very few companies pay particular attention to how they and their employees make their customers feel. Many service encounters leave the customer with negative feelings toward the firm. Some encounters, probably a smaller number, make the customer feel very good. Many of the things that elicit these positive and negative *feelings* are understandably remote from the provision of the core product or service and may therefore escape the notice of senior marketing and customer service managers. Many, it would seem, have paid little attention to the potential for damage or for improved customer relationships.

As we consider these five levels of the drivers of customer satisfaction, we should keep the following observations in mind.

- Things that the company and its employees provide and do at each level take on progressively more importance in terms of their influence on customer

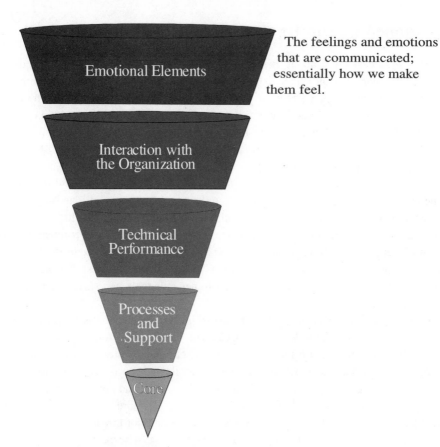

The feelings and emotions that are communicated; essentially how we make them feel.

Figure 3-8 Drivers of Customer Satisfaction—Level 5

satisfaction as we progress from the core product or service to the emotional elements of the interaction.

- As we move from the core product or service to delivery to interpersonal interaction and on to delivering positive emotions, we are addressing progressively higher-order customer needs, similar to human needs in general as described by Maslow.

- Also, in this movement, we are adding progressively more value for the customer.

- It is far easier to differentiate one's company from the competition by competing at the higher levels of the drivers of customer satisfaction model than at the levels of core and process.

Evidence of the Importance of Feelings

Customers interviewed about their perception of the quality of service provided by a particular company or their level of satisfaction with their dealings with that firm will often comment on how they are made to feel. An examination of such incidents supports the importance of feelings in customers' evaluation of service provision and suggests the need to define more clearly the impact of such reactions on relationships. One retail customer I interviewed spoke of her feelings of *injustice* when, having stood in line at a supermarket for several minutes behind other shoppers, she is left standing when people behind her in the line rush to move to a new cashier when the next lane is opened. The shopper is genuinely upset by such a process and feels the supermarket should institute a system that is more *fair*. The same customer indicated that she feels much the same when she stands in a line at an ATM to make a deposit, only to find, partway through the transaction, that the ATM is out of envelopes. Despite the absence of any human interaction, the customer still feels very *frustrated* and that she *has been let down*.

Feelings of inequity or *injustice* were also expressed by customers of a heating oil company in the example I gave in Chapter 1, who were told that some of their neighbors had been offered a discount of four cents a liter simply because they had threatened to switch to a discount supplier who was offering a lower price. Some of the "loyal" customers felt that their value had not been acknowledged as they had been customers of the company for more than 30 years but had been denied the discount simply because they had not threatened to leave. They were disappointed that their loyalty had not been respected or valued. These feelings are related to violation of the human need for justice. It seems inevitable that these feelings will trigger some sort of customer reaction, the exact nature of which may be based on a trade-off between the intensity of the feelings and the relevance or importance of the service.

A lady with teenaged children returned a pair of cotton slacks to the store where she had purchased them because the dye had run on the first washing. The employee to whom she spoke called the manager and he proceeded to "make a spectacle of me right there on the floor of the store." The manager pointed out the washing instructions on the garment and questioned whether the customer had washed the slacks properly. The customer's reaction: "He made me feel like a fool. I have been washing for 30 years. I have told hundreds of people about that incident." The lasting damage from this encounter seems to have been caused by a violation of the customer's need for self-esteem. Her problem with the store rapidly escalated well beyond the initial problem with the jeans; it was soon elevated to the point where the manager was questioning her competence as a mother.

Contrast this experience with that of the customer who said she felt that a store *trusted* her. "I brought a toy back to a store. They did not ask any questions or even look at it; they just refunded the money, no questions asked." This is the sort of encounter that provides the organization with an opportunity to prove its potential as a quality service provider, to build trust, and to increase loyalty. All of this can be quickly diminished or destroyed when customers feel let down because companies do not live up to their promises. "There is nothing worse than calling and being promised that a service person will come on Tuesday afternoon; you stay home waiting for this person and he does not come." In both of these situations, the customer's reaction was outside his or her zone of tolerance. In the latter case, negative feelings were elicited when the service was delivered at a level below the implicit threshold of the zone of tolerance. In the former situation, the evaluation of service was at the upper bound of the zone and resulted in a "Wow!" response by the customer.

Positive and negative feelings about a service encounter are not limited to those involving face-to-face interaction between the customer and service provider. Customers feel frustrated when they are unable to contact their suppliers, either because the phone is busy or because they have to deal with voice mail or other call-management systems. "I hate being answered by a machine; I want a personal touch." "I hate being put on hold when I am calling a supplier for assistance." "Service is when they return your call right away." "I like to reach people on the phone who know what I am talking about, rather than being handed around from person to person." "I want to talk with a real person. The computer can't answer all of your questions."

While the ability to add value and differentiate may be low at the core and support levels of the drivers of satisfaction model, it is easier at these levels to measure satisfaction with the core product or service and control the service delivery. Because the control and measures of success can be determined in exact numbers with little or no room for subjective interpretation, this is often where management focuses its attention. As well, the processes for measurement at these levels have been in existence and accepted for longer periods of time than those used to measure satisfaction at the higher, softer, more emotional levels. For this reason, most managers continue to rely upon those measures of customer satisfaction and organizational success that they have always used and that will be readily accepted by others, including senior managers and directors.

There are few instances when customers do not expect something more than the core product or service from a business transaction. Even when a person stops for a cup of coffee on the way to work, he or she expects the person serving the coffee to be courteous and polite. However, something as simple as a smile or thank you from the person behind the counter can improve a customer's perception of a firm. Sometimes it is the advice from a waiter or waitress regarding a menu selection or choice of wine that increases a customer's level of satisfaction by exceeding his or her expectations.

Researchers conducted surveys with more than 900 participants who were asked to evaluate different service failure recoveries for a restaurant or hotel they had recently patronized. The respondents were asked about process and outcome failures. (A process failure occurs when the company provides the core service but in a flawed way; an outcome failure occurs when the company fails to provide the core service.) It was found that the respondents were less satisfied after a process failure than after an outcome failure. The implication of this is clear: while it is important to get the core service right, the delivery of the service is important to the overall satisfaction of the customer.[13] Mistakes can provide an opportunity to demonstrate concern and commitment to satisfaction.

The service provider has the potential to make or break a situation based on how the customer is made to feel during the service encounter.[14] Focus group research that I have conducted over the past 20 years has proven to me that *customer dissatisfaction often has nothing to do with the core product or service or the support systems and performance.* Rather, the interactions with staff and how the customer is made to feel are often the elements that ultimately satisfy or dissatisfy customers. Unfortunately, few service companies seem to pay attention to the feelings of their customers, despite their importance to customer satisfaction and the establishment of customer relationships.

Merely Satisfied Is Not Enough

Thomas Jones and Earl Sasser make the very revealing point that "except in rare instances, complete customer satisfaction is the key to securing customer loyalty and generating superior long-term, financial performance."[15] The especially pertinent point that Jones and Sasser make is that *merely satisfied is not enough.* Businesses must strive for total customer satisfaction because that is where the rewards lie.

Many companies carry out customer satisfaction surveys to measure how well they are doing in this very important area. Customers are asked to rate their satisfaction with various aspects of the business, its products and services, or overall interaction with the firm, often on a 10-point scale, with 10 being completely satisfied. Many managers and business owners are understandably

---

[13] Katharine Zoe Andrews, "Satisfied Customers: Recovering from Service Failure," *Insights from MSI* (Winter/Spring 1998): 3–4.

[14] Judith A. Cumby and James G. Barnes, "How Customers Are Made to Feel: The Role of Affective Reactions in Driving Customer Satisfaction," *International Journal of Customer Relationship Management* 1(1) (1998): 54–63.

[15] Thomas O. Jones and E. Earl Sasser, Jr., "Why Satisfied Customers Defect," *Harvard Business Review* 73 (November–December 1995): 88–99, at 89.

pleased when they see average scores between 8 and 9. After all, isn't that pretty good? When we achieve 80% or 90% on a test, we feel pretty good about ourselves. Only when we dig below the surface do we realize that pretty good is not good enough.

Unfortunately, almost is not good enough where customer satisfaction is concerned. Research that I have conducted with clients in recent years shows conclusively the implications of scoring only 8 or 9 on customer satisfaction surveys. Customers who report their satisfaction levels at 8 or 9 are more likely to take part of their business elsewhere and less likely to refer the business to others than those who report satisfaction levels at 10. Yet most managers with whom I have come in contact over the past 20 years or more would be quite delighted with their performance if they registered average scores of 8 or higher on customer satisfaction surveys.

The results shown in Table 3-1 offer conclusive evidence to support Jones and Sasser's point that merely satisfied is not good enough.

First, note that more than 30% of the customers of telecommunications companies indicated that they are "completely satisfied" (10 on the 10-point scale) with their dealings with their local telephone company. Almost 30% of banking customers and more than 20% of grocery customers expressed similar levels of satisfaction. Now let's look at how committed the "completely satisfied" customers are to their respective suppliers compared to those who were quite satisfied at 8 or 9 and those who were less satisfied at a level of 7 or less.

The most satisfied customers also feel significantly closer to the company. (We will examine the importance of closeness in relationships when we delve more deeply into the nature of relationships in Chapter 5.) They also have much stronger relationships, ones that are more likely to last. But it is the slightly more tangible payback variables that are most likely to gain the attention of managers looking for a reason to spend money on programs and systems designed to satisfy customers and encourage the development of relationships.

Those customers who rate their satisfaction with the company at 10 give that company significantly more of their business (the share of wallet result), are significantly more likely to indicate that they are very likely still to be customers of the company two years from now (retention), and are significantly more likely to recommend the company to others (referrals).

Strategic Lessons to Be Learned

Results such as these should be sufficient to demonstrate two very important points to even the most short-sighted manager: (1) customer satisfaction pays dividends in the form of greater share of spend and long-term customer patronage and support—it leads to the development of relationships; and (2) customer

Table 3-1 The Impact of Total Satisfaction

Respondents from three industries (telecommunications, banking, and retail grocery) were divided into three groups, based upon their present level of satisfaction with their main telephone company, bank, or grocery store. The groups were as follows:

Group #	Description	Telecom	Banking	Grocery
Group #1	"Generally Satisfied or less" (Rated their satisfaction as 1 to 7)	22.9%	28.0%	34.2%
Group #2	"Quite Satisfied" (Rated their satisfaction as 8 or 9)	42.5%	43.0%	43.6%
Group #3	"Completely Satisfied" (Rated their satisfaction as 10)	34.6%	29.0%	22.3%

As shown below, very significant differences were found, in each industry, across the three satisfaction groups on all of the critical relationship and loyalty variables. Note that, for the telcom industry, *share of business* is the percentage of customers who also buy their long distance telephone service from their local telephone service provider.

	Telecom	Banking	Grocery
*Relationship Closeness****			
Group #1	4.4	6.0	4.7
Group #2	5.8	6.7	6.7
Group #3	6.8	8.0	7.9
*Relationship Strength****			
Group #1	8.2	8.6	7.5
Group #2	9.4	9.1	8.9
Group #3	9.6	9.5	9.3
*Share of Business***			
Group #1	78.4%	89.9%	76.0%
Group #2	92.4%	92.1%	79.3%
Group #3	91.3%	94.6%	85.2%
*Very Likely to Be with Main Telco/Bank/ Grocery Store Two Years from Now****			
Group #1	71.0%	78.7%	49.0%
Group #2	87.3%	89.0%	83.5%
Group #3	87.8%	94.5%	86.0%
*Very Likely to Recommend Main Telco/Bank/ Grocery Store to Others****			
Group #1	31.5%	50.0%	30.4%
Group #2	75.3%	69.0%	73.7%
Group #3	89.9%	91.9%	92.1%

** = significant differences exist at level 0.01
*** = significant differences exist at level 0.001

satisfaction is achieved by focusing on satisfying higher-order customer needs—having a great product and a low price is not enough. In fact, these may not be all that important in achieving customer satisfaction.

Jones and Sasser conclude that the objective of a business is to turn as many customers as possible into "apostles" who are extremely satisfied with how they are treated by the company, demonstrate a high level of loyalty, and become strong supporters of the company by remaining customers and spreading the word to others.

Susan Fournier and David Glen Mick recently drew five particularly salient conclusions about customer satisfaction.[16]

1. Customer satisfaction is an active, dynamic process.

2. The satisfaction process often has a strong *social* dimension.

3. *Meaning* and *emotion* are integral components of satisfaction.

4. The satisfaction process is *context-dependent* and *contingent*, encompassing multiple paradigms, models, and modes.

5. Product satisfaction is invariably intertwined with *life satisfaction* and the quality of life itself.

The implications of these conclusions are significant for managers wishing to achieve higher levels of customer satisfaction and thereby some of the payback that, as we have demonstrated in this chapter, is possible from higher average levels of customer satisfaction.

The achievement of satisfaction is a dynamic process and therefore an unending one; the job is never done, the rules change, the environment is turned upside

Table 3-2 Individual Customer Satisfaction, Loyalty, and Behavior

	Satisfaction	**Loyalty**	**Behavior**
Loyalist/apostle	high	high	staying and supportive
Defector/terrorist	low to medium	low to medium	leaving or having left and unhappy
Mercenary	high	low to medium	coming and going; low commitment
Hostage	low to medium	high	unable to switch; trapped

Source: Thomas O. Jones and E. Earl Sasser, Jr., "Why Satisfied Customers Defect," *Harvard Business Review* 73 (November–December 1995): 88–99, at 97.

[16] Susan Fournier and David Glen Mick, "Rediscovering Satisfaction," *Journal of Marketing* (October 1999): 5–23.

down by new competition, and what was a "Wow!" experience a short time ago is now commonplace.

The achievement of customer satisfaction is very much dependent on how we interact with customers at an interpersonal level. We achieve satisfaction by creating meaning in people's lives and touching them at an emotional level. Great products and superior technical service are not enough. How we make customers feel is paramount.

One of the most valuable lessons to be learned in business, and in marketing and customer service in particular, is that most questions can be best answered, "It depends." What will satisfy customers in a particular situation very much depends on who the customers are and what they bring to the interaction with the firm. What will satisfy that group of customers in one situation will not satisfy them in another. Customer satisfaction is very much a moving target.

The purchase and consumption of products and services is an integral part of our lives as consumers. To achieve satisfaction in the commercial exchange of products and services is to assist customers in achieving greater satisfaction in their lives. Some purchases are more salient and important than others, but helping customers achieve satisfaction in their purchase and use of products and services goes a long way to helping them be happier people.

To ensure total customer satisfaction, management must first gain an appreciation for the customer needs that exist at different levels—from the core products and services to the emotion elicited by an encounter. Then management has to focus on the customer's higher-order needs and determine how best to satisfy these since this is where a company can differentiate itself and its products and services from others.

Management must understand what leads to customer satisfaction. If they think that customers are going to be completely satisfied with a good product at a fair price, they are not acknowledging the complexities of the customer–business interaction, nor are they heeding the diverse needs each customer brings to the purchase or service situation. When management stays focused on the product and price, they miss the opportunity to create value for customers through the "softer" aspects of the encounter. Thus, management also fails to communicate the importance of service to its employees who work most closely with the customers.

Customers expect value and will not be completely satisfied until they perceive that value. The value is not created by lowering prices or adding features to the product or service. It is not even added by improving warranties or fulfilling promises for service. Value is created by doing all of these things right every time, in a way that makes the customer feel good about doing business with us and good about themselves after they do business with us.

4

The Customer's Definition of Value

How Can We Add Value?

The concept of value is of critical importance to marketing success, an essential building block in the quest for customer satisfaction. Quite simply, it is value that drives customer satisfaction, and the concept of creating and adding value is a solid one that demands management attention. The fundamental issue that must occupy managers if they are to attract and retain customers is knowing *how* to create and add value for the customer. Companies must examine value from the customer's point of view and not assume that they know what value means to the customer. It is also critical to get beyond a focus on value for money. Customers want much more than low prices. In fact, many managers seem surprised to find that customers often are prepared to pay more to get what they really want.

Over 30 years, through hundreds of projects that examined the extent to which customers are satisfied with companies in North America and Europe, I have learned a great deal about what creates value in the customer's mind. I have also learned how customers define value. What continues to surprise me is that very few managers seem to have a solid understanding of the critical importance of value in driving customer satisfaction. Even fewer have a broad view of how value may be created for the customer.

Value Creation: The Essential Responsibility of the Firm

Peter Drucker has observed that the new definition of the function of business enterprise is *the creation of value and wealth*.[1] The creation of value is the

---

[1] Peter F. Drucker, "The Next Information Revolution," *Forbes,* 24 August 1998.

essential responsibility of the firm—value for employees, for customers, for shareholders, and for the communities in which they operate. From the perspective of ensuring their long-term viability and prosperity, creating value for their customers has become an appealing, even essential, prospect for many firms. The creation and addition of value takes on many different forms as companies—both services and product based—try to increase customer satisfaction, loyalty, and retention by addressing the issue of delivering value. But "adding value" has become something of a catchphrase as companies introduce added-value features to their credit cards, or seek to add value for customers by making their products easier to use, or add value by bundling telecommunications and cable television services together.

All of these may represent value addition; *but they may not.* The customer must be the final arbiter; the customer alone must determine whether he or she perceives value to have been added. If not, he or she won't buy. Unless value continues to be perceived and experienced, customers won't be satisfied, and will drift away to the competition.

Let's remind ourselves that value is like service and quality among marketing terms, in that it must be defined by the customer. It is an individual thing, one that can be defined only from the perspective of the individual customer. It exists, as do service and quality, only in the mind of the beholder. It is easy, therefore, for companies to fall into the *value trap*—designing product and service features that are intended to add value, only to find that customers do not perceive them to add value at all. The key word is "perceive." It is perceived value that we are seeking. And it is only the customer who can determine whether the added product or service features are valuable.

Adding value may involve improving the quality of a product by using higher-quality materials and workmanship. It may also mean reducing the risk associated with purchasing a product or service by offering better guarantees and promises of post-purchase service. *When a business attempts to add value for its customers, it must first determine what those customers value.* While management of an airline may perceive greater value for customers in improving the in-flight service, customers may feel that shorter check-in lines would increase value. Similarly, flight attendants may know that travelers value comfortable seating while management focuses on improved meal quality.

What Do They Value?

How do we find out if a planned product feature or a service improvement would be considered a valued addition to the range of products and services that the company offers its customers? While there are many sophisticated research techniques that would allow us to measure the relative attractiveness of various proposed improvements, one qualitative technique that I have used for many years actually reveals a great deal about what customers value. First, it is important to recognize that value can be created in the customer's mind by either adding something that is felt to be of value or reducing or diminishing some aspect of the product or service that is viewed to be negative. *Value creation does not always have to involve the addition of something.*

I learn a lot about what customers value by asking them to describe in detail their interaction with a company or with its products and employees. I ask them to tell me about the interactions, the processes, the detailed steps they pass through as they buy the product or avail themselves of the service. I ask them to tell me what could go right or what could go wrong at each step along the way. And I ask them to tell me what they like to have happen and what they hope does not happen. I get them to talk about why they would buy this company's product or service rather than a competitor's and what it would take to draw them away to another supplier. By asking a series of questions such as these, I can build up a detailed understanding of the interaction between the customer and the company and of what aspects or elements of that interaction are satisfying and what are potentially or actually dissatisfying. It is then a rather short step to conclude that we can create value by doing more of the things that the customer finds attractive and fewer of those that are potential dissatisfiers.

Creating value for the customer, then, is not only about adding product features and benefits or lowering prices. While it is important to add benefits and remain competitively priced, the customer often expects this. Genuine or meaningful value creation takes place only if customers perceive an improvement in value and feel more satisfied as a result.

Views of Value

There are many definitions of value. Axiology is a branch of philosophy that is dedicated to the study of the nature and types of value. It addresses the issue of how people place a value on things. I agree with Morris Holbrook, who has observed that axiology has a great deal to teach consumer researchers and marketing practitioners.[2] It offers superb insights into how people place value on things, and by extension into how value may be created. It allows us to see that value can be created and enhanced in many different ways. It makes it very

---

[2] Morris B. Holbrook, "The Nature of Customer Value: An Axiology of Services in the Consumption Experience," in *Service Quality: New Directions in Theory and Practice,* ed. Roland T. Rust and Richard L. Oliver, (Thousand Oaks, Calif.: Sage, 1994), 21–71.

clear that value has been and continues in many organizations to be viewed in a very narrow sense, as value for money.

Before we proceed, let's distinguish among the several ways in which the term *value* may be applied in the context of relationship marketing. Specifically, we are focused on the creation of value *for* the customer. What can we offer the customer or what can we design into the offer that the customer will perceive to be adding value? Or, stated another way, what value does the customer place on the things that we are offering? The premise behind this approach is that by creating or adding value, or by offering things to which the customer attaches value, we are likely to increase the extent to which the customer is satisfied with the offer.

Contrast this with the view of value that we introduced in Chapter 2, where we were interested in the value *of* the customer, that is, the long-term value that the customer represents for the company. The premise here, of course, is that the longer we are able to retain a customer, the more valuable he or she will become to the company, for all the reasons outlined in that chapter. The two concepts are, of course, related. By creating additional value *for* the customer, we increase that customer's satisfaction level, thereby contributing to greater likelihood of retention and therefore greater value *of* the customer to the company. We can further extend our reference to the concept of value by observing that the creation of long-term customer value will lead in the end to the creation of additional shareholder value, a concept to which we will return in greater detail in Chapter 8.

Some views of how value might be created for customers are based on simply providing the core product or service at a better (i.e., lower) price than the competition. While this may represent value creation for some customers in some situations, it does not usually create the long-term satisfaction and retention that most firms are looking for. Even with value being added through the enhancement of processes and support services, there is often little that the competition can't replicate. Some authors have said that the key elements of the value package include quality, features, branding, packaging and labeling, product safety, customer service, and warranties and guarantees.[3] While these are indeed elements of the value package, particularly if one takes a very product-focused view of the offer, other authors and researchers correctly include additional elements such as the availability of the service, the types of support service provided, and the responsiveness of the firm.

[3] William G. Nickels and Marian Burk Wood, *Marketing: Relationships, Quality, Value* (New York: Worth, 1997), 258.

What Is Value?

Such divergence of opinion as to what constitutes value is not surprising, as value is a very personal thing. What represents value for one will not necessarily represent value for another. Just as we look for different things when we buy, we attach greater or lesser value to many of the components of the value package, and do so in different situations. Thus, to return to our earlier analogy, what we consider to be of value when we are traveling on a business trip to a major city will not be what we value when traveling with the family on a holiday to Disney World.

Valarie Zeithaml and Mary Jo Bitner have identified through their research that consumers view value in many different ways. They observe that what constitutes value is highly personal and idiosyncratic.[4] Their view of value is very much connected to price and to what the customer gets for his or her money. They observe that consumers define value in four ways: (1) low price; (2) whatever I want in a product or service; (3) the quality I get for the price I pay; and (4) what I get for what I give. This last definition comes closest to what I consider to be a holistic view of how consumers view value, at least in a subconscious sense. I agree that if you simply ask consumers to comment on the value they are receiving in a certain situation, they will usually couch their answer in monetary terms. But if you probe beneath the surface, they actually place considerable value on things that are well removed from the price they are paying.

Morris Holbrook observes that value is *a relativistic (comparative, personal, situational) preference characterizing a subject's experience of interacting with some object.*[5] Value involves a preference—a favorable disposition, a liking, positive affect, or a judgment as being good. It also involves an interaction between subject and object, the subject here being the customer and the object a product or firm. Value is also relativistic in three respects—it is comparative (involves rating one option against another), personal (differs across individual consumers), and situational (varies widely from situation to situation). Holbrook's final and very important point is that value is associated with an *experience* in that it pertains not to the acquisition of an object but to the consumption and use of its services. This is an especially useful exposition of what value entails when defined by the customer. It is not at all limiting and does not focus on price or on tangible objects. Rather, it gives value the scope it deserves and

---

[4] Valarie A. Zeithaml and Mary Jo Bitner, *Services Marketing: Integrating Customer Focus Across the Firm,* 2d ed. (New York: Irwin/McGraw-Hill, 2000), 441.
[5] Holbrook, op cit., 27.

which customers intend. Customers do define value very broadly, even though they may not use the terminology. They know, in very broad terms, what they get in dealing with a firm, and they know roughly what it "costs" them to get it.

In this chapter we will examine the many elements that are critical to value creation. We will look at the link between value and customer satisfaction and at how the drivers of customer satisfaction model presented in Chapter 3 can be used to help us better understand how we can enhance value for customers.

The Customer's View of Value

The title of this chapter was chosen because it is the customer's perception and definition that determines whether real value has been created. Many organizations attempt to add value, but if the customer does not feel he or she is getting value, a company's efforts will not pay off with increased levels of customer satisfaction. As well, as we have just observed, different things are valued by customers and in different contexts. We cannot make blanket statements about value and expect them to apply to all customers. Because each customer brings a unique background, value system, and level of expectations to the interaction with a firm, each one's notion of value and what adds value is also unique.

Value is a predictor of customer choice and loyalty. Buyers who are considering a purchase in a particular product or service category will scan their options and develop a consideration set consisting of all the brands or models that they will consider purchasing. The customer will purchase the product or service that he or she perceives to deliver the most value.[6] This assessment of value in the products or services being considered, and the post-purchase evaluation of value received, may take place at a very subjective or even subconscious level. The customer will likely not weigh each element of the product or service offer and mentally calculate which offers the best value or whether value has been received. He or she may not even use the term value, but may simply decide to buy one product or another. However, the customer is making an implicit determination of value whenever he or she faces the inevitable trade-off that characterizes a purchase situation or a decision whether to stay with a supplier. It will be a judgment call—very appropriate terminology for a situation that is highly judgmental. The customer will weigh anticipated benefits against current and anticipated costs, and the conclusion may be, "I didn't get good value there. I won't be back."

[6] William D. Neal, "Satisfaction Is Nice, But Value Drives Loyalty," *Marketing Research* 11 (Spring 1999): 21–23.

The customer must determine whether value is being created or added, and customers define value in many different ways—some see value in the lowest price possible. But Mercer Management has estimated that only about 30% of customers are price sensitive.[7] This leaves 70% who by definition are more value conscious and care about more than price alone. While this percentage is almost certainly a rough estimate, and the measurement of something as ephemeral as price sensitivity is subjective and prone to variability across product categories and situations, the principle is nevertheless an important one. Regardless of the actual percentage, *some large percentage of customers is indeed not particularly interested in price.* They want value, and they define it on their own terms.

Give vs. Get

The simple definition of value as what customers get for what they give is broad enough to allow for the incorporation of many different types of benefits and costs. The concept of *give vs. get* goes far beyond the basics of money and core product or service. The costs that the customer might give in the exchange situation with a firm include money, time, energy or effort, and psychological costs. To these, Christopher Lovelock has added sensory costs—putting up with noise, drafts, uncomfortable seats, or other negative aspects of the physical setting in which the interaction takes place.[8] The money and time costs are easily measured, but, the energy, sensory, and psychological costs are less evident to the company and are measured subconsciously in the mind of the customer. These are subjective concepts, and customers do not usually calculate these costs consciously. However, they do from time to time make judgmental observations that what they are getting from the exchange or relationship with the firm is not worth the time or bother. What they are saying is, "We're not getting value."

The concept is useful when we wish to examine the impact of customer satisfaction on customer relationship creation. In Figure 4-1 we examine the various scenarios that might be involved when customers interact with a company or service provider. We look at those situations where a customer might perceive that he or she is getting more or less from a relationship than he or she is contributing. Again, this is a judgment call on the part of the customer, who weighs all of the costs associated with dealing with the company against all of the benefits that are received as a result.

---

[7] Simon Glynn, Simon Caulfield, and Jacques César, "Making Customer Relationships Make Money," *Mercer Management Journal,* no. 9 (1997): 11–20.

[8] Christopher Lovelock, *Product Plus: How Product + Service = Competitive Advantage* (New York: McGraw-Hill, 1994), 60–61.

SERVICE PROVIDER (SP)

GETS +   GIVES+

	GETS +	GIVES +
GETS +	C: gets > gives SP: gets > gives C and SP are mutually satisfied – win-win! C feels good about staying with SP, which enjoys satisfying C	C: gets > gives SP: gets < gives Customer is satisfied. SP is looking for ways to reduce what it gives or increase what it gets.
GIVES +	C: gets < gives SP: gets > gives Customer is a cash cow and is dissatisfied. SP wants to keep C around, milking the relationship. C is probably trapped.	C: gets < gives SP: gets < gives Both want to end the relationship; some situations may trap C and SP in such a setting.

CUSTOMER (C) appears to the left between the GETS+ and GIVES+ rows.

Figure 4-1 Value Model of Customer Relationships

In the upper left quadrant, both the customer and the service provider perceive that they are getting more from the relationships than they are contributing. This is the classic win-win situation, although, as we discussed in Chapter 2, the company is most likely defining its benefits and costs in purely current monetary terms. The customer is more likely to be weighing more intangible aspects of the interaction. In any event, there is satisfaction in both camps and the relationship is likely to go on.

In the upper right quadrant, the customer perceives that he or she is getting a great deal out of the relationship—more than he or she is contributing. However, the service provider is less than satisfied, having determined that the customer is actually costing more to serve than he or she is worth. This is also the classic case that many banks and some other companies appear to face where the course of action that they have chosen to increase the value of the customer is to charge for services that were previously offered free, or to encourage the customer to avail of services that cost the company less to deliver; that is, services that are for the most part delivered via technology.

In the lower left quadrant, the customer is trapped, feeling that he or she is getting less from the relationship than he or she is contributing. On the other hand, the service provider is satisfied because the customer costs less to serve than the revenues he or she contributes. The customer is a cash cow. But the customer may also be a terrorist, frustrated in his or her inability to exit the relationship.

Finally, in the lower right quadrant, both customer and service provider are likely frustrated and dissatisfied. Neither feels particularly comfortable in a relationship that generates less in benefits than it does in costs. It's a lose-lose situation. Neither party derives perceived value. The customer would prefer to find another supplier but may be trapped, and the service provider may be unable to divest itself of the less than valuable customer because of some regulatory restriction which precludes the cutting off of service.

Not Worth the . . .

When I want to demonstrate to managers the range of factors that customers take into consideration when they subjectively and subconsciously assess whether they are receiving value, I ask them to think about how customers would complete the following statement: "I'll never go back to that company again. It's just not worth the _____." I use the same technique when interviewing customers in focus groups. They tend to complete the statement with words like "hassle," "time," "trouble," "bother," "effort," and "grief." It is still surprising to me, and to most managers behind the glass in the focus group facility, how few customers say "price." Evidence such as this that has led me to a very revealing conclusion, one that many business people find difficult to accept: overall, *price is often just not that important in determining the customer's perception of value.*

What do customers mean when they use words like those above to complete the statement? They have made a judgment that what they are getting out of their interaction with the company is simply not worth what they have to put into the interaction. This is a judgment about value. They are consciously or subconsciously weighing benefits against costs. When they use such words, what kind of message are they sending to management? Essentially: I'm not going back unless you make it easier for me to deal with you; unless your employees treat me better; and unless you speed up your service delivery. Those are a few of the things that management can focus on if they want to add genuine value for their customers.

A Progressive View of the Value Proposition

The *value proposition* is a useful concept. It focuses the attention of the firm on what it can offer the customer that would be valued and would, as a result, contribute to increased customer satisfaction. But, like many words that creep into the lexicon of business, value proposition is now used rather loosely to refer to many different aspects of what the company is offering the customer. Consistent with our earlier discussion of value, companies must have a holistic view of their value proposition: that it is literally everything that the company offers or is capable of doing for its customers. Conversely, the value proposition may be viewed as the collectivity of tools that the company can use to create or add value for existing or prospective customers.

Many people—most likely those who define value very narrowly—apply a limiting definition of the value proposition. There appears to be a tendency to limit the scope of the term to a product-related view. Eric Almquist and Adrian Slywotzky of Mercer Management Consulting comment on the rapid growth in the number of "value propositions" being offered to consumers in the developed world.[9] They use the term *value proposition* to refer to "a product, service or combination of products and services that offer some value for a price." They go on to give examples of the glut in value propositions, including the number of SKUs in the modern supermarket, the number of mutual funds that investors can choose from, the number of magazines on newsstands, and the number of credit card options that can be created.

The problem with such definitions is that they imply that the only way to create value for the customer is through modifying or improving the core product or service or manipulating the price. Such is, of course, not the case. As we will see in the next few pages, there are many ways to create value for your customers.

Consider for a moment how online retailers create value for their customers. They do so not only by providing a variety of products for sale, but also by making it convenient for customers to buy from them. They also create value by offering various delivery and payment options, allowing customers to track the progress of their orders online, offering book reviews, virtual dressing rooms, and joint shopping trips with a friend, and making suggestions on what would look good with that pair of slacks, or what book by that same author you might like to read.

As this example suggests, when we examine the value proposition, we must look at the entire offering a firm provides or is capable of providing to its customers. This offering goes beyond the core product or service. It has the potential to meet higher-order needs of customers and to create value at a level much higher than product features, price discounts, and support services. However, many companies stop at this level, for various reasons. Some do not see

---

[9] Eric Almquist and Adrian Slywotzky, "The Emerging Glut of Products and Services: Implications for Managers," *MMC Viewpoint* (Fall 1999) (http://www.marshmac.com/views/99fall.almquist.shtml).

any long-term benefit in trying to meet their customers' higher-order needs. Others see the benefit but are unwilling to spend the money in the short term. Some firms simply fail to recognize all of the needs that a customer brings to the purchase situation and the opportunities that are presented.

Adding More Value

Joseph Pine and James Gilmore argue that considerable value is added for consumers as organizations move through various stages of development, from the offering of commodities so that consumers can create their own products, to the manufacture of those products for the consumers, to the delivering of services, and finally to the staging of experiences.[10] Their concept of *progression of economic value* deals with the fact that an organization that develops in this way adds progressively more value for the customer, is able to differentiate itself better from its competitors, and is able to command higher prices.

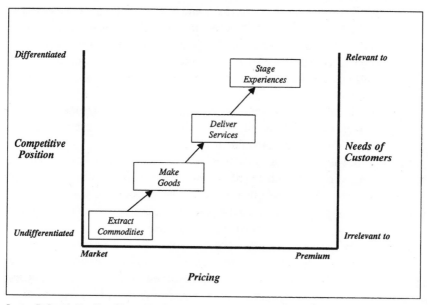

Source: B. Joseph Pine II and James H. Gilmore, *The Experience Economy* (Boston: Harvard Business School Press, 1999), 22.

Figure 4-2 Progression of Economic Value

[10] B. Joseph Pine II and James H. Gilmore, *The Experience Economy* (Boston: Harvard Business School Press, 1999), 22.

This same argument can be made with respect to the various levels of our drivers of customer satisfaction model, discussed in Chapter 3. I suggested there that a company is able to add progressively more value for the customer as it moves from focusing on the core product or service offering to focusing on service delivery and accuracy and the interpersonal contact between customers and the company. Ultimately the greatest value is added when the company is able to create an environment where there is a strong emotional connection between the company and its customers; in other words, a genuine relationship.

To illustrate how a company can get beyond the basic levels of customer satisfaction and add value to its offerings, let's return to the drivers of customer satisfaction model. We will consider each level and examine its potential to add value and to move the company's customers to a higher level of satisfaction.

The Commoditized Core

This is the basic element of the firm's offer to its customers. It has to be right in order for customers to consider the other elements. The core of the offer is exemplified by a product or service in its simplest form: the long-distance telephone call, the bank account, the hotel room, the flight to New York. Because, as I have stressed before, there is often little in the core product or service that distinguishes one company's offer from another's, gaining any form of competitive advantage at this level is particularly difficult. In the case of tangible products, the quality of a company's product may, because of technological advances, be easily replicated by competitors. An example is the electronics industry where most consumers are unable to tell any real differences across brands of stereo systems, television sets, or laptop computers.

The situation is compounded in those situations where there is *in fact* no difference in the offerings of competing companies. In many industries today, *at the level of the core product* their offerings are indeed all the same. AT&T's long-distance telephone call is indistinguishable from Sprint's. A savings account at Bank of America is identical to a savings account at Citibank. The quality of the television signal from one cable operator is the same as another's.

This situation where gaining a competitive advantage at the level of the core product is widely known today as *commoditization* because the products and services involved have been reduced to the status of commodities. Whenever we have a situation where the customer does not perceive any difference across suppliers, we have commoditization.

Such a situation brings about two important results. First, it becomes extremely difficult to convince the customer that our product is better than the competition's. Secondly, when nothing is done to differentiate the core product or service, customers will default to using price as the differentiating factor. This situation is obvious in many industries where the customer simply does not see any value in the core product, because it is indistinguishable from those offered by others. In the classic definition of commodities, that is why consumers will often buy household products like flour and sugar based on the lowest price. That is why we have gasoline price wars and why a very large percentage of customers will shop around for the lowest rates on auto insurance and home mortgages.

In these commoditized situations, for firms to attract and retain customers without lowering prices, they must add value. If they do not, their products and services will become commodities where only price is important to the customer. Long-distance telephone competitors have experienced this in every market where competition has been allowed in recent years. Customers switch from one company to another in order to take advantage of the latest price promotion.

To add value and to create satisfied customers at this core stage, many companies will simply reduce price. This often leads to price wars, where one or more of the competitors will also lower prices. Margins will be reduced, and often the company will have to reduce the amounts spent on customer service personnel. This serves only to dissatisfy the customer who measures value by components of the offering other than price. Dropping price in an attempt to create value for the customer is often a futile exercise. Generally this tactic attracts the price conscious, builds no customer loyalty, and results in the firm leaving money on the table by missing opportunities to attract less price-motivated customers who would have been prepared to pay more had the firm been able to create value in their minds.

Another strategy that some firms have used to combat the commoditization of the core service is to charge for services that were once offered free. This has occurred where advances in technology and deregulation have contributed to reduced margins. Because those services had been free, customers had not attached value to them, and their outcry has been loud and angry. "Excuse me! Let me see if I understand. You are charging me a fee to deposit my money into my bank account?!?"

Other firms will attempt to increase value for the customer at this stage by improving product quality and features. While this is recommended for any business that wants to remain competitive, in many industries it will not set the product or service apart from the competition for very long since any improvements or modifications that convey value are usually replicated easily and in a short time. This is especially the case where companies have fallen victim to the results of applying advancing technologies. By adopting new technology, many organizations have tried to gain a competitive advantage, only to find it fleeting at best. It didn't take long, once Hertz adopted hand-held terminals that allow employees at airport locations to check-in a customer's car in seconds, before Avis and most of the others had them as well. One of the easiest ways to enhance the core product or services and its delivery is through its technol-ogicalization. But because technology by its very nature is very easily replicated, the result is not so much *de-commoditization* as *e-commoditization*.

Take, for example, the many e-commerce retailers that are selling books, CDs and videos on the Internet. Essentially, their core products are the same. This book is the same book whether you buy it from amazon.com, barnesandno-ble.com, chapters.ca, or your neighborhood independent bookseller. How then can the Internet retailers compete? They all have essentially the same technology and the same access to inventory. Some will be able to ship more quickly, but for the most part they have been competing on price and the offering of free shipping, essentially falling into the e-commoditization trap. Their challenge, as it is for all firms, is to seek to de-commoditize through the creation of more value for the customer at the higher levels of the drivers of customer satisfaction model.

Move to Support Services

This is the level where firms add services which are intended to create value for the customer by reducing nonmonetary costs. Services such as deliveries, repairs, installation, warranties, and payment plans help to differentiate the com-pany and provide added value for customers by reducing psychological, time, and energy costs. A customer who buys a home theater system will appreciate the delivery of the components, the warranty, repair service, and other support services. Because the technology and features are quite similar in a given price range, the manufacturer will differentiate its products by these added service features. The customer will then choose a specific brand or vendor based on the support services provided and how important these are to him or her. These services too are easily replicated by the competition, and what was a differen-tiating factor now becomes a commodity in the marketplace.

Enhancing the core product through the addition of services is a very sound strategy, but many of the services and enhancements that we may consider add-ing are very easily copied by the competition and have in fact become standard equipment in the value proposition of many companies. We all expect furniture retailers to deliver and auto and appliance manufacturers to offer warranties. As our example from Chapter 3 of the iron and ironing board in the hotel room illustrates, such service enhancements are easily copied and end up as expected and standard.

We observed earlier that value may be created at each level of *the drivers of customer satisfaction* model through the addition or deletion of something. The objective at the support services and processes stage is to use the addition of valued services and support systems to create value. By so doing, we are creating

ADD   REDUCE

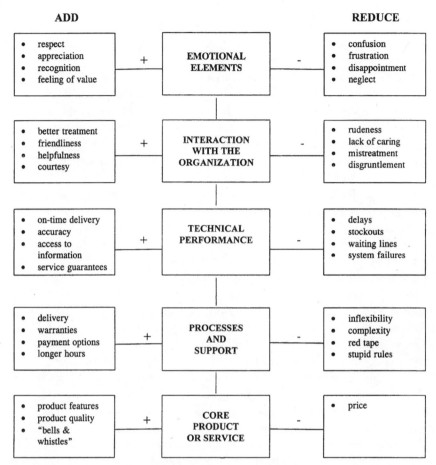

Figure 4-3 Value Creation at the Stages of the Drivers of Customer Satisfaction Model

value by making it possible for customers to get in touch with us and generally making it easier for them to deal with us. We add value by having longer opening hours, constructing a well-designed website, and providing customers with the kind of information they need to make purchase decisions.

But we also can also create value at this level by taking away those elements of service that customers find frustrating. Many firms would be well advised to remove barriers to exit which cause the customer to feel trapped, or to install more customer-friendly telephone systems that actually make it possible for them to talk with real live employees. For many customers, these would represent genuine value additions.

Getting It Right

At the technical performance level, companies strive to deliver on their promises and establish themselves as leaders in "service excellence." Companies are becoming more aware of this level as a driver of customer satisfaction because it is more difficult to achieve and for the competition to replicate. There is a positive relationship between customers' evaluations of service quality and assessments of service value.[11] Customers evaluate service quality in five underlying dimensions: tangibles, reliability, responsiveness, assurance, and empathy.[12] Four of these five are dimensions of relationship growth and are directly related to the customer's overall perception of value.

Achieving excellence at this level depends on many factors. Top management commitment is essential since time and money must be spent in order to develop processes and technologies as well as to attract, retain, and train staff to perform at the highest level. The payback from this investment comes from the customer's perception of increased value. Customers who value excellence in service will be more satisfied and will tend to remain loyal.

To create value at this level, we can improve our performance and provide superior service. This increases what the customer gets because he or she can rely on the company to deliver on time and produce exactly what was promised. Thus, value is added through the addition of controls and systems to ensure that service is completed as and when we said it would be. We do whatever it takes to get it right. Some companies are now so confident of their ability to deliver for their customers that that are offering service guarantees.

In addition, we can reduce the psychological cost to customers by making it easier for them to obtain information and advice. Many businesses now offer toll-free customer telephone lines which allow customers to request service, seek advice on the use of a product, or obtain information about where to take it for servicing. Others, such as FedEx and UPS, offer Internet-based services that allow customers to trace the shipment of packages so that they know precisely when they will be delivered. This reduces the anxiety, time, and money associated with owning and using a product and accessing a service, thereby increasing value for the customer.

The converse of value addition at this stage is, of course, that value can be created through the reduction or elimination of delays, errors in order filling, systems failures, or employee mistakes. Anything that a firm can do to reduce such errors will enhance service delivery and reliability. The result is that cus-

[11] Ruth N. Bolton and James H. Drew, "A Multistage Model of Consumers' Assessment of Service Quality and Value," *Journal of Consumer Research* (March 1999).

[12] Valarie A. Zeithaml, A. Parasuraman, and Leonard L. Berry, *Delivering Quality Service* (New York: Free Press, 1990), 26.

tomers will be much more confident that they can rely on the firm to deliver and will tend to have a much higher level of trust.

Meeting the Staff

This level of our model focuses on satisfying some of the customer's higher-order needs. These needs may not be satisfied at the lower levels, where emphasis is placed on the core product or service and on its delivery, but they are important in the customer's overall view of the firm and perception of value. Customers will decide whether to continue their patronage of some firms based largely on how they are handled by members of staff. Even when all aspects of the core product and its delivery are quite acceptable or even superb, poor treatment by staff can cause a customer to go elsewhere. For obvious reasons, customers prefer employees who are friendly, helpful, understanding, personable, courteous, and empathetic. The interaction with staff influences the customer's assessment of the psychological costs associated with the interaction. Customers who are treated with respect, empathy, and genuine concern will perceive psychological costs as low and benefits high and have a better view of the overall value of the interaction.

The solution to creating value at this level, therefore, is in the decisions relating to the employment of people. The firm's ability to create value for customers through their interaction with staff is very much dependent on its human resources policies and programs—hence my earlier comment that the most important decision made in services marketing is the hiring decision. To that we can add staff training, motivation, rewards and recognition programs, compensation, and other HR tools. The key to creating value for the customer lies in creating value for the employees, which leads to the delivery of superb interpersonal service.

The converse, of course, is to create value for the customer by reducing or eliminating situations where the customer is likely to encounter employees who are rude, uncaring, unhelpful, disgruntled, unfriendly, and so on. Such encounters, which are too common, serve only to undo all of the company's good work and planning in creating a great product and an efficient delivery system. Many sales are lost and customer relationships ended, despite excellence at the lower levels of our model, because of an upsetting encounter with an uncaring employee.

How We Make Them Feel

This is the fifth driver of customer satisfaction and the highest level at which to add value. When customers are treated with respect and courtesy, they will feel better about their encounter with a firm. Businesses and their employees who place greater emphasis on the core product, price, and support services do not always consider the importance of the customer's feelings throughout his or her dealings with the company. Even those firms that reach a very high level of technical excellence will often overlook the customer's feelings. On-time delivery is important, but if the delivery people are rude, the customer's perception of value will be diminished.

But let's consider the fact that the creation of positive customer emotions does not take place in isolation from the activities and strategies at each of the four lower levels of our model. Companies must be aware that customer feelings and emotions are often deeply held and will have a profound influence on whether a customer will continue to do business with us in the future. But where do these emotions come from? From each of the four previous levels. We can badly confuse a customer by making it difficult for him or her to assemble a piece of garden furniture or failing to include the wrench needed to attach the bolts to the frame—both product problems. We can create a sense of undervaluing our loyal customers by offering lower prices to switchers to return to the fold. We can create considerable frustration with difficult-to-use telephone answering and messaging systems.

Websites can be very frustrating if not well designed. When I recently hit the "contact us" button on the website of a well-known European services company, I was instantly provided with the postal address of the company, with an invitation to "write us a letter." What kind of feeling did that leave me with concerning that company? That they are high-tech enough to have a website, but act very low-tech in asking me to resort to the postal system to contact them. I have been similarly frustrated by the websites of a number of American companies that ask me to register in order to obtain information but have designed their system *not* to accept my alphanumeric Canadian postal code—only a five-digit numeric zip code will be accepted.

Firms can obviously add emotional value for their customers by designing and implementing customer rewards and recognition programs and developing programs that make the customer feel important, valued, appreciated and impressed. Avoiding situations, whether caused by products, processes, systems, performance or employees, that make customers feel disappointed, neglected, let down, unimportant, or ignored is always a good strategy.

This view of value in the context of the *drivers of customer satisfaction* model illustrates a number of very important points:

- Value can be created or added at each of the five levels of the model as we strive to satisfy progressively higher-order needs for the customer. Conversely, we can do things at each level that will interfere with value creation and actually drive the customer away.

- We can create value successfully at the lower levels of the model, only to see it destroyed at a higher level. Simply put, we can have the best product but fail to deliver it on time and thus make the customer very disappointed.

- The most important kind of value is that which reaches the emotions of the customer. While we place this appropriately at the top of the model, we must acknowledge that emotions, both positive and negative, can be generated at each of the four lower levels.

A Broader Value Proposition

I observed earlier in this chapter that many managers appear to have a rather limited view of value and how it can be created in the minds of customers. For them, value means value for money, and adding value means product improvements or price discounts. It is sufficient, they think, to add some feature to the core product, while holding price the same, or to bundle together two or more products or services and charge the customer an attractive price for the bundle. This strategy has been followed in financial services for many years, where a number of features are offered as part of the package of services that come with a credit card. The customer pays one flat monthly fee, or no fee at all, and has available this range of services, which might include travel insurance, no-fee travelers checks, trip planning services, or access to airport first-class lounges. Banks offer a number of services and accounts to their customers for a flat monthly fee. Telecommunications companies now bundle local telephone service with long distance, satellite television service, Internet access, and cellular telephone service.

But offering such bundled services, while they may very well represent perceived higher value for customers, is still a rather blunt-instrument approach to value creation. It still amounts to price discounting because the customer is being offered a package of products or services for a lower overall price. Reducing price is clearly the least attractive form of value creation. First, it is the most easily copied strategy. Competitors can usually drop their prices just as quickly as we can. Secondly, the company often ends up leaving money on the table because customers are in fact often ready and willing to pay *more* if we would only give them what they really want. Thirdly, if we make a practice of discounting with any degree of predictability, some customers will simply wait for the sales and will never pay full price if they can avoid it.

Companies that define their value propositions very narrowly often have an equally narrow view of how they can create value for customers. I delight in demonstrating to such companies how their customers define value. These companies, in my experience, are typically looking for ways to save the customer money by shaving a few dollars off the price, or trying to run a predictive model that says that sales will increase by a certain percentage if services A, B, and C are bundled together, and if customers would be prepared to pay $39.95 a month, and if only a certain percentage of the customer base will switch to this new bundled service. Meanwhile, customers are often sitting at home thinking that what they would really appreciate is if it were easier to pay the bill, or possible to talk with a real live person when calling the 1-800 number, or possible to send an e-mail message through the website. All of these examples represent the creation of value too. They simply represent the customer's definition of value, rather than the company's.

Different Value for Different Folks

Different segments of customers perceive value in different ways. Customers combine various elements of the value proposition in order to define the value from their perspective. As a result, what is considered valuable or an important element of the value proposition by one customer is not considered valuable by another. Value may be created in different ways, and it is critical that marketers really understand what forms of value are considered most important by the segments of the market in which the firm is interested. In fact, an extremely lucrative way in which to segment markets is on the basis of the forms of value that contribute to satisfaction for the various segments. But it is critical first that marketers and others understand how the customer defines value.

In an attempt to break away from the narrow interpretation of value as a function of what is received for the price paid, the Conference Board in a 1997 report identified four sources of value:[13]

1. *Process:* optimizing business processes and viewing time as a valuable customer resource

2. *People:* employees are empowered and able to respond to the customer

3. *Product/service/technology:* competitive features and benefits of products and services, lowering productivity interruptions

4. *Support:* being there when the customer needs assistance

Morris Holbrook talks about the three key dimensions of consumer value: (1) extrinsic versus intrinsic value; (2) self-oriented versus other-oriented value; and

---

[13] Conference Board, "Seminar Profile: Developing and Sustaining Customer Relationship Excellence," Members' Report No. 11, New York, July 1997, 6–7.

(3) active versus reactive value.[14] This framework for understanding value is extremely useful and reinforces my own view of value as perceived by customers.

The following represent components or forms of value that I have identified in my work with the customers of many organizations. They reflect the fact that value can be created in many different ways, some of which are not generally acknowledged by managers in some companies. We will start with the easiest form of value creation, that involving altering the core product and the price charged. Unfortunately, this happens to be the most easily copied and the least likely to result in the creation of genuine, long-lasting value for the customer.

Product-for-Price Value

This is the most basic source of value. It is characterized by customers who will switch to the competition for a lower price. Customers who equate value with price are classic price switchers. The implication is that they perceive value in nothing else that the company offers. They are also likely to perceive the product as a commodity and think that all suppliers are the same. These customers perceive little value in what is offered by competing firms and have determined that other characteristics of the offer are not important or attractive enough to outweigh the importance they place on price. This price-based view is likely to prevail when the customer is focused on the core service rather than the entire offering from the company, especially when the core is virtually indistinguishable from that of the competition. We see this in utilities and increasingly in financial services, where, primarily because of the increased use of technology to deliver services, core products are often viewed as commodities. This is the reason for the level of price competition in long-distance telephone service and financial products such as mortgages.

Access or Convenience Value

This form of value is created when firms make it easy for customers to access their products and services and to deal with them. Access and convenience value is created by being open for business when the customer is available, providing convenient locations, and offering a variety of means to access services. This aspect of value creation has been enhanced by technology through such services

---

[14] Morris B. Holbrook, "Introduction to Consumer Value," in *Consumer Value: A Framework for Analysis and Research,* ed. Morris B. Holbrook (London: Routledge, 1999). 9

as Internet banking and shopping. This form of value also has an information component because customers are often in need of certain information and want to obtain it at their convenience. Technology has made this possible with the introduction of e-mail and Internet access to account information, for example.

Choice-Based Value

Giving customers a variety of options in the selection available to them or in how they access those options creates value for them. The customer is allowed to stay with that company while being able to choose from a varied selection. This creates value in that it provides the customer with lower time, energy, and psychological costs. Choice does not extend, however, only to the selection of products or service on offer. Value is created for customers every time we give them an option with respect to how they can deal with us, how they can pay for their purchases, how they want them shipped, or how they receive information.

Employee-Based Value

This form of value relates to the level and type of service a customer receives from the employees of a firm. Quality service will often bring customers back to the firm, and this quality is often attributable to the actions and attitudes of employees. The general definition of service includes various aspects of the service encounter, such as response times, length of waiting lines, speed of service delivery, and friendliness and courtesy. These aspects, which are associated directly or indirectly with staff, include the factors that drive satisfaction at the level of technical service delivery and interaction with staff. The way in which employees greet and deal with customers certainly has the potential to add value to the purchase situation or service encounter.

Information Value

Providing customers with more information can increase value for them. Often customers are not aware of the choices and options available to them. When customers are informed, they can make choices based on knowledge, which increases their level of comfort in their decision making. The provision of information is especially important in companies whose services are closely related to technology. Many customers do not know all of the capabilities of the technology at their disposal, and they appreciate learning new and useful ways to use technology. A focus group participant was asked why he did not use the ATM to pay his utility bills, to which he replied, "Can I do that?" Customers of a telephone company for which I consulted were most impressed when they were shown many of the features of their voice mail system that they had not been using but that were included in the base monthly price. They immediately perceived greater value in the service. Knowing the capabilities of the technology and understanding how to use it to its full potential reduce anxieties for the customer and increase the perception of value.

Association Value

Customers sometimes derive pleasure and a certain amount of comfort from being associated with a certain service provider with whom they associate positive attributes or values. This is especially true when companies are perceived as being good corporate citizens or convey a positive image within the community. Some customers are actually proud to say that they are customers of a certain company because others hold that company in high regard. Others perceive positive associations in certain services brands and may experience value when they stay in a Four Seasons hotel, for example. The positive image of the brand is perceived to rub off on its customers.

Enabling Value

Many service providers are valued not so much for the core product or service as for what is made possible because of it. For example, customers value an airline not only because it gets them from one point to another, but also because it allows them to reunite with their families or get away for a relaxing weekend. A paging service allows parents to know where their children are at all times. By focusing attention on the effects of the service, rather than on the service itself, a company can also increase the benefits perceived. This form of value is very much related to Holbrook's concept of *extrinsic* value, where consumption is valued for its "instrumentality in serving as a means to accomplishing some further purpose, aim, goal, or objective." [15]

Relationship Value

This refers to the value created when a firm makes its customers feel better about dealing with the company. This type of value is not directly related to the products of the company or to its prices, but rather to the more subtle aspects of the interaction with customers. It really relates to the many ways that a

[15] Ibid., 10.

company can increase feelings of closeness and ownership. Customers, when asked about companies they like to deal with, will invariably refer to those firms that treat them special, that seem to understand them and value their business. Ultimately, in the case of some service providers, the customer will feel so close to the service provider that he or she will personalize the relationship with expressions like "my hairdresser" or "my mechanic." The customer feels a part of the organization, with all of the emotions that this entails.

Customer-Unique Value

This form of value is created for customers when firms treat them as individuals. By tailoring the service offering to the individual customer, a company sends all sorts of messages that the customer is noticed, that he or she is known and valued, and that his or her business means something to the company—that the customer is more than a mere number. Creating such value may be as simple as recognizing the customer and calling him or her by name.

Surprise Value

This refers to the benefit that comes from surprising the customer with good news or with special treatment—the "Wow!" experience. It requires that a service provider look for opportunities to impress the customer with actions and programs that are unexpected and that send the message that the company has noticed and genuinely cares about meeting customer needs. Many customers are pleasantly surprised when they receive a call informing them of a sale. They are impressed when an employee goes out of his or her way to solve a problem or to obtain information. In a number of client companies, when programs were launched to place calls to customers occasionally, not to sell them things but to enquire whether there was anything the company could do for them, many expressed genuine surprise and were impressed that the company cared enough about them to make such a call. This form of value is also created when employees engage in what I call "planned spontaneity"—when employees set out to do the unexpected, to impress the customer with service or a gesture that was not expected but is very much appreciated. The result is value creation and customer delight.

Community Value

This refers to the contribution that a company makes to the local economy and the communities in which it operates. It is the benefit created indirectly through donations and sponsorships and through the fact that the company employs large numbers of people. This represents value created not through direct contact with customers or carrying on the company's core business, but through altruistic and charitable activities. Through its sponsorship of arts activities and sporting teams and donations to the local college building fund, a company gains a deserved reputation that carries over indirectly to its image among customers. Some will choose to do business with such a firm because of what it is giving back to the community. Thus, companies create value for their customers at a level that is very far removed from the products and services that they sell and has nothing to do with the price being charged. In fact, at the height of the long-distance price wars, a core group of customers of one Canadian telephone company chose to stay with the firm, and to pay higher rates for long distance service, because the company was, after all, "our telephone company."

Memory Value

This is the value created when the customer is involved in an event or experience that remains in his or her memory for many years—when a customer hears Pavarotti at the Met for the first time, for example, or enters St. Mark's Cathedral or the Sistine Chapel. Family vacations have the same effect. Joseph Pine and James Gilmore have observed that families don't take their children to Disney World for the event itself but for the shared experience that will remain a part of family conversations for years. They note that the value of the offering lies *within* the customer, where it will remain for a long time.[16]

Experience Value

Very much related to the concept of memory value is the creation of an experience for the customer. Pine and Gilmore relate the creation of experience value to the staging of an event or to the entertainment that is associated with plays, concerts, theme parks, and stage shows. They are quick to point out, however, that entertainment is only one part of an experience; experience value is created whenever the customer is *engaged*.[17] Firms can create experience value for their customers by adding some form of entertainment to the service offering or value proposition, as is common in theme restaurants, boat tours, and whale-watching expeditions, but they can also do so by turning the service experience into a memorable experience, by creating such a pleasant service environment, and delivering such exceptional service that the customer will never forget and will spread the word among friends and colleagues.

---

[16] Pine and Gilmore, op. cit., 13.
[17] Ibid., 3.

Adding Value: What Gets in the Way?

One of the most obvious conclusions that I have drawn from the research that I have conducted with consumers over the years is that different customers place different levels of importance on different components of value. Simply put, different customer segments value different combinations of things in assessing the attractiveness of a service offering. In addition, customers will place different weights on various components of value in certain circumstances, buying principally on low price in some situations and paying more in different circumstances to buy from a company that offers superior service or makes it easier for the customer to buy. Much of what may be considered to be impediments to value creation stems from the fact that customers view value in many different ways. They clearly know when value has not been added, or when some aspect of service that they did value has been removed. Customers are able to identify situations where they feel that no value is being added by the firm or where they perceive value to have been decreased. The following represents my view of situations that contribute to value reduction.

Management View of Value

An aspect of service provision that certainly impairs the customer's view of the value being created is the failure of some firms to realize that the customer's definition of value is so complex. There is a tendency in some firms and in some situations for service providers to assume that the customer is always looking for the lowest price. Such firms are constantly striving to lower prices and to offer customers the "best deals." Meanwhile, many customers are simply not interested in obtaining the lowest possible price and will forsake a service provider that stresses the lowest prices in order to obtain added service or other components of value. Many openly admit to being prepared to pay even higher prices if they could obtain the level of service they want.

Introduction of Technology

One of the most striking aspects of service that interferes with value creation, from the customer's perspective, is the introduction of technology into service provision. Throughout my research, many customers make reference to the fact that they resent having to interact with technology in order to access service. Many dislike the impersonality of service provided by technology and perceive its introduction as a means for the firm to reduce costs. Having the option to do one's banking through an ATM or by phone or Internet is perceived by some to be value-adding in that it creates both choice and convenience value; but for many others it diminishes value because it reduces relationship value and increases psychic costs.

The Customer's View of Cost

Increasing the application of technology in service provision also leads to another customer view that compromises the firm's ability to create or enhance value for its customers. Because service is today often delivered by technology, much of it below the line of customer visibility, the customer is led to believe such service costs the company little or nothing to provide. Thus, banks are soundly criticized when they impose a charge to transfer funds from one account to another. The customer's view is that such a transaction merely takes a couple of computer keystrokes and the transfer is complete. Service providers make it difficult for their customers to understand why they have to charge for such services. The customer tends to associate service provision with people—they are prepared to pay for services that are people-delivered, in part because there is the prospect of employee-created value. They tend to appreciate much less the value associated with technology-delivered service.

Commoditization

We addressed earlier in this chapter the concept of "commoditization": the view that the products or services being provided by competing firms are all alike. Possibly unwittingly, many marketers are contributing to this view, thereby encouraging the customer to focus on price as the sole differentiator. In some industries there is in fact little or no difference in the core offering of the competing firms. Other industries that are relying increasingly on technology to deliver their core service are in danger of becoming commodities in the eyes of their customers—many financial services are moving in this direction. Similarly, as we observed earlier, many processes and amenities that have been introduced by service providers in certain industries have, because virtually all competitors now offer them, themselves become commoditized. Marketers in such situations must look to different ways to set themselves apart from the competition. They must look to new value creators and enhancers that are more likely to be at a higher level of value creation. If they do not, they are likely to be faced with an ongoing situation where customers view all competing firms as alike and resort to separating them only on the basis of price.

Charging for Services That Were Once Free

There is considerable evidence from my research that customers perceive reduced value when firms begin to charge them for services that were in the past offered for free. Customers encounter such situations regularly in banking, where charges are now imposed for a number of services which employees routinely delivered at no charge. They are also encountering this phenomenon in the travel industry, where travel agencies, because of commission caps imposed principally by airlines, are now charging fees for services that had been performed free. These service providers have already sent a message to their customers about what the service is worth—nothing. Now they charge for it, and because customers are unable to understand the costs incurred by the firm, they perceive reduced value.

Insufficient Emphasis on Employees

A rather obvious conclusion to be drawn from the comments made by customers is that many firms simply do not understand the importance of employees in the creation of value. Customers inherently understand and appreciate the importance of people in service provision. They comment when employees are unhelpful, when there is insufficient staffing at busy times, or when employees are constrained by rules and regulations from spending time with customers. Managers in service organizations often appear not to appreciate the importance of human resources principles in the provision of customer value. To create genuine value for customers, management must ensure that sufficient emphasis is placed on the employee component of value.

Systems and Processes Interfere

Finally, customers often comment on the little things that get in the way of value creation. They comment that companies make it difficult for customers to get through on the phone, don't call back when messages are left, put in place systems and processes that get in the way of efficient service delivery, provide inadequate procedures for notifying customers when service will be impaired or delays encountered, and so on. These irritants are impediments to service delivery, and they reflect a situation where management has given inadequate attention to access and convenience value.

How Well Do We Create Value?

Before a firm can improve on its delivery of value to its customers, it must understand two aspects of value: which forms of value are most appropriate for the market segments of interest and how well the company is currently performing in creating those forms of value. In much of the customer relationship analysis work that I do with clients, we incorporate a value measurement component that essentially looks at these two aspects. With this information, we can not only determine the comparative role of each form of value in influencing customers' overall satisfaction with the firm, but also determine the effect that improving value perception can have on customers' relationships with the firm. Such an analysis allows us to prepare a grid such as in Figure 4-4, which plots the importance of each form of customer value against the company's performance in delivering that form of value to its customers.

This presentation allows management in the client firm to determine how well the company is performing in increasing those forms of customer value that are of the greatest importance to customers. Obviously, separate versions of this grid may be prepared for various key customer segments, as the relative importance of the forms of value may vary across segments.

Interpretation of the value importance–performance grid is quite straightforward. Those forms of value that fall in the upper right quadrant represent those that the company can feel very good about; they are of relatively high importance to customers and the company is perceived to be performing well in delivering them. In the case of the results presented in Figure 4-4, this company appears to be doing well in creating value for its customers in those important areas of making its products and services accessible and conveniently available (B), providing employee service (D), making information available to customers (E), and making it possible for them to accomplish things (G).

Those in the upper left quadrant are forms of value that are of high importance to the customer but that the company is not seen to be delivering. These should be flagged for action. In the case presented in Figure 4-4, this company should

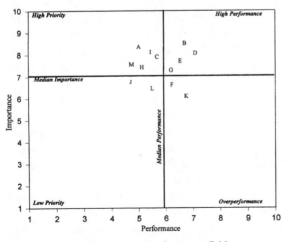

A: Product-for price
B: Access-convenience
C: Choice
D: Employee
E: Information
F: Association
G: Enabling
H: Relationship
I: Customer-unique
J: Surprise
K: Community
L: Memory
M: Experience

Figure 4-4 Value Importance–Performance Grid

direct its attention toward the creation of additional value in such important areas as product-for-price (A), treating customers as individuals (I), offering customers a variety of options (C), creating a memorable experience for customers (M), and generally making customers feel that they are a part of a genuine relationship (H).

Those forms of value that lie below the median on the vertical importance axis are those that customers do not consider particularly important in delivering overall value. As a result, it may be argued that the company should not pay particular attention to improving its performance in these areas. One proviso, however, may merit consideration. Those forms of value that fall into the lower right quadrant in the grid represent forms of value that customers do not feel are of particular importance, yet that the company is seen to be delivering very well—possibly overdelivering. These may represent wasted effort on the part of the firm, and its efforts in these directions may be better assigned to creating value on those forms of value that lie in the upper left quadrant. In the case of the results in Figure 4-4, this company appears to have been overinvesting in matters relating to the building of associations (F) and strengthening community ties (K), both of which appear not to be of particular importance to the customer segment which participated in this research project.

Value: The Essence of a Relationship

In this chapter we have examined the concept of customer value in some detail. This is necessary because of the critical role of value creation and maintenance in customer relationships. Managers must realize that unless they create and regularly add value for their customers, they will not succeed in creating any reason for the customer to stay. Without value being regularly provided, customers will perceive no differential advantage for one company over another, and thus no competitive advantage will have been created. Without value being created, there is no customer satisfaction, because customers do not willingly continue to do business with companies that provide them with little of value. And without sustained customer satisfaction, relationships do not develop.

Thus, an understanding of and appreciation for the creation of value for customers are critical components in a company's quest to establish genuine relationships with its customers. Other important messages from this chapter include the fact that value may be created for customers in many different ways, a number of which have been outlined briefly in this chapter. Undue emphasis on creating value for money is often misguided and may well succeed in turning away some potentially valuable customers. Finally, different customer segments attach different degrees of importance to different forms of value in different contexts. Like so many aspects of a company's striving for long-term customer satisfaction, this too is a moving target. Creating value for customers is not an easy task. It is one that demands management's constant attention.

5

The Nature of Relationships

The Emergence of a Relationship Orientation

The term *relationship marketing* began to find its way into the academic marketing literature and onto the pages of trade publications only in the late 1980s. In fact, my research suggests that the first use of the term is attributable to Professor Leonard Berry of Texas A&M University, in an American Marketing Association presentation in 1983.[1] From its inception, there has been little consensus concerning how the term should be used and to what form of marketing it should be applied. My view, as I expressed in Chapter 1, is that while the concept is new to the professional marketing lexicon, it is an approach to doing business that has been practiced for hundreds of years by enlightened business people who thought it was nothing special to treat their customers well so that they would come back again and again.

As the concept of relationship marketing became more mainstream in the early 1990s, and as more and more books and articles were written on the subject and more companies established a relationship marketing function or embarked upon relationship marketing programs, I became progressively more disillusioned with the concept as it was being discussed by some authors and speakers and applied in many organizations. My concerns centered around the use of the word "relationship." I had a clear view in my mind of how most people would use the term and the contexts in which they would think that they had a relationship with someone else or with an organization. My view was and still is that the word "relationship" has special meaning for most people and is reserved for those special situations where there is a genuine feeling and an emotional connection between—in most cases—two people.

---

[1] Leonard L. Berry, "Relationship Marketing," in *Emerging Perspectives on Services Marketing,* ed. Leonard L. Berry, G. Lynn Shostack, and Gregory D. Upah (Chicago: American Marketing Association, 1983), 25–28.

They Know When Relationships Exist

My view of what constitutes a relationship was buoyed by the feedback I received from real live consumers when I asked them in focus groups and depth interviews to describe for me those companies with whom they enjoyed dealing and to which they would go back time and time again, where they felt comfortable dealing with the firm and its employees and felt good about the interaction. Most consumers have no difficulty bringing such companies to mind as soon as they are asked to describe them. The companies with which customers have genuine relationships tend to be smaller firms with whom customers have been doing business for years; companies where they are greeted by name and are made to feel special.

Conversely, when customers are asked to talk about those companies with which they refuse to deal or those where the relationship is strained, they can name these as well. When they are asked to talk about why they won't deal with these firms or deal with them under duress, the reasons for their disappointment, many managers are surprised to learn, have little to do with the products and services sold by the company or the prices being charged, and a great deal more to do with the interaction with the company and its employees and with how the customer feels about how he or she is treated.

Consumers are protective of the word "relationship." They don't use it indiscriminately. When asked to talk about their relationships, regardless of context, not surprisingly they talk about family, friends, and neighbors. The closest relationships are with family, loved ones, and special friends. Generally less close, but still strong and lasting, are relationships with workmates, members of the soccer team or gardening club, or neighbors.

Consumers are also comfortable with the use of the word "relationship" in a business context, but its application is similarly limiting. Many consumers acknowledge having a relationship with retailers and service providers with whom they have been doing business for some time: hairdressers, neighborhood grocery stores, drugstores, and health care professionals. But when asked to describe their relationships with large companies such as major retail chains, banks, telephone, and electrical utilities, they are most likely to respond with comments such as: "that's not a relationship; I have no choice" or "it's entirely one-sided; I never talk with them," or, even worse, "to me, they're just a bill!"

Comments and observations such as these indicate that consumers do indeed acknowledge the existence of relationships with commercial entities, but that they reserve their use of the word itself for those special, close relationships they have with firms they trust, with whom they feel comfortable dealing and where they get something special from the interaction. With such firms, customers develop a genuine relationship, an emotional bond or loyalty that stands the test of time. They keep going back, not because they have to or have a financial incentive to so do, but because they feel rewarded in an emotional way.

Customers also acknowledge that not all business relationships are positive ones. Just as in our personal lives, there are some interactions or relationships that we are forced into; certain companies or organizations we have little or no choice but to deal with them. Similarly, consumers can speak eloquently about business relationships that were once strong and close but are now "at risk" or "on the rocks."

The literature on relationship marketing in the early 1990s for the most part did not approach the subject from the consumer's perspective. There are, of course, notable exceptions. In 1990, John Czepiel, Professor of Marketing at New York University, observed that a marketplace-based relationship is "the mutual recognition of some special status between exchange partners."[2] More recently, Susan Fournier and her colleagues, writing in the *Harvard Business Review*, refer to what relationship marketing is *supposed to be:* "the epitome of customer orientation."[3] They also write of their concern that the term *relationship marketing* has lost its meaning since going mainstream. They suggest that marketers, in their attempt to get closer to customers, have lost sight of what a true relationship is. This is evidenced, for example, in the use of customer databases, where there is often a lack of concern for privacy and intimacy.

I was quite disillusioned with what I read on the subject of relationship marketing in those early years. The approach generally taken by writers and practitioners focused primarily on database marketing, data mining, loyalty programs, and the creation of barriers to exit, none of which reflected the concept of a relationship as I envisioned it. I decided, therefore, that the best way for me to understand relationships in a business or marketing context was to try to understand the roots of interpersonal relationships. I discovered the work of researchers and authors in social psychology who have been conducting fascinating research on interpersonal relationships for 50 years or more. Much of what I read confirmed what I had suspected: that there is a great deal more to genuine relationships than providing attractive incentives to "target" individuals to enter the relationship, or making it impossible for them to leave. In fact, such activities are clearly contrary to the essence of a genuine interpersonal relationship.

I decided to borrow heavily from the work of these social psychologists, and in doing so I benefited greatly from the compendious work of Steve Duck, a

[2] John Czepiel, "Service Encounters and Service Relationships: Implications for Research," *Journal of Business Research* 20 (1990): 13–21.

[3] Susan Fournier, Susan Dobscha, and David Glen Mick, "Preventing the Premature Death of Relationship Marketing," *Harvard Business Review* 76 (January–February 1998): 42–44, at 44.

Professor of Psychology and Communications at the University of Iowa, who has written many articles and books on the subject of interpersonal relationships.[4] I concluded very early on that the principles inherent in the establishment and maintenance of relationships between two human beings could be applied more or less intact to the relationship between a company and its customers. The following is a short overview of what I learned.

What Is a Relationship, Anyway?

One of the drawbacks inherent in much of what has been written on relationship marketing is the lack of consideration given to what actually constitutes a relationship. Unfortunately, the social psychology literature does not provide a definitive answer, since most authors in that field begin by discussing the complexity and diversity of relationships and the resultant difficulties that occur in defining or classifying them. We are, therefore, missing a clear conceptualization of when a relationship can truly be said to exist. Conceivably, some people may term a certain interaction a relationship, while others may perceive the same interaction to be merely that, an interaction, devoid of the elements or characteristics constituting a relationship. Given that there is at best an arbitrary distinction between an interaction and a relationship, it may be useful to examine the various components or dimensions of interaction on which most relationships are based.

The customer, as the object of the firm's attention, must be considered when the concept of relationship building is discussed. *The objective must be to build a positive relationship from the perspective of the customer, not of the firm.* Surely a customer will not wish to return to a firm where the relationship is negative or where he or she does not perceive that an acceptable relationship exists. It is, therefore, quite likely that firms may feel that they have a relationship with their customers when no such relationship exists in the customers' minds. It continues to surprise me to encounter companies who feel that they have a relationship with their customers when that "relationship" is entirely defined by the amount that the customer spends with the firm.

Many companies seem to have embraced relationship marketing, and devoted sizeable resources to their efforts, with little examination of the bases of genuine relationships. Without this critical examination, many relationship marketing efforts will likely be off target. As a result, most of the initiatives companies are

---

[4] See, e.g., Steve Duck, *Friends, for Life: The Psychology of Close Relationships* (New York: St. Martin's Press, 1983), and id., *Meaningful Relationships: Talking, Sense, and Relating* (Thousand Oaks: Sage, 1994).

presently touting as relationship marketing are anything but. Many relationship marketing programs are not customer-focused but are based on either raising the switching costs for customers—locking them in with service contracts, security deposits or penalties for reopening—or relying on database-driven information to market "at" customers, whether or not they are interested in a relationship. The missing link that these companies do not understand is that having a relationship with a customer requires that there be a two-way interaction. There has to be a desire on the part of both parties to want to develop a relationship. However, even this is insufficient, as the desire to maintain the relationship must be grounded in emotion and feelings.

There's No Emotion

Something fundamental is missing in what is currently described by many authors and in many firms as relationship marketing: the emotional component of the relationship. Nowhere in many programs that fall under the relationship marketing banner is there any evidence of care or concern on the part of companies for how the customer is *made to feel* by the interaction. Companies may indicate that they are customer-focused, that they want to get closer to their customers, and that they want to develop a relationship with their customers. But all too often they are only paying lip service to these concepts. Once you get past the buzzwords and start to assess what companies are trying to do, you realize that they really have no concept of what it means to have relationships with their customers.

The emotions elicited from an interaction between a customer and a company or brand can take many forms and in many cases are independent of the core product or service delivered. Negative emotions result from the company failing to meet the expectations the customer brings to the interaction with the firm. On the other hand, positive emotions are aroused when the company succeeds in exceeding those expectations. As we observed in Chapter 3, most interaction with customers will likely elicit nothing special by way of emotions, as expectations are merely met. To put it in the terminology we introduced in that chapter, the performance of the company falls within the customer's zone of tolerance. The service is tolerable and does nothing to provoke an emotional response.

The company has the ability to arouse emotions in the customer because of the customer's experience in dealing with the company. As an example, a customer who has continuously had a very positive experience with a particular company will come to expect this high level of service each and every time he or she comes in contact with the company. If during the interaction the customer's expectations are not met, negative emotions are elicited that take the form of anger, regret, frustration, humiliation, or embarrassment. On the other hand, a customer whose expectations are exceeded by a particular company will have a positive experience and thus will feel positive emotions such as satisfaction, pride, and even surprise—the customer will be made to feel important and valued. While the company's level of service may cause the arousal of these feelings, it is more often the result of interaction with the company's employees, systems, and processes.

A good example of how a customer is made to feel in his or her dealings with a company relates to the all-too-often-experienced situation of having to wait for something. In a classic article written in the mid-1980s, David Maister addressed the "psychology" involved in making the customer wait.[5] His conclusions are well worth reading. He addresses the customer's perception of how long he or she has been waiting and the factors that contribute to that perception and to the eliciting of (mainly) negative emotions at having been made to wait longer than expected. While Maister was commenting principally on the physical process of waiting in a queue, much of the waiting that the customer of the 21st century does is virtual waiting—waiting for an e-mail response or for a Web page to load. Often we are put on hold by some automated telephone system and are exposed to "elevator music," unsolicited advertising for the firm we are calling, or regular reminders of how important our call is to them. What is the impact of such treatment on customer relationships?[6]

I can't help but think that many developing relationships are ended (or never get a chance to start) because the customer simply can't wait any longer and gives up in frustration and disgust—both emotions which are frequently voiced by customers. I have often observed that I would very much like to see the results of a research study to examine just how much business is lost with the introduction of interactive voice response telephone systems. They are a classic example of a corporate focus on cost reduction at the expense of customer service and relationship building, often cloaked in the argument that they are enhancing customer convenience. I recently met with senior marketing executives at Hong Kong and China Gas who told me that they had done such a study three years ago. This very customer-focused company concluded that their IVR system was getting in the way of their delivering superior service. So they took it out. Now, all callers reach a real live person. A great example of customer focus triumphing over technology and cost reduction.

While the thinking that customer satisfaction is linked to performance against customer expectations is certainly not new, emphasizing it is important. I suggest

[5] David Maister, "The Psychology of Waiting Lines," in *The Service Encounter,* ed. J. A. Czepiel, M. R. Solomon, and D. F. Suprenant (Lexington, Mass.: D.C. Heath, 1985), 113–23.

[6] Deborah K. Unzicker, "The Psychology of Being Put on Hold: An Exploratory Study of Service Quality," *Psychology and Marketing* 16 (July 1999): 327–50.

that a company that is able to elicit positive feelings from a customer's inter-actions with that company will place itself at a competitive advantage because the customer will be encouraged to continue the connection. The same customer will also want friends and family to have the same experience that he or she had and will be inclined to tell others.

Is a Relationship with a Supermarket Possible?

Much of the writing on relationship marketing has left important questions un-answered. For example, few marketing authors have addressed the question of when a relationship truly exists. What is the true nature of a relationship? Where does transactional marketing end and a customer relationship begin? Under what circumstances is it realistic for a marketer to consider establishing relationships with customers? Can a relationship be said to exist with a bank or an airline or a supermarket, or is the relationship necessarily with the employees of the com-pany?

Some marketing authors have questioned the authenticity of customer rela-tionships.[7] The decision to initiate what is considered a customer relationship is usually one-sided in that the company decides unilaterally to build a relationship with its customers. Thus, many companies purport to be building relationships through the creation of customer databases, generally without the consent of customers. The data maintained on customers are often shared throughout an organization (and occasionally outside), usually without the consent or knowl-edge of the customer, with attendant issues of privacy and confidentiality of information.

The building of customer relationships has particular relevance for firms op-erating in service industries. While it may be argued that all organizations are service providers to greater or lesser degrees, those firms that deliver services as their core "product" would appear to have the potential to benefit most from the application of the concept of relationships. This is so because such firms depend on people for the delivery of services and because a "relationship" is essentially a people-centered concept. In fact, one of the characteristics of ser-vices most often pointed out is the *inseparability* of a service from the person providing it. This notion of inseparability breaks down somewhat when services are increasingly delivered by technology, but the provision of most forms of service still depends greatly on the involvement of people. Therefore, the op-

---

[7] M. K. Hogg et al., "Touch Me, Hold Me, Squeeze Me: Privacy—The Emerging Issue for Relationship Marketing in the 1990s." in *Emerging Issues in Marketing,* Proceedings of the 1993 Annual Conference of the Marketing Education Group of the United King-dom, Loughborough University, July 1993, 504–14.

portunity exists for genuine relationships to be established between the people who represent the service providers and the people who are their customers.

It appears obvious that, as individuals, we tend to develop relationships with other individuals; that is the context in which the term *relationship* is most frequently applied. We tend not to use the term *relationship* to apply to our interaction with inanimate objects. As an "interpersonal" concept, the idea of establishing a relationship with a customer would appear likely to work best in situations where there is a considerable interaction between customers and staff; where customers have the opportunity to establish relationships which are not particularly different in form from those they have established with other people: family, friends, neighbors, and coworkers.

Many firms appear not to appreciate the fact that relationships are principally interpersonal interactions, with a considerable emotional component. This raises many issues, including the fundamental question whether it is possible for a company, as an essentially impersonal entity, to form a genuine, close relationship with a customer. It is valuable to examine the social psychology origins of the concept of relationships in an attempt to determine the extent to which the concept can be applied in a customer–firm context. What conditions must be present in the interaction between a firm and its customers in order for a relationship to be said to exist? Can a fleeting, technology-based interaction be said to be a relationship? What if it occurs frequently or on a regular basis? What distinguishes a relationship, in the mind of the customer, from a series of interactions? What conditions are necessary for the interactions to be considered a relationship?

The point is that the principles of relationship establishment are the same, regardless of whether the individual's relationship is with another person, a company, a brand, a sports team, or other organization. The relationship has to be felt; the customer knows when it's more than a transient event or interaction.

Characteristics of Strong Relationships: Why They Last

Relationships are "extremely complex entities that need careful management and demand skills from their participants at all times." *Relationshipping,* as Steve Duck terms it, is actually "a very complicated and prolonged process with many pitfalls and challenges. Relationships do not just happen; they have to be made—made to start, make to work, made to develop, kept in good working order and preserved from going sour." [8]

---

[8] Steve Duck, *Understanding Relationships* (New York: Guilford Press, 1991), 3.

One of the most interesting features of a relationship is that it is a continuous process. Every interaction has the potential to change it. Another observation from Steve Duck. "Relationships are at least not permanent stations or states so much as temporary transitions."[9] Accordingly, once a relationship is formed, a great deal of effort must be expended on maintaining it as a healthy, viable alliance. Throughout most of the social psychology literature, two key factors emerge as vital to the maintenance of relationships: commitment and trust. Many other factors, of course, have been linked to the establishment and maintenance of close relationships. Some of these "dimensions of relationships" are presented in Figure 5-1. This list has been developed in part from a review of the social psychology literature on interpersonal relationships and in part from my research with the customers of many companies over many years.

Roger Bennett of London Guildhall University makes the very important observation that "to initiate a relationship, one of the parties (invariably the supplying firm in a marketing situation) must present an attractive proposition [the value proposition] to the other side and, crucially, has to be liked."[10] Bennett goes on to comment that likeability is closely related to sincerity, dependability, truthfulness, thoughtfulness, and consideration, all of which are connected to trust. Other factors commonly associated with attraction and attractiveness of a relationship partner are ease and frequency of interaction; propinquity—feelings of closeness, familiarity, and nearness; similarity—possessing similar values, attitudes, and perspectives; mutuality—sharing of goals and a sense of "being in this together"; and interdependence—the sense of relying on the other party in order to achieve certain goals.

• trust, ethics	• dependability
• commitment	• awareness of history
• reliability	• two-way communications
• attachment	• warmth, intimacy
• understanding, empathy	• interest in needs
• mutual goals	• knowledge
• shared values	• responsiveness
• reciprocity	• keeping of promises
• respect, sincerity	• social support, community
• caring, affection, liking	• competency

Figure 5-1 Dimensions of Relationships

[9] Ibid., "Relationships as Unfinished Business: Out of the Frying Pan and into the 1990s," *Journal of Social and Personal Relationships* 7 (1990): 5–28, at 9.

[10] Roger Bennett, "Relationship Formation and Governance in Consumer Markets: Transactional Analysis versus the Behaviourist Approach," *Journal of Marketing Management* 12 (1996): 417.

These characteristics or dimensions of relationships all point to the existence of feelings as the basis for genuine relationships. These are present in different proportions in different relationships. This supports the contention that relationships are exceedingly complex concepts, which differ across individuals and in different settings. Clearly, different things are important to different people in establishing and maintaining relationships with other people and, it may be suggested, with companies, organizations, and brands. Different customers will want different experiences and different treatment in dealing with a firm and may want to be treated in one way by a firm in one industry or one situation and differently again by other firms in other settings. The challenge to a marketer who wishes to create an atmosphere conducive to the establishment and maintenance of positive customer relationships is to learn what is important to customers and to segments of customers in dealing with firms in their industries. Individual differences of customers notwithstanding, the following are generally considered to be the more important elements of interpersonal relationships.

Trust

This is the factor that has probably received the most attention in the literature on interpersonal and customer relationships. Several definitions of trust have been proposed, including "confidence that one will find what is desired from another, rather than what is feared"; the idea that trust involves a willingness to act in a certain manner because of confidence that the partner will provide the expected gratifications; and "a generalized expectancy held by an individual that the word, promise, or statement of another individual can be relied on." [11] In most of the social psychology literature, trust is often mentioned in conjunction with love and commitment as a cornerstone of the ideal relationship. Several critical elements of trust are:

1. Trust evolves out of past experience and prior action.
2. Dispositional characteristics are attributed to the partner, such as reliability and dependability.
3. Trust involves a willingness to put oneself at risk.
4. Trust involves feelings of confidence and security in the partner.

These components of trust may be labeled as predictability, dependability, and faith.[12] Predictability is reflected by customers saying they deal with a certain

---

[11] J. K. Rempel, J. G. Holmes, and M. P. Zanna, "Trust in Close Relationships," *Journal of Personality and Social Psychology* 49 (1985): 45–112, at 95.
[12] Ibid, 97.

firm because "I can count on them." Dependability results when a relationship progresses to the point where emphasis shifts away from specific behavior toward an evaluation of the qualities of the individual—trust is placed in the person, not the specific actions. Faith reflects a sense of security on the part of customers that they can have some confidence that the relationship partner will "look after them."

From a marketing point of view, this suggests that the development of trust, and especially faith, should be a fundamental component of any marketing strategy that is intended to lead to the creation of genuine customer relationships. The customer must be able to feel that he or she can rely on the firm; that the company can be trusted. However, trust takes time to build and can only be developed after repeated encounters with customers. More importantly, trust develops after an individual puts himself or herself at risk with the partner. This suggests that the building of trusting relationships with customers may be more possible in certain industry sectors—principally those that involve some risk for the customer in the short term or necessitate a long-term obligation.

Commitment

Not surprisingly, one of the key factors that determines the success of a relationship is each individual's commitment to it. Robert Morgan and Shelby Hunt observe that "commitment and trust are 'key' because they encourage marketers to (1) work at preserving relationship investments by co-operating with exchange partners, (2) resist attractive short-term alternatives in favor of the expected long-term benefits of staying with existing partners, and (3) view potentially high-risk action as being prudent because of the belief that their partners will not act opportunistically." [13]

Given the importance of commitment to a relationship, perhaps the most appropriate question to ask is, "What is commitment?" Commitment is "a psychological state that globally represents the experience of dependence on a relationship; commitment summarizes prior experiences of dependence and directs reactions to new situations." [14] It represents a long-term orientation to the relationship, including a desire to maintain the relationship, both in good times and bad. While the importance of commitment is obvious in close personal relationships, it is less so in relationships between firms and their customers, where, not uncommonly, customers will cease doing business with a particular company

[13] R. M. Morgan, and S. D. Hunt, "The Commitment-Trust Theory of Relationship Marketing," *Journal of Marketing* 58(3) (1994): 20–38, at 22.
[14] C. E. Rusbult, and B. P. Buunk, "Commitment Processes in Close Relationships: An Interdependence Analysis," *Journal of Social and Personal Relationships* 10 (1993): 175–204, at 180.

in order to take advantage of a "deal" or a business will decide that it no longer wishes to do business with particular customers because they have been deemed to be in a "less valuable" segment.

Two key attributes have been identified that determine the magnitude of a person's commitment to a relationship: satisfaction level and level of investment. Two main components of satisfaction exist: (1) the degree to which a relationship provides valued outcomes by fulfilling important needs, and (2) the *comparison level of alternatives,* which is based on a qualitative expectation of what a relationship's outcomes ought to be in an ideal involvement, as well as a comparison of one's own outcomes to partner's inputs and outcomes.

The notion that "individuals feel more committed when they believe they have poor quality alternatives to their relationships"[15] is an interesting one. For the business that is dealing in a highly competitive environment, it implies that the firm's ability to create a lasting relationship with a customer is determined not only by its own actions, but also by the actions of its competitors. The firm that can differentiate itself successfully from its competitors may have a better chance of creating relationships than the firm that cannot. On the other hand, having customers who are "loyal" merely because they perceive no attractive alternatives suggests a vulnerable state and borders on the situation where the customer feels that he or she is "locked in."

Investment

The size of an individual's investment in a relationship also influences his or her commitment to it. Generally, investment resources include time, emotional energy, personal sacrifice, and other indirect investments, such as shared memories, mutual friends, and activities or possessions that are uniquely linked to a relationship. A sense of having invested a great deal in a relationship inspires a commitment in the individual to making it work; abandoning it would mean wasting the investment. If one applies this to marketing, organizational attempts to increase the barriers to exit, such as the development of rewards programs, are consistent with this theory of relationship commitment, although such a definition may not be consistent with the customer's view of what constitutes a genuine relationship.

I have observed in my research that some customers who have several thousand points accumulated in a frequent-flyer program or other loyalty program may express their preference to leave for another service provider but feel that

[15] Ibid., 182.

they cannot because of their "investment" in the program. Can we term this a close relationship?

Similarly, small business people often comment in negative terms about their relationships with their banks. Yet when I ask them why they do not switch their business to another financial institution, they are likely to comment, "What, and have to break in a new banker?" The implication is that they have developed a relationship with "their" banker, who knows their file and that it has taken a certain amount of time and effort to get to this stage. To abandon this, however difficult the relationship may be at present, would mean abandoning the investment that has been made.

Many companies see evidence of the concept of the customer's investment in a relationship when they receive complaints from customers. How many complaint letters begin something like this? "My family has been a loyal customer of your company for more than forty years. . . ." The implication here is simple—I've got a lot invested in this relationship and I expect a payback in the form of good service; we don't deserve to be treated like this!

Dependence

Relationships are undoubtedly characterized by a certain degree of dependence. Without it, there would be no relationship. Insofar as the relationship is formed in the first place to satisfy certain needs for both parties, each party relies on the other to satisfy certain of those needs. It may be correct to observe that the nature of the dependence in a customer relationship is different than it is in an interpersonal relationship. While the customer relies on the company for the satisfaction of a series of needs, both functional and emotional, the needs that are being satisfied for the company tend for the most part to be related to revenues and profits. The same may not be true, however, for the individual employees of the firm, who may rely on their customers for the satisfaction of more personal needs.

It is also useful to distinguish between nonvoluntary and voluntary dependence. According to research in social psychology, those individuals who are voluntarily dependent on their partners and who perceive poor alternatives to the relationship are both dependent and *satisfied*. On the other hand, those individuals who are dependent on a relationship, yet see better alternatives to their present situation, are not voluntarily dependent and are therefore somewhat dissatisfied or entrapped. Thus, forcing dependence may actually decrease an individual's commitment to that relationship, not increase it. Companies that do business with customers in an environment characterized by nonvoluntary dependence have a real challenge to engender in their customers a genuine feeling of relationship. This is the case in monopoly situations or environments that customers perceive to be near monopolies.

Two-Way Communications

One of the most fundamental characteristics of a relationship that is working is two-way communications. We have all seen that when communication is not ongoing, the state of a relationship is likely to deteriorate. The same is true of a relationship between a company and its customers. The strongest relationships, as we will discuss in Chapter 7, are those between small businesses and their customers, where there is frequent contact and relaxed dialogue.

Customers regularly refer to the existence of communications as evidence of a relationship. When a customer complains that "I never hear from them" or "They don't return my calls" or "All they even send me is a bill," he or she is really saying that there is no regular flow of communications between the company and the customer. The same is true of those "relationships" that are built on a direct mail program, where communication with the customer is almost completely one-way. The company sends things in the mail, or increasingly by e-mail, and the customer disregards them. This is certainly not a relationship from the customer's perspective, even though the company may think it is.

Attachment

While communications is a behavioral or action dimension of a relationship, a sense of attachment is much more emotive. Most researchers will agree that a close relationship is characterized by genuine feelings toward the other party: feelings of attachment, liking, or affection. We deal with a company because we like it or the people who work there; we feel a certain attachment toward them or share certain values or goals. This attachment contributes to the sense of closeness which is so fundamental to a relationship and which we will discuss later in this chapter. Customers will comment on this regularly in focus group sessions. They may refer to their having a certain "comfort level." Or, as the telephone technician commented in Dublin, referring to the staff and students of the business school where he is permanently assigned: "We're all like family here."

Reciprocity

Within solid interpersonal relationships, reciprocity is the norm, and it serves an important function. Steve Duck points out that the relationship between two people is most often defined by what the people in it provide for one another, the resources that they distribute and the exchange that takes place.[16] In the context of customer relationships, this implies that the nature of the firm's relationship with the customer is determined by what the customer receives in return. Therefore, we can expect that a customer would wish to have a different form of relationship with different service providers. For example, a customer is unlikely to wish to have the same relationship with an auto mechanic or a travel agent that he or she has with a bank or a medical doctor.

What form of reciprocity exists between a service provider and its customers in a client relationship is an important question. Many interactions that some marketers consider to be relationships with customers are decidedly one-sided. If a relationship is characterized by reciprocity, we need to examine what each party provides for the other and the nature of the exchange that takes place. Clearly, for a relationship to exist, what is exchanged must go beyond the obvious goods and services, on the one hand, and money on the other; these are the stuff of transactions, not relationships.

Relationships that are mutually regarded and that both parties wish to perpetuate must, of necessity, convey reciprocal benefits to both sides. It might be useful to consider what the firm must receive for it to acknowledge that it is in a relationship with a client. Presumably the firm wishes to experience the obverse of the things that the customer desires, the benefits of long-term patronage: retention of the client's business; the stream of earnings associated with repeat purchasing; even the associated results of referrals and positive word-of-mouth. But what of the employees of the firm? Do they feel that they are in a satisfying relationship with a customer if all that is received are the fruits of repeat business? Might they also wish to experience something of the feelings that are experienced by customers themselves, such as feelings of trust, commitment, and being appreciated.

Shared Benefits

Consideration of the relationship benefits that the firm derives from its involvement with its customers has for the most part been limited to the financial reasons, or at least the business case, for fostering customer relationships. There has been very little reference in the literature to the more emotional benefits to be gained by the firm and its employees.

In a study of the relationship benefits experienced by customers, researchers identified three sets of benefits over and above the performance of the core product or service: (1) *confidence benefits,* relating to reduction of risk, trusting the firm, increased confidence in the service, and reduced anxiety; (2) *social*

---

[16]Duck, *Understanding Relationships.*

benefits, associated with recognition by employees, familiarity and friendship with employees, and being called by name; and (3) *special treatment benefits,* linked to receiving special deals and discounts, preferential treatment, little favors, and faster service.[17]

What the firm gains from being in close relationships with its customers might be expected to parallel what the customer gains. Just as the customer wishes to receive more than just the tangible, financial aspects of transactions, so might the firm (or at least some firms) be interested in the more emotional side of dealing with its customers. For example, it may be valuable to consider the effect of close customer relationships on the morale of employees and on their productivity. Where close customer relationships are present, what benefits does the employee derive? Probably greater job satisfaction, a sense of being appreciated, even greater loyalty to the firm. Such results may represent additional benefits to be derived from close customer relationships that have not yet been studied in any depth in the relationship marketing literature.

Mutuality

One social psychologist observes that

> a relationship implies first some sort of intermittent interaction between two people, involving interchanges over an extended period of time. The interchanges have some degree of mutuality, in the sense that the behavior of each takes some account of the behaviors of the other. However this mutuality does not necessarily imply "co-operation" in its everyday sense: relationships exist between enemies as well as between friends, between those who are forced into each other's company as well as between those who seek it."

In addition, there is "the further implication that there is some degree of continuity between the successive interactions. Each interaction is affected by interactions in the past, and may affect interactions in the future." [18]

This observation suggests that relationships are not necessarily positive, that situations in which participants in the relationships are forced together against their will (or possibly against the will of one of them) are still relationships. But this is precisely the situation in what I refer to later in this book as "taken-for-granted" service situations. Often, where customers have no choice but to

---

[17] Kevin P. Gwinner, Dwayne D. Gremler, and Mary Jo Bitner, "Relational Benefits in Services Industries: The Customer's Perspective," *Journal of the Academy of Marketing Science* 26(2) (1998): 101–14.

[18] R. A. Hinde, *Towards Understanding Relationships* (London: Academic Press, 1979), 14.

deal with a particular service provider, as historically has been the case with some public utilities, for example, they tend to take the provision of the service for granted and generally do not perceive that any relationship exists between them and the service provider. In fact, some voice the wish to be released from the "relationship" if only some viable alternative existed.

Genuine Customer Relationships

Examining the foundations of interpersonal relationships, as documented in the social psychology literature, provides marketers with true insight into factors that can add value in developing customer relationships. In consumer markets, the importance of taking the customer's point of view is vital, for in most cases it is the customer who is being courted. It is also usually the customer who decides that the relationship is over. How should relationships be defined in order to convey the customer's perspective? First, for a relationship to exist, it has to be *mutually* perceived to exist; that is, acknowledged to exist by both partners. Secondly, a relationship has to go beyond occasional contact to some *special status,* suggesting that a relationship is difficult to define but the partners will know when one exists. Obviously, relationships involve more than these two characteristics, but in their absence, it cannot be said that a true *relationship* exists. As evidenced by the parallel that organizations have drawn between loyalty programs, database marketing, and relationship marketing, it appears that these characteristics of genuine relationships have yet to be fully recognized.

A relationship is more than repeat buying or retention. While the behavioral components are an indication that a relationship may exist, they do not define the relationship. A relationship implies loyalty, emotions, and positive feelings toward something or someone. When a customer speaks of "her hairdresser" with a sense of ownership, pride and positive feelings, it is apparent that a relationship exists. As well, relationships vary in how close and intimate they are. For example, what may be mistaken for a relationship may really be a sense of familiarity or rapport. A customer may shop at the same convenience store for years and be familiar with the staff, but the nature of the interaction does not necessarily mean that a relationship has been created.

Just as people know the extent and form of their personal relationships, they also know whether they have a relationship with a business and, if so, how close that relationship is. Many authors and researchers have attempted to define customer relationships in behavioral terms that are based on frequency of contact, length of time the customer has been dealing with a vendor, and how much information is in the database. Although these elements will provide insight into the dynamics of the interaction, they cannot be used to define the relationship. In order to do this, we must first look at the dimensions in Figure 5-1 that are based on personal relationships but hold meaning in customer relationships as well.

Participants in many focus group interviews that I have conducted have discussed companies and organizations with which they have positive relationships. The results from these focus groups have confirmed that relationships with companies do exist and that they can take the form of relationships in a social context. Participants have offered comments such as "You really feel that they are telling the truth," "They go out of their way to help you," "When trying to contact them, it is always busy; very frustrating." Statements such as these that have led me to conclude that it is the emotional link that makes a relationship possible in a consumer context.

Levels of Relationships

Relationships between companies and their customers may be considered to exist at four different levels. The closest are *intimate* relationships. These are characterized as personal, friendly relationships and generally involve the disclosure of personal information. Many are high-involvement situations, where the customer places his or her trust in the service provider. Intimate relationships may actually involve physical touching such as customers experience with hairdressers, dentists, and doctors. These are the relationships that we would normally associate with the traditional definition of a relationship, one that is very personal and intimate.

Face-to-face customer relationships involve a broader series of interactions for most consumers. We have such relationships most often in a retail context, where customers may become well known to retail clerks, bank employees, hotel managers, and receptionists. Such relationships, although they involve face-to-face meeting and conversation, do not deal with the same subject matter as the intimate relationship. They will often develop in retail situations, in hotels and banks, or with auto mechanics. While there is face-to-face contact, the interaction is not of a personal nature and does not involve the disclosure of personal information.

Distant relationships include interaction that is likely less frequent, is carried on via technology, and involves few if any physical meetings. Examples include the customer's relationships with utility companies and Internet service providers. This type of interaction is becoming increasingly more prevalent as technology becomes more closely interwoven with our daily lives. Customers are increasingly interacting with employees or with IVR systems over the telephone or conducting their business with a company through the Internet. Interaction that in the past would have required a meeting or at least a telephone conversation can now be conducted through touch-tone telephone systems, e-mail, and interactive websites. Such relationships raise many issues for business organizations. In Chapter 10 we will discuss issues such as whether it is possible to develop and sustain meaningful customer relationships entirely or even primarily through a technology interface.

The final category of relationships that customers have with business organizations involves situations where a customer may rarely or never have occasion to make contact directly with a company or its employees. We all have hundreds of such relationships. Most of us will go through life never having met a representative of Pepsi-Cola, Heinz, Michelin, or Levi's. The physical contact with a company that makes some of the world's best known products is usually conducted through agents: distributors and retailers. Does that mean that we do not feel a certain attachment to these brands and even to the companies that manufacture them? Such *brand* relationships do exist. They are a special kind of customer relationship that does not require physical contact or even a personal meeting to be strong. What is important is the connection established between the customer and "his" or "her" brand and what the brand stands for in the customer's mind. We will examine the concept of brand relationships more completely in Chapter 11.

Consumers often describe certain relationships, such with their hairdressers and doctors, as close and personal. They maintain contact on an ongoing basis and often refer to them as "my hairdresser" or "my doctor." A sense of "ownership" evolves over time out of trust that is built between customer and service provider. The customer trusts the hairdresser or doctor to deliver consistent, personal, high-quality service, and the service provider trusts the customer to maintain contact through repeat business and referrals.

People will often say that they feel guilty when they try a new hairdresser. Why guilty? After all, it is the consumer's choice. The guilt comes from feeling that they have let someone down by not upholding their part of the relationship, by seeking out another person to fulfill that need. Often, as well, the hairdresser will feel disappointed or even betrayed when a customer goes to someone else.

This sense of guilt is not often reported when people choose an alternative long-distance telephone provider or a different airline. The customer seldom feels the same sense of loyalty to these businesses. As well, customers will seldom feel guilty about changing brands of laundry detergent, shampoo, or breakfast cereal. But many consumers do develop such strong attachment to particular brands that are very disappointed when for some reason they are no longer available. The relationships that customers have at this level are genuine relationships, and although they are not characterized by the same high levels of personal involvement as the relationship with a doctor or dentist, they nevertheless elicit strong feelings and emotions. "Building the brand" has become a common phrase, but only a limited number of brands truly understand what it means to have a genuine relationship with their customers.

The Transaction–Relationship Continuum

It is useful to view the contact between businesses and their customers on a continuum, ranging from discrete, one-off transactions at one end to relational exchanges at the other. Near the transaction end are exchanges that are discrete, short-term, and often mechanical, with little commitment on either side. The purchase of a chocolate bar from a machine is an example. At the opposite end is a relationship that is ongoing, complex, highly personal, and characterized by trust and discretion. The relationship between patient and physician is an example. At some point along this continuum, a transaction approach to marketing ceases to be appropriate and the possibility for the establishment of a genuine relationship begins.

Once a true relationship is said to exist, it becomes more than a one-sided attempt on the part of the seller or marketer to tie in the customer to a longer-term commitment; the customer may actually take "ownership" in the company to the point that he or she will begin to refer to it as "my bank" or "my supermarket," in much the same way that customers refer to "my" doctor, lawyer, or hairdresser. An important question is when the conditions are appropriate for such ownership to take form and whether many marketers can ever expect their customers to get to "my." [19]

Even though a relationship continuum exists, this is not to say that relationships can be placed along the continuum from intimate relationships to brand relationships. It is possible to increase the closeness and strength of a relationship regardless of the level at which it exists. For instance, an electrical utility has a distant, technology-based relationship with its customers. This leaves the company in a vulnerable position if competition enters the market. In order to improve its relationships with customers, the company must increase its communication with them and convey its concern for customers. A well-executed

Figure 5-2 Transaction—Relationship Continuum

[19] James G. Barnes, "Close to the Customer: But Is It Really a Relationship?" *Journal of Marketing Management* 10 (1994): 561–70.

communications plan that adds value for the customer is one way to strengthen the relationship. While challenging, it is possible for an electrical utility and other organizations that typically are not "close" to their customers to develop genuine relationships.

Relationships, regardless of whether they are intimate, face-to-face, or distant, may exist at any point on the continuum. While relationships with hairdressers will likely be closer to the warmer, "relationship" end of the continuum, some people never establish close relationships with hairdressers, preferring to go from salon to salon, possibly because their physical appearance is simply not a particularly important or high-involvement matter. By the same token, the kinds of relationships that we describe as "distant" are more likely to be farther along the continuum toward the transaction end. Yet we do find in our research customers who will describe their relationships with their telephone company as very close, and we do encounter customers who have developed lasting, loyal relationships with companies over the Internet.

Conditions Conducive to Relationship Growth

Firms that try to form relationships with customers will find that it is not easy to move customers towards a relationship. Customers can sometimes be wary of a firm's motives when suddenly they receive phone calls, letters, and displays of concern. Just as in personal relationships, people tend to pull away from sudden advances by those to whom they have not been close in the past.

Conditions that are conducive to relationship building do exist. These include frequent contact, face-to-face interaction, two-way communication, knowledge and information, familiarity, customer involvement, and the ability to add value. While not all of these are available to every firm, any firm can take some steps to increase contact with customers, solicit their opinions and concerns, and add value for them by improving service. By doing these things in a systematic, nonintrusive manner, firms can build trust with their customers, thereby addressing one of the fundamental dimensions of a genuine relationship.

Out of the research I have completed over the years in customer relationships and their growth, I have identified several conditions conducive to this growth. Some of these I have already discussed, but it is important that management and employees recognize these conditions when building customer relationships. Figure 5-3 lists some of these conditions.

The nature of the interaction is an obvious factor in the growth of the relationship. For instance, a customer who has divulged personal information will be less likely to switch suppliers, which would mean having to divulge this information again. Because that customer has invested time and energy in the

- physical proximity, access
- extent of personal contact
- length of time invested
- complexity of the task
- ease of two-way communication
- added value through service
- dealing with the same people
- frequency of contact
- continuity of contact
- perception of high risk
- customer lacks expertise
- level of involvement
- intimacy
- switching costs

Figure 5-3 Conditions Conducive to Relationship Growth

relationship, the switching costs for changing companies are great. Thus, the customer's level of involvement in the relationship will affect his or her willingness to seek out other suppliers.

The more accessible the company, the greater the opportunity for communication to occur. However, not all customers want to communicate with a company in the same manner. Thus, companies must have multiple channels in place for customers to access the company, such as toll-free numbers, e-mail, and the Internet.

The extent of the personal contact necessary relates to the personalization of the contact. If a customer of a large corporation tends to deal with an individual employee or a small group of employees, that customer is better able to begin to develop a relationship with the firm. Customers may come to perceive these individuals as experts in their field. This provides a certain comfort zone because customers know that their welfare with the company is in good hands.

Closeness in Customer Relationships

The concept of closeness has considerable value in relationship marketing. Relationships which consumers deem to be "close" are, by implication, those which are likely to endure. According to social psychologists, some relationships are closer than others, and different groups of individuals may be more or less prone to establishing of close relationships. I would suggest that the closeness concept captures many of the emotional aspects of relationships. Relationships cannot exist without emotional content—close relationships are characterized by positive affective ties. The intensity or strength of the emotions present in a relationship tend to determine the likelihood of the relationship continuing. Strong, close relationships are less vulnerable and more likely to continue into the future.

In a series of research studies that I conducted, participants were asked to rate how close they felt to service providers in three industries: banking, grocery, and telecommunications. Customers were asked to base their ratings on their main provider of financial services, their main supermarket, and their main telephone company. Most scores were in the medium range, indicating that few people felt very close to either of these service providers. Of the three industries, respondents answered that they were closest to their main bank. Figure 5.4 shows the distribution of the closeness scores.

The difference in closeness across the three industries is not surprising. Customers feel closer to their banks (or at least did so) in part because of the level of involvement and the salience of financial matters. More recent research that takes into account the growth in the use of technology in banking, with the near-universal use of ATMs in many countries and the rapid diffusion of telephone banking and Internet banking, indicates that banking relationships are currently much less close than they were even five years ago. The relationship with a customer's main supermarket is almost as close as the banking relationship, likely because of the frequency of interaction and the growth in familiarity over time. Finally, telecommunications companies suffer from the classic taken-for-granted effect. As we will discuss in greater detail in Chapter 9, these companies are victims of their own success. Because of the advances made in technology, the service almost always works and there is no need for most of their customer ever to interact with installers, service personnel, or even operators.

The Impact of Closeness

As customers become closer to a firm and its employees, there is a positive effect on the customer's interactions with the business. For instance, customers

Table 5-1 Distribution of Closeness Scores

Score	Banking	Grocery	Telcom
Low (1–5)	32.5%	38.9%	54.5%
Medium (6–8)	50.0%	45.0	35.7
High (9–10)	17.3	6.1	9.8
Mean	6.540	6.279	5.494

who are very close to a business (rate their closeness at 9 or 10 on a 10-point scale) are more likely to have a greater share of their business with that firm. As well, they are more likely to refer other customers and stay with the firm than those customers who feel less close to the firm. As indicated in Table 5-2, the likelihood to refer and the likelihood to stay are dramatically affected by the closeness score, especially in the retail banking and grocery industries. Even small improvements in closeness have a large impact on a customer's behavior with respect to referrals and retention. The conventional wisdom is correct that "getting closer to the customer" is a good thing. The problem many companies and organizations encounter is that management has no idea how to increase that closeness or is not committed to providing the resources needed to increase the customer's sense of closeness.

The results of this research suggest that management should be very interested in the closeness of their customer relationships and should set out to measure and manage that closeness. Closeness does vary from one industry to another and across segments of customers, and some customers prefer less close relationships. However, closeness contributes to longer-lasting, more valuable relationships and is a leading factor in the referrals of new customers.

There are steps an organization can take to achieve greater closeness with its customers. First, it is usually necessary to increase the frequency of contact. Customers are more likely to feel close to a company that makes regular, meaningful contact, regardless of how that contact is made. Secondly, whenever possible, a company has to make face-to-face or personal contact with the customer. This is difficult to do in organizations where technology is used to deliver the service. However, periodic phone calls can boost the customer's feelings about the human content of the service.

While some situations and particular industries are conducive to forming close personal relationships that are intimate or face-to-face, in others the restrictions

Table 5-2 The Impact of Closeness

	Banking	Grocery	Telecom
Share of business			
Low (1–5)	88.4%	76.6%	83.9%
Medium (6–8)	93.2	80.1	92.8
High (9–10)	94.0	84.5	92.1
Very likely to stay			
Low (1–5)	64.0%	63.0%	80.3%
Medium (6–8)	88.4	79.4	84.1
High (9–10)	94.1	83.1	86.8
Very likely to refer			
Low (1–5)	36.0%	48.3%	57.5%
Medium (6–8)	75.5	68.6	64.9
High (9–10)	88.4	81.0	97.2

of distribution channels and customer interaction make this more difficult. In this case, companies should focus on establishing brand relationships. By doing so, they can reduce the likelihood that customers will defect when employees leave. We will discuss this important idea in greater depth in Chapter 11.

The *closeness gap* is an important concept in determining where to place resources to strengthen the relationship and increase closeness with customers. The gap identifies the current level of customer closeness as compared with how close the customer would like to feel towards the company. I will discuss this in greater detail in Chapter 8, but for the moment it is important to understand that the closeness gap for each customer segment can be determined. This is accomplished by first asking customers to rate how close they feel to a particular company compared to other companies with which they deal. They are then asked how close they would like to be to that company. For instance, if a customer segment has a mean closeness score of 5.8 but only wants to be a 6.0, this suggests that the closeness level is fairly close to where customers want it to be, and that perhaps resources should be placed on other segments where there is a greater desire for closeness. Another customer segment may have a mean closeness score of 6.2. This may sound better than the 5.8, but if the segment would like to be at a closeness level of 7.5, clearly there is a very long way to go, and the company should probably put in place programs to get closer to its customers.

It may even be possible to have a negative closeness gap. We see this in a small percentage of customers, where the customer feels closer to the company than he or she would like to be. In this case, the company needs to understand that the customer does not desire a close relationship and treat him or her accordingly. Such customers will say that they do not want frequent contact from, for example, their financial institution or telephone company. They want the service available when they need it, and nothing else. The company has to recognize this through a customer's response to the company's attempts to build the relationship. If repeated attempts to get closer to the customer are rejected, ignored, or met with hostility, then the company has to accept that this customer is not open to a close relationship and wants to build a relationship on his or her own terms. It would be better in this case for the company to focus its efforts on other customers rather than risk driving these customers to a competitor in search of the anonymity or distance they desire.

What the Customer Wants (and Says)

The best way to learn whether a genuine relationship exists between a company and its customers, or if one is possible, might be to listen to what customers have to say about their interactions with firms. In my research with customers of many companies, I have found that customers use similar language to describe their business relationships and their interpersonal relationships. They regularly refer to how they are treated and how they are made to feel by businesses. Comments such as "They are almost like family," "They are honest with me," and "They deliver on their promises" show that some companies are closer to establishing positive, long-term, close relationships with their customers than are others. Comments such as "They try to avoid me," "They talk down to me," and "They never apologize" indicate that some companies still have a long way to go before they create the value and satisfaction that is associated with relationship building.

The key ingredient in the cultivation of mutually rewarding customer relationships is that firms must place considerable effort into getting to know the expectations of their customers regarding the development of a relationship. Not only is it important to become closer to the customer, the firm must understand the types of customers with whom they should be developing closer relationships, how close they can expect to get, what constitutes closeness for the customer, and how the firm can best become closer. These questions and more are critical to the development of a closer relationship. Without knowing the answers to these questions, firms will find it nearly impossible to become closer to the customers.

Basically, customers know how they want to be treated. The dimensions that are important to personal relationships are also important in customer relationships. Only by asking customers appropriate questions through well-developed research can firms expect to understand and be able to track whether their efforts to become closer are being rewarded.

Eliciting positive feelings from customers is an integral component in developing relationships with them. This chapter should illustrate that customer relationships are nothing more than a special category of human relationships. We can and do develop genuine, close, long-lasting relationships with companies and brands as we do with friends and family members. In some cases, in fact, our relationships as customers are stronger and longer-lasting than some friendships and associations that develop in a nonbusiness context. The key from a management perspective is to apply the principles that guide the establishment and maintenance of human relationships in general to the special case of customer relationships. We will turn our attention to this challenge in Chapter 6.

6

Building Long-Term Relationships

Getting to Know Them

In Chapter 5 we introduced a more conceptual view of relationships, building upon the nature of interpersonal relationships as discussed by social psychologists. We now know something about how relationships are established and how they work in an interpersonal context. The challenge now is to put into practice an approach to develop genuine customer relationships.

We will build upon the framework we have established and discuss how companies can go about establishing strategies to create genuine, long-term relationships with their customers. This can only be accomplished if the relationship develops from the customer's perspective. As we will see, genuine relationships cannot be created simply by establishing a customer database or setting up a customer loyalty program. These approaches may form components of an integrated customer relationship strategy, but alone they do not create genuine relationships.

It may be useful at this point to remind ourselves that we are interested in the formation and maintenance of *genuine* customer relationships. The distinction is important between those relationships that are genuine and those that are not—the artificial or spurious relationships. Genuine relationships are characterized by an emotional attachment, a sense of commitment to the other party (in this case the company), and a shared sense of values and goals. In short, genuine customer relationships demonstrate the same dimensions of relationships that have been identified by social psychologists. These relationships are deeper and much more likely to last.

By contrast, artificial or spurious relationships tend to be devoid of emotional connection. They involve parties being thrust together by virtue of market circumstances or the lack of an alternative. Or they tie the customer to the company because an incentive or reward is involved—the more you buy from us, the more "points" you will receive. Or they involve essentially one-way communications, whereby the company directs communications at the customer, much of it customized to have greater appeal. This form of relationship is thought to be more efficient from the marketer's perspective; *and it is*. But it does little to bond the customer to the company in an emotive sense.

Too many companies think they know exactly what customers want. Management may think that the price of products is what drives customers to continue to do business with a company or that if the company is accessible 24 hours a day, 7 days a week, the customers will be satisfied. These components of what we offer customers—the value proposition—will indeed be valued by some of our customers. Some may even consider them to be among the most important things that we can offer them. But not all customers are looking for convenience or lower prices. Some are prepared to pay more if we can craft the right value proposition to make it worth the money.

What is important to the customer is not always obvious. Lurking beneath the surface are many things that customers feel are important that management hasn't even begun to think about. Or, even more elusively, there are things that influence customer satisfaction and the customer's perception of value that the customer doesn't even realize are important until they happen. Different situations evoke different expectations and needs. Managers and employees must realize that understanding what will deliver the building blocks of lasting customer relationships is an extremely difficult and complex process. Getting to know customers and their likes and dislikes is fundamental to building relationships.

It sounds trite to say that a company has to know its customers. In fact, many managers will tell you that they do. But I'm talking about *really* understanding the customer. This goes well beyond knowing where they live and what they buy. It's even more than knowing the demographic and psychographic characteristics of their household. It means truly understanding what they like and dislike, what they want to see happen, what's important to them, how they want to be treated. Finding out these things about individual customers, and even about segments, is not easy. Much of the knowledge comes not from formal research, but from working with customers over time and from paying attention to what works and what doesn't. That's why small firms have an advantage, as we will see in Chapter 7.

Take Their Perspective

To fully understand the needs of customers, we must view the situation from their perspective. What customers want has to be defined well beyond the conventional bounds of marketing. As we know, satisfying customers involves a great deal more than giving them great products, attractive prices, compelling advertising and convenient locations. We also have to address what they want to happen when they interact with the company. Customers want, among other things, to be made to feel that their business is valued and that the company actually cares about them. One of the dangers is focusing on the product or core service and not thinking enough about how customers want to be treated. To really get at what will drive customer satisfaction and lay the groundwork for the establishment of a genuine relationship, companies have to stop focusing only on the obvious or what they have been reading about in marketing books.

How do we know what customers want? One of the obvious answers is that most companies will need a program of ongoing customer research. Without it, we risk trying to decide what's important for the customer from our own perspective. Management all too often makes decisions on what it would personally like, rather than on what the customer would like. In many cases, management may not be in a position to be close to the customer. Certainly, most of us are not in our desired target markets; that is, the customers we are targeting are not usually mirror images of ourselves. As managers, we don't know how they live, how they think, what's important in their lives, what appeals to them. Research is thus a necessary component of any decisions that impact the state of the relationship with the customer. Management, if it is not in a position to listen directly to the customer, must listen to the research.

The topic of measurement will be addressed in greater detail in Chapter 8, but a number of aspects of a research program will be mentioned here. Participants in focus groups are often surprised that a company cares enough about them to ask them to participate. Responses often include comments such as "I didn't know they cared" and "Wow, you mean my opinion counts!" Simply asking customers to participate in such research often does wonders to establish goodwill with the participants.

I often use focus groups to address what's important to customers, as a preliminary stage to measuring the state of the relationship. We also need to define the essential dimensions of the relationship, what the customer likes to have happen and not to happen, and how these affect how he or she feels toward the company. For instance, this form of qualitative research can allow us to explore what causes customers to return to a company again and again. Is it convenience, is it the employees that make them feel special, or is it something completely different? How do they want to be treated? What kind and frequency of contact with the firm would work best for them? What would cause them not to go back? Once we know the answers to questions such as these, we are well on our way to understanding what it will take to build a solid relationship with our customers.

Demonstrating the Value of the Customer

One criticism that I often hear from customers is that they are not made to feel important. Obviously this gets in the way of forming a positive customer relationship. In managing the relationship with customers, it is critical that we constantly show them how important they are to the firm. This message must be evident every time the customer comes in contact with the company. At each "moment of truth" the potential exists for the customer to be impressed or disappointed. If the new furniture is not delivered on time as promised, if a retail employee chooses to ignore a customer looking for service, if telephone messages (and increasingly e-mail messages) go unreturned, the customer is made to feel undervalued and unappreciated. Deeper feelings of resentment or anger will result, and a formerly positive relationship will be soured or a fledgling relationship never get off the ground.

We know that all customers are not created equally, at least in the eyes of the company. But it is important to treat customers as if they are important, even if their financial value to the firm may be low. We need to acknowledge the value of customers and take every opportunity to send them the right messages. Doing so requires that the attitude that the customer is important must permeate the organization. All employees must buy into the idea that every customer has the power and influence to bring us a certain volume of business and probably even greater power to cause us to lose business. The message that each customer represents a certain level of buying power and profitability must get through to staff. If it does not, then customers are likely to encounter situations where they *are* made to feel unimportant and unappreciated. Customers encounter such situations all the time, and they vote with their feet; or in the case of the Internet, with their mouse.

It's easy to understand how companies send the wrong message when they don't pay enough attention to customers, when commitments are not met, and when calls are not returned. But how do we take a positive approach to creating the kind of positive feelings and emotions that will cause a customer to *want* to come back? How do we show them that we really do know them and appreciate how important they are to our business? How do we send the message that we do care whether they stay or go?

One of the easiest ways is to reward customers periodically for giving us their business. This tells customers that we've noticed that they do come back to do business with us over again, and that we appreciate that. The element of recognition is important. It satisfies a fundamental human need for appreciation. Smaller firms are able to greet regular customers by name, but so too are large businesses through the intelligent use of technology. The restaurant that rewards a regular customer with a complimentary drink or entrée is telling the customer that they know how much business he or she represents and that they want him or her to continue doing business with them. This represents *unanticipated recognition* on the part of the customer.

But larger firms can do the same. Using the database of guests in its Hilton HHonors program, Hilton Hotels occasionally places a basket of fruit or flowers in the room of a returning regular guest. Interestingly, the gift may be more appreciated if it is not there *every time* the guest stays at a Hilton hotel. If it is, then the surprise element is not present and the guest may come to expect it at every visit. The database system can tie the gift into the frequency of visit and may tailor the gift to the length of stay. For example, there may be little point in providing a large basket of fruit if the guest is arriving late at night and leaving before breakfast the next morning. On the other hand, the same gift may be much more appreciated if the guest will be at the hotel for three or four days.

One of the most effective programs that I have seen in this regard involved a letter sent by the President and CEO of NewTel, a regional Canadian telecommunications company, to its top 2000 residential customers who had remained loyal to the company in the face of heavy price competition from long-distance suppliers AT&T and Sprint. The letter simply said "thanks"—thanks for staying with us rather than switching to the new competitors. Each letter was individually hand-signed and included a $20 gift certificate. The response from customers was overwhelmingly positive.

The Importance of Delivering Extraordinary Service

Delivering extraordinary service is one of the ways in which a company can endear itself to its customers—by providing a positive service experience every time. This involves performing beyond the customer's *zone of tolerance;* adding value for the customer by exceeding expectations and surprising him or her with service. The service itself, though, cannot create the desired emotional attachment between the customer and the company. However, as customers continue to receive exceptional service every time they come in contact with the company, they come to accept this as the norm. For instance, customers may come to know that each time they visit a particular restaurant, they will be greeted with a smile, the order will be correct, and it will be served promptly. This is the initial stage of trust and commitment. The customers trust that they will have a quality experience each time they visit the restaurant and know that the restaurant is committed to providing this high-quality service. This level of service may begin the process of establishing relationships, but it is insufficient by itself.

Merely satisfying the customer is not enough. We have to get beyond satisfaction to surprise and delight the customer, as there is a great deal of difference between satisfied customers and completely satisfied customers. Research conducted in the United States showed that, among retail banking customers, those who were completely satisfied were nearly 42% more likely to be loyal than merely satisfied customers. The same holds true for customers of airlines, hospitals, and personal computer vendors.[1] Keeping this in mind, it is important for firms to concentrate on exceeding their customers' expectations in order to move them from being satisfied to completely satisfied.

To exceed expectations, companies must demonstrate their appreciation of the customer. This can be done in many ways, including thank you notes and rewards for loyal customers. Although we have already said that loyalty programs should not be misconstrued as relationships, when a relationship does exist, rewards for loyal customers represent one way of showing them that their business is appreciated.

I have always felt that spontaneity is best. Customers seem to be more impressed by the fact that they are recognized, that an employee will call them by name, that a small gesture sends the message that the company knows who they are and appreciates their having been customers for some time. They refer to such events as the "little things" that make so much difference in making customers feel welcome and valued.

Such examples of showing appreciation have a very positive influence on customers. They are made to feel that the company cares about them and that their business is actually valued by the company. This, in turn, results in the customer developing a more emotional attachment to the company. In all, it is a win-win situation for both the company and its customers.

Surprising customers with extraordinary service does wonders to cement loyalties and stimulate positive word of mouth. They appreciate it when employees go out of their way to make them comfortable and to do things that are not necessarily part of the service being paid for. We should not underestimate the power of the "Wow!" factor, where the company shows that it is willing to go out the way to help and to do the unexpected. This surprise-based value creation, discussed in Chapter 4, is important in exceeding customer expectations and turning them into completely satisfied customers. These surprises send the message that the company has noticed customers' needs and genuinely cares about meeting them. For example, your regular clothing store, when a new shipment of belts has arrived, may call to tell you they have kept a belt aside for you that would look great with the new suit you bought last month. Most customers will appreciate the initiative taken by the employee and the fact that he or she remembers what you had bought and had cared enough to watch for a belt to match. The most likely responses are "Wow! I wasn't expecting that" or "Thanks! You didn't have to do that."

To the customer, actions such as these by companies and their employees appear to be spontaneous or "out of the blue." They don't have to be. In fact,

---

[1] Thomas O. Jones and W. Earl Sasser Jr., "Why Satisfied Customers Defect," *Harvard Business Review* 73 (November–December 1995): 88–99.

the best approach is what I refer to as *planned spontaneity,* whereby employees are trained to watch for opportunities to surprise customers with service such as this, to send the message that we care about them and appreciate their business. Planned spontaneity works in an informal or anonymous context by having employees recognize situations where a little gesture or action would be noticed by the customer and appreciated. Staff must be trained to watch for opportunities to impress.

The second approach to planned spontaneity relies more on databases, or at least on remembering the details of the business done by individual customers. Records are kept which prompt the company to do something occasionally that will send a message to customers that they have not been forgotten and that their business is appreciated. For obvious reasons, the more personal the contact, the better.

In order to create positive feelings among their customers, companies must look for ways to impress, to get beyond the ordinary. It is important that employees be selected based on their ability to recognize opportunities to impress. Then management has to give employees the freedom to make the decisions to create such surprises. Training employees to look for ways to create these "Wow!" moments will increase the likelihood that the surprise value will be created.[2]

In My Experience

Let me share with you an experience that exemplifies the kind of spontaneous service excellence that stays in the mind of a customer and leads to the cementing of a customer relationship. After such an experience, a customer will likely not even consider a competitor and will talk about it to all who care to listen.

For the past 10 years, the Conrad International hotel has been my favorite destination in Dublin, a city that I visit five or six times a year. The Conrad, part of Hilton Hotels Corporation in the United States, is a friendly hotel, characterized by employees who are especially attentive to the needs of guests. I have come to know many of the employees rather well, to the point that now, when I arrive, Christy Barrett, the senior doorman, greets me by name and welcomes me back.

A few years ago, I learned by telephone late on a Friday afternoon that a close friend and business associate of mine had passed away rather suddenly in

[2] James G. Barnes, "Close to the Customer: But Is It Really a Relationship?" *Journal of Marketing Management* 10 (1994): 561–70.

Dublin. Wishing to send flowers for the funeral, which was to be on Monday, I called a number of local florists to enquire whether they could arrange an international delivery to Dublin. They all said they could, but it would take three to five days. Not having five days to wait, I decided to call a florist in Dublin to arrange the flowers, and to have the cost put on my Visa card. But how to locate a capable Dublin florist? Especially when in Dublin it was now 9 PM on a Friday evening.

I decided to call the Conrad, thinking that I would ask one of the staff to suggest a florist I might call on Saturday morning. The phone at the bellman's desk in the lobby of the Conrad was answered by John Parkinson, who immediately identified who I was and enquired how he might be of assistance. I explained the situation and asked whether he might be able to recommend a florist nearby whom I might call in the morning. He said that he would recommend the florist who provides the flowers for the hotel and does the floral arrangements in the lobby. I indicated that I thought that was an excellent suggestion and asked if he could give me with their telephone number. John then asked if he might call the florist on my behalf and arrange the delivery of the flowers. I told him that that was not necessary, but he insisted that it would be easier and that he would know how to make the local arrangements. I accepted his kind offer.

John then suggested that the florist would want to know the name of the funeral director and the church from which the burial was to take place, neither of which I knew. He said "Not to worry," that he would find the necessary information and call the florist in the morning to make the arrangements for me. I thanked him, gave him my credit card number, and indicated the kind of flowers and arrangement that I wanted and what to have written on the accompanying card. Next day, Saturday, at noon, the telephone at my home rang. It was John from the Conrad, indicating that the flowers were at the church.

On my next visit to Dublin, about a month later, John Parkinson greeted me at the door of the Conrad as I arrived, reached into the top pocket of his uniform, and handed me the press clipping announcing my friend's death, saying, "I thought you might like to have this."

I have discussed with Michael Governey, the General Manager of the Conrad, this and similar service experiences I have had at his hotel. How is he able to train his staff to be as responsive as they are? His very simple explanation: "it's all in the selection."

Building the Relationship Dimensions

A number of dimensions are typically associated with interpersonal relationships. We know that certain characteristics must be present for the customer to feel that a relationship exists. This is true whether that relationship is with another individual or with a business entity or organization. Some or these characteristics are more central or critical to a relationship than others, and different individuals will attach different levels of importance or salience to each. While only some of them are necessary for a relationship, the more that are present and the more strongly they are felt to exist, the greater closeness the customer will feel with the service provider or company.

The challenge facing a business lies in understanding how the principles of relationship building can be applied in dealing with their customers. What makes a strong, solid, genuine relationship between two individuals is precisely what makes a strong, solid, genuine relationship between a company and its customers.

Let's now turn to how these dimensions of genuine relationships can be turned into a positive component of the relationship between the customer and the company and how companies can avoid behavior that diminishes the experience of the dimensions.

Trust

How can we demonstrate to the customer that we trust him or her, or make sure that we don't send the message that we don't trust him or her? In Chapter 5 we spoke about trust being one of the most important characteristics of a genuine and long-lasting relationship. But how does trust develop? And where do you start to cultivate the trust of your customers? In many aspects of the interaction between customers and companies, trust becomes a critical element. Customers must perceive that companies are committed to their welfare; that they can be trusted to come through for the customer.

Trust is involved when the home-delivery grocery retailer is allowed to enter the customer's home to deliver the groceries that have been ordered that morning, or the clothing store takes back a sweater that doesn't fit, even though the customer does not have a receipt. Lack of trust is involved when young people speak of not wanting to even enter certain retail stores because they feel they are being watched by staff. It is surprising, in fact, just how often customers will speak of trust in their dealings with companies. It is also important to realize that the feeling of not being trusted is enough to ensure that a relationship never begins.

Consider the insurance company that quickly makes restitution with a family who has recently lost their home to a fire. It would be all too easy to start quibbling over how the fire started, who is at fault, and so on. These are certainly important questions that need to be answered, but in the short term the insurance company must ensure that the customer's emotional needs are met. At this traumatic time, the client does not need any additional stress. By dealing with it quickly, the company sends the message that it trusts the customer and can be relied upon.

Reliability

Companies that demonstrate reliability are also more apt to develop enduring relationships with customers. This means doing what you said you would do, when you said you would do it, for the price you said! Take the electrician who shows up at the job site when he said he would and if he has to be late, phones ahead to let the customer know; or the company that, if there are cost overruns, swallows the costs, even if profitability is reduced or a loss incurred.

Customers also need to know that the companies they deal with understand their needs. Take the daycare that is willing to stay open just a few minutes later than normal because their clientele is primarily young professional couples who may on occasion be unable to pick up their children at the scheduled time—doing this, of course, without charge and with a smile. The customers appreciate the extra effort given by the daycare and are more than willing to tell their friends and colleagues of the great service they receive.

Sense of Community

Community-based value is the benefit in terms of strengthened customer relationships that a company derives from its contribution to the local economy and the communities in which it operates. Indirect benefits to the customer include donations and sponsorships to arts activities and sporting teams, but the more direct benefit to the relationship is the shared sense of community that results. This endears the customer to any firm that adds this type of value because the company gains a deserved reputation that carries over indirectly to its image among customers. Some will choose to do business with such a firm because of what it gives back to the community. I have encountered a number of instances where a company is able to command a price premium with certain segments of customers principally because of the commitment that it demonstrates to the local community. A residual pride is involved, and a genuine sense of wanting to support our own.

Mutuality

Mutual goals—"we believe in the same things you believe in"—and shared values—"the same things are important to us"—are related to the concept of community-based value. Companies can capitalize on these by positioning themselves as the "Home Team," as was done effectively by NewTel Communications, the Canadian telecommunications company. Faced with deregulation in the long-distance market and a declining market share, NewTel developed a communications strategy that focused on positioning the company as the "Home Team": a company is committed to and supportive of the local economy and community. The strategy worked extremely well: the relationships NewTel customers have with the company have been strengthened since the introduction of the communications plan. Advertising that appeals to the emotions of a local community, coupled with an active sponsorship program, has contributed to NewTel's having the highest customer retention rate in the Canadian telecommunications industry and in more than 75% of customers agreeing that they are "proud to be a NewTel customer."

Respect

Respect is more than "do onto others as you would have them do onto you." For instance, companies like The Gap and Wal-Mart place greeters at the entrance of stores to give a warm smile and polite hello to all visitors. At The Gap, employees are instructed to approach all store visitors within 60 seconds of their entering the store to offer assistance and encourage dialogue.[3] The objective is to make the customer feel welcome and more comfortable shopping in the store. It also serves to personalize the otherwise impersonal self-service shopping experience.

While this may be a very reasonable approach to conveying a friendly atmosphere in the store, many people just don't like it. They find the greeters overbearing and too much "in your face." Some people simply do not want this type of friendly approach. They want to get in the store, shop, and get out. Companies that do not recognize this form of customer behavior are at risk of alienating these customers. But what can companies do to negate this risk? First, company policy must be flexible enough to allow greeters not to greet store visitors if they detect any resistance. Secondly, employees must be sufficiently trained to recognize when store visitors are exhibiting signs of wanting to be left alone.

Dependability

As I related in an earlier chapter, one customer recently told me of her feelings of *injustice* when, having stood in line at a local supermarket for several minutes

---

[3] John Heinzl, "In-Your-Face Service Leaves Customers Cold," *Globe and Mail* (Toronto), 16 January 1998, B23.

behind other shoppers, she was left standing when people behind her in the line rushed to move to a new cashier when the next lane was opened. The shopper was genuinely upset by such a process and felt the supermarket should institute a system that is more *fair*. The same customer indicated that she feels much the same when she stands in a line at an automatic teller machine to make a deposit only to find when she is partway through the transaction, that the ATM is out of envelopes. Despite the absence of any human interaction, the customer still feels extremely *frustrated* and even *let down* by the inconsistency of service.

Contrast this experience with that of the customer who said she felt that a store *trusted* her. "I brought a toy back to a store. They did not ask any questions or even look at it; they just refunded the money, no questions asked." This is the sort of encounter that provides the organization with an opportunity to prove its potential as a quality service provider, to build trust, and to increase loyalty. All of this can be quickly diminished or destroyed when customers feel let down because companies do not live up to their promises. There is nothing worse than being promised that a service person will come on Tuesday afternoon, then staying home waiting for this person, who doesn't come.

In all of these cases, the customer is angered by not being able to count on or rely on the service provider. By treating people unfairly, a company is telling you that you can't be sure they will deliver what they promise.

Communications

Two-way communications, for something so obvious and necessary, it is all too often missing. Take the feedback cards, available at many restaurants and hotels, that provide customers with the opportunity to offer advice and to make complaints. Often the customer is given the option of leaving his or her name and contact details so that the company can follow up. An individual who has recently had a bad experience fills out a feedback card in the hope of preventing a similar experience in the future or of receiving some compensation, or at least an explanation. Will that customer receive a reply from the company indicating that they have received the feedback card and are taking steps to remedy the problem? If not, how is the customer made to feel, knowing that he or she took the time to provide the company with feedback but that this has obviously not made a difference? The customer's negative feelings toward the company are now compounded.

The same observations apply to those companies that are slow to respond to e-mail messages or to voice messages left on answering systems. Many customers speak of calling a company to request information or even to make a purchase. They leave a message, or possibly more than one, and "never hear from them again." These customers are left with a plethora of emotions. They are *confused* ("Why didn't they even call back? I was trying to buy something"), *frustrated* ("I really wanted that item"), *undervalued* ("I'm obviously not a very important customer"), and *angry* ("That's the last time I'll try to deal with them").

The absence of two-way communications is obvious in many frequency marketing programs, in many of which the communications is decidedly one-way. A friend of mine wryly observed recently that he thought he had a close, personal relationship with the President and CEO of a major airline who writes to him regularly. A letter from the CEO is enclosed in every monthly statement from the airline's frequent flyer program, and several times a year he receives a "personal" letter from the CEO in connection with a special promotion or offer. But when he recently experienced a negative service encounter on the airline, he wrote the CEO. No response! He then sent a second copy of the letter. Still no response!

Knowledge

As we will discuss later in this chapter, knowledge of the customer does not mean collecting as much data as possible and storing this in a database for future use. Companies need to be sending messages that say, We know you, We've been listening to you, and We understand your needs. This may come in the form of something as simple as customer service representatives using a customer database to contact customers who have made purchases in the past month to thank them for their patronage.

Genuine knowledge of customers—knowledge that extends far beyond the amount they spent with us last year or how much of a certain product that have bought from us—is a tremendously valuable tool in creating and solidifying close customer relationships. The challenge is to collect the right information and use it in a way that will impress the customer, to create that "Wow!" experience that endears the customer to the company. For example, realizing that cellular or mobile telephones operate on a different technological platform in North America and Europe, I advised a telecommunications client of mine a couple of years ago to identify their valuable business customers who travel to Europe on a regular basis and equip them at no cost with GSM phones that they could use as soon as they landed in Europe. By making such a gesture, the company is sending a number of messages: We understand your business. We know some of the challenges you face. We are there to help you when you need us.

The creation of customer emotions is an essential component of relationship building. Without such emotions, there is no relationship, only a series of transactions. The few examples cited in these paragraphs should serve to illustrate one of the most important lessons of marketing and customer service: that *the factors that drive customer satisfaction and that ultimately affect whether or not a customer will form a meaningful, genuine relationship with a company often have absolutely nothing to do with the products that the company is selling or the prices that are charged.* This is an entirely different side of marketing, one that demands management's attention. I am convinced that a very large percentage of business is lost simply because companies have no idea what negative emotions are being generated. Conversely, important opportunities to create positive emotions are not acted upon.

What Relationships Are NOT

Many businesses in recent years have turned to techniques to increase repeat buying behavior. Many of these have been termed "relationship marketing" programs. I will now examine a number of these approaches that have become associated with the concept of customer relationships, and I will suggest why they do not in fact lead to the creation of genuine customer relationships at all but are really aimed at producing repeat business. This is, of course, not a bad thing. But let's not confuse the stream of repeat business that results from a frequency marketing program or the ability to target customized messages to "loyal" customers in our databases with *genuine* customer relationships. What's missing in most of these cases is the next step, the transformation of these connections into relationships that see customers continuing to do business with us because they really want to, not because they are tied to us by some artificial means.

Why Databases Are Not Enough

More and more companies have begun to use sophisticated databases as a means to get closer to their customers. While many have been successful at gathering information about their customers, few have used the information to build strong close relationships. Some have used customer databases to become more cost effective by segmenting customers based on attributes in the information base and identifying segments of customers who are more profitable and have greater potential. However, these are only small steps in the development of genuine relationships with customers. While the database may contain a great deal of information, it has to be put in a usable format so employees can access the information when serving customers and use it to add value.

Databases represent a barrier to relationship formation in that they generally involve only one-way communication. A firm may use its information about customers to customize literature and promotional material or stimulate outbound telephone calling, but gives the customer no avenue to influence how the information is used or have input into the types of information in the database. Thus, a database may impede the formation of a relationship because the company uses it to market *at* customers rather than exchange information and ideas *with* them.

In addition, most company databases are designed to capture data on customers automatically as they shop or transact business with the company. Some companies have data on the customer and his or her household that may have been collected when the customer first started doing business with the firm and not have been updated since. The data in the database pertain to the demographic characteristics of the household and the purchasing behavior of the individual. These data may be very detailed, including every unit in every product category that the customer has bought, how it was paid for, time of day purchased, account payments, total spending, and so on, and may automatically incorporate internal data relating to the company's margin on the items purchased and an estimate of customer profitability. *Nevertheless, these are still transactional data, relating entirely to the behavioral side of the interaction.* Such data tell us virtually nothing about the really important side of the customer's relationship with the firm, how he or she feels toward the company, what emotions characterize that relationship, and how strongly felt they are.

Few marketing authors, researchers, and managers seem to approach customer relationships from the perspective of the customer. More prevalent is the view that relationship marketing is all about creating customer databases so that we can be much more efficient in directing sales initiatives at targeted consumers. Direct marketing, data mining, frequency marketing, loyalty programs, locking in the customer—these are all concepts that are generally discussed in the context of relationship marketing. Some or all of these marketing tools and techniques may be appropriate components of an integrated approach to relationship building, but they do not, in and of themselves, constitute a set of components that most customers would consider essential to genuine relationship building. In fact, as we will discuss later in this book, for many customers they may represent the antithesis of a genuine relationship.

Database Marketing: Better-Targeted Mail Shots

Relatively few companies that deal with end consumers have historically maintained detailed records of all customer purchasing. Even those that have, such as financial institutions, telephone companies, and other public utilities, have used them mainly for accounting and billing purposes and rarely to plan marketing strategies.

However, as technology has become more widely available and companies have recognized the value of tracking and understanding the behavior of their customers, the use of customer databases has become commonplace in many companies. This has led to many companies drawing a close link between relationship marketing and database marketing, thereby suggesting that the technological capabilities of customer databases *allow* them to form relationships with customers. This view of relationship marketing is far too one-sided, no evidence of caring for the customer or even of asking the customer for input, short of collecting information that is automatically generated and easily obtained. When we collect data in this way, we end up with "data" in the true sense of the word. We don't really know customers when we only know what they buy, where they live, and how many kids they have at home. What's going on in their lives and in their minds is infinitely more important.

The purpose is to market *at* them, with little concern for whether they are willing participants in this relationship or view it as satisfying. In addition, databases are limited in the degree to which they can help manage relationships that do truly exist. For example, from a customer's point of view, a relationship can end long before a database indicates this to be the case. Databases, for the most part do not, however, have the capability of tracking or managing this type of information.

Databases are great tools and valuable additions to relationship marketing programs. They provide businesses and their employees with information about a customer's spending patterns, lifestyle, and various other factors that are useful in initiating and maintaining contact with a customer. As well, in a large corporation, the technology will allow employees around the world to be linked to the same customer database. This provides opportunities to contribute to the satisfaction of customers, regardless of where they are located. But a database view of and approach to managing customer relationships falls short of our goal of establishing genuine relationships. The maintenance of a customer database in and of itself does not render a customer relationship artificial or false, but it certainly does not guarantee that a genuine relationship will be formed.

Customer Relationship Management (CRM)

One area that has received a tremendous amount of interest in recent years is a branch of the software industry labelled Customer Relationship Management (CRM). The CRM industry has positioned its software products as having the ability to create stronger relationships with customers by integrating every aspect of the contact with the customer, including sales, marketing, and customer service. While the concepts upon which CRM is based—focusing efforts on recruitment and retention of customers—can certainly be justified, there is nevertheless a piece of the puzzle missing: CRM is data driven and product driven and can be used primarily to understand the customer's behavior, not the emotional bond between customer and company.

CRM deals with the mechanics of building relationships, including data capture and analysis and business process simplification. Proponents of CRM argue that many benefits can be derived from implementing CRM; including sales functionality by developing customer profiles and history; customer service support through warranty management, tracking, and problem resolution; cross-selling and upselling higher-margin products or services to targeted customer segments; and attracting additional customers by offering personalized service such as direct mailouts. Another key benefit claimed by the CRM industry is that customers are segmented and communication programs are developed to retain the most profitable customers.

With CRM, emphasis is placed on selling more products and services through data mining to determine the types of customers that would be most likely to buy a particular product. This is achieved by developing sophisticated predictive models that assess a segment's propensity to purchase products based on the purchasing behavior of individuals with similar demographic and other profiles. Thus, as I noted above, segmentation is product focused rather than customer focused and does not consider any element of the emotional connection with the consumer. The "relationship" is driven entirely by historical behaviors.

CRM does have the capability to allow companies to better understand customer purchasing behavior, or at least that portion that is captured in the system, and to determine the type of communications that should be undertaken with the customer. However, simply knowing how often a customer has purchased a particular product in the past six months, or whether he or she is spending a certain amount of money with your company, does not tell you anything about *why* the customer is behaving this way. Is it because there are no competitors within a convenient area? What share of wallet is the customer spending with you? Is the customer likely to recommend you to his or her friends? What are the customer's true feelings toward the company? CRM cannot answer any of these questions.

Contractual Links: Locking Them In

Companies often use barriers to exit as a means to develop "relationships" with customers. A structural bond between a customer and a company can often make it difficult for the customer to change suppliers. The customer is locked in because the costs involved in making the break cannot be justified. Mortgages are one of the best examples. Banks and other providers of financial services set up structural barriers when they provide residential mortgages of a fixed term and charge customers a penalty for reopening before the term has expired. Financial institutions may naively believe that because the customer has had a mortgage with the company for several years a relationship must exist.

Technology provides another example of a structural bond that some companies may incorrectly interpret as a relationship. The use of a particular type of software or the existence of a service contract may preclude customers from switching computer suppliers because the costs of doing so cannot be justified. Thus, the customer may be forced to continue using the software or equipment even when he or she would prefer to be extricated from the "relationship."

The most successful relationships, however, appear to be characterized by mutual trust, which is based upon exchange of information, commitment, and satisfactory performance of the partners' respective roles. This cannot exist when the bond between the customer and the company exists only because of a contract that increases the barriers to exit.

Frequency Marketing: Clubbing Them to Death

The approach to building relationships by raising the switching costs can be seen in the bevy of "loyalty" programs in today's marketplace. This is not a new concept—trading stamps, such as S&H Green Stamps, have been around for over 100 years.

A vast number of companies have implemented such programs. A very large percentage of North American customers and their households are members of loyalty programs or frequency marketing programs offered by companies in many different industries, including hotels, airlines, grocery retailers, gasoline retailers, and department stores. These programs are all designed with the purpose of "getting closer" to the customers and locking them into programs that will encourage repeat business. The programs allow their owners to collect volumes of purchasing data about customers and to develop predictive models of their future spending patterns so that they can be targeted with communications messages. On the surface, these programs work. They do result in customers continuing to buy from specific companies that offer such clubs. Club members do give the card issuer a larger share of their total category spending.

But the proliferation of loyalty programs has resulted in an ongoing discussion about the effectiveness of card-based or club-based programs and what they actually achieve. It is suggested that companies that develop or participate in these programs do so to stimulate customer purchases with the company and build loyalty. However, with so many companies now participating in similar programs, the question arises whether they do indeed offer some form of competitive advantage and whether the relationships customers have with participating companies are really strengthened.

In Canada, for instance, over two-thirds of Canadian homes participate in the Air Miles program. Shoppers are awarded points for purchasing products and services from participating companies by swiping the Air Miles card whenever a purchase is made. Points can be redeemed for air travel, arts and entertainment tickets, and merchandise. Companies participating in the Air Miles program include Shell Canada, Bank of Montreal, Holiday Inn, American Express, and Blockbuster Video.

Nicholas Clarke suggests that loyalty programs designed to stimulate loyalty towards specific brands may in fact only stimulate purchasing behavior, regardless of the brands involved in the program.[4] As Clarke asks, "Loyalty to what?" If a participating company such as Shell were to leave the program, perhaps to establish their own loyalty program, would the subscribers to the Air Miles program be dramatically affected? He suggests that if another gasoline retailer were to become an Air Miles partner, the consumer would simply switch gas stations to continue to receive Air Miles. In this situation, he argues, the loyalty is towards the program rather than towards the brands that participate. Brand loyalty does not exist, and a relationship with the customer has not been developed. In essence, the brands have commoditized their existence.

Such so-called loyalty programs—more correctly labelled frequency programs because they do stimulate repeat purchase behavior—are somewhat myopic in that they are behaviorally driven and thus do not lead to the creation of a genuine relationship between company and customer. In addition, much like core product attributes, these tactics can be easily copied by competitors. The result is the raising of switching costs in that customers may feel locked into dealing with a company because they do not wish to forfeit the rewards they have accumulated. As illustrated by recent developments in the passenger airline business in many parts of the world, loyalty programs appear to do little to provide competitive advantage because companies do not forge true relationships with customers and no company ends up any further ahead than its competitors. Colgate, Stewart, and Kinsella make an insightful comment regarding the problematic nature of equating relationship duration with true customer loyalty: "[L]oyalty is more than a set of behaviors. It is recognized that loyalty has a behavioral dimension but that it also has an attitudinal aspect."[5]

Clearly, many companies have implemented loyalty programs and have begun to create and manipulate customer databases in efforts to build closer relationships with their customers. While each of these tactics may form a component of an integrated relationship marketing program, neither represents a strategic, customer-focused approach to relationship formation. Such tactics will do little

---

[4]Nicholas Clarke, "The Limits to Air Miles," *Marketing Magazine,* 13 April 1998.
[5]M. Colgate, K. Stewart, and R. Kinsella, "Customer Defection: A Study of the Student Market in Ireland," *International Journal of Bank Marketing* 14(3) (1996): 23–29.

to bolster the relationships a company can have with its customers if the company does not examine how the customer defines a relationship; whether the conditions under which the company interacts with customers are conducive to relationship formation; and the factors which contribute most to genuine, quality relationships.

A loyalty program does undoubtedly establish or strengthen the relationship between some customers and a company using the program. However, many consumers do not participate in only one program. Consider a customer who participates in your company's loyalty program along with similar programs of your biggest competitors. What value is the loyalty program creating for that customer? Is there really a competitive advantage? More likely the loyalty program represents a price of entry. To be a competitor at all today, at least in the airline, supermarket, and hotel businesses, one must have a frequent-flyer/shopper/guest program.

The points, travel miles, discounts, coupons, and so on that companies use as rewards in their loyalty programs can dilute the value of the service or product offering. The rewards are extrinsic to the service offering and do not reinforce the value derived from dealing with a particular company. Should another company with similar products or services introduce a better rewards program, customers will be inclined to switch suppliers because the relationship between the customers and the company in question is behaviorally driven, with no emotional bond. The incentive to remain a customer has nothing at all to do with the level of service provided or the emotional tie to the customer. It isn't even connected to the value of the core product or service. The program is entirely based on incentives that encourage the customer to buy more, to increase his or her share of wallet, not because we do things better than the competition, but because our rewards are more attractive.

Loyalty programs are efficient in bringing customers back as repeat buyers, but the relationship is an artificial rather than a genuine one, based in the customer being rewarded for repeat business or for giving the company all of his or her business. Indeed, something is missing from the equation: the emotive side of a true relationship.

Complicate the Connection: Sell Them More Stuff

Another naive view of relationship marketing focuses on developing so-called relationships with customers by selling more products or services to them. I am amazed at the views of some bankers towards building customer relationships. Some of them believe that if customers have four or five products with them, a relationship must exist. They think that if customers are willing to have this many products with a particular bank, the customer must want to have a relationship. What they do not consider is that in many cases a bank will not provide a mortgage without also having the customer's credit card, car loan, and traditional banking business. The customer may have no choice but to place all of his or her financial business with a particular bank in order to receive approval for a mortgage. This can hardly be called a true relationship. A true relationship may indeed exist when a customer has many products with a particular bank, but simply buying a certain number of products or services from a company is not an indicator of one. The customer, as I noted, may have no choice, may continue to deal with a particular bank or other company because of convenience or sheer inertia. Our research in Canada suggests that many customers stay with their bank and even give that bank all of their financial services business, not because anything approaching a genuine relationship exists, but simply because they feel that all banks are alike.

Overcoming Barriers to Relationship Formation

To develop genuine customer relationships, companies must identify and develop ways to overcome the barriers to forming these relationships. The barriers most often cited are infrequent contact, absence of direct contact, the introduction of technology, and the fact that customers are anonymous. The introduction of technology is a factor today in many interactions between companies and their customers. Technology, and the Internet in particular, has enormous potential to facilitate relationship formation through improving access and availability. But technology also makes it possible for customers to do business without ever meeting the service provider, resulting in less dialogue and contact between customer and company. Companies must recognize the limitations of using technology and work toward creating contact with customers in other ways that allow for closer customer interaction.

To implement a relationship marketing plan, companies need to determine whether they are ready to build relationships with their customers. Asking people at various levels and areas of the company a few simple questions will allow the company to assess where barriers to relationship building exist and what needs to be done to overcome this.[6] Don Peppers and Martha Rogers suggest the following four questions:

1. How well can your company identify its end-user customers?

[6] Don Peppers, Martha Rogers, and Bob Dorf, "Is Your Company Ready for One-to-One Marketing?" *Harvard Business Review* (January–February 1999): 151–60.

2. Can your company differentiate its customers based on their value to you and their needs from you?

3. How well do you interact with your customers and do they ever hear from you?

4. How well does your company customize its products and services based on what it knows about its customers?

By analyzing the answers that various managers and other employees give these questions, a company can determine where it needs to focus its effort in order to become closer to its customers through increased value and satisfaction. By examining its own barriers to relationship formation from the outset and working to overcome them, a company is much more likely to succeed in building meaningful customer relationships.

Some companies have been working very hard to overcome the barriers to relationship formation created by the increased use of technology and by the customer's connection with the company having been through buying its products at the retail level. Major Internet-based retailers such as Amazon.com, L.L. Bean, Lands' End, and J. Crew are building closer relationships between themselves and their customers by making use of the interactive properties of the Internet. By customizing the interaction and making the communications two-way, these companies have moved toward creating of something more closely resembling a genuine relationship.

Similarly, many companies in the grocery products and other consumer products industries, whose contact with end consumers in the past has been largely limited to the sale of their products through retail stores, have taken major steps toward the creation of major brand relationships by reinventing themselves in part as service providers. Using technology as old as 1-800 customer help lines and as new as the Internet, companies such as Kraft, Pepsi-Cola, and Levi's have now made it possible for customers to interact directly with them. The barriers of distance and lack of contact have been removed. By establishing recipe clubs, kids' Internet sites, in-store displays, and interactive websites, the firms are able to solidify their brand relationships.

How Do We Do It?

In this chapter we have attempted to apply some of the principles of genuine customer relationships. We have considered what is essential in the establishment of relationships that the customer will feel are real. We have also identified a number of approaches that businesses take to establishing what they may consider relationships but really are not, at least in the minds of customers. These approaches may well be effective at stimulating repeat business, they are not genuine relationship builders. They may deliver on the behavioral definition of a relationship, though they do not produce the emotions that are characteristic of genuine customer relationships.

Note that we have not talked in this chapter about establishing relationship marketing programs. That is because the most genuine, longest-lasting customer relationships do not develop as a result of formally designed programs at all. They are more likely to occur naturally, simply because of the way the company treats its customers. In Chapter 7, we will examine how some the best of the natural relationship creators, small businesses, accomplish this.

7

What Small Firms Can Teach Us about Relationships

Nothing Out of the Ordinary

Just about everyone has a story to tell about an experience dealing with a small business. Whether it's the corner store, the deli, or the neighborhood service station, most of us deal with small businesses for a variety of goods and services. We've all had positive experiences with small companies, particularly with retail stores in small towns and neighborhoods, where the owner or one of the employees has treated us special or done an unexpected favor for us. What is very interesting is that most of the small business owners and managers with whom I have discussed this seem surprised that I even raise the topic. Their reaction is that there is nothing special about how they treat their customers; they are just doing things naturally, the way they have always done them; treating customers as they themselves would like to be treated. Small firms are the natural relationship marketers—and they often don't even know it.

A small firm is in the best position to develop a genuine relationship with its customers. There are many reasons for this, which we'll explore later in this chapter. Suffice it to say here that small businesses are by their very nature in a better position to get to know their customers and meet their higher-order needs than are large companies who deal with their customers in a very different way. In this chapter we will examine the special place of small companies in the marketplace and the advantage that they have in establishing relationships with their customers.

That is not to say that all small businesses are successful in developing strong, close relationships with their customers. In fact, most of us have also had experiences with small firms where we have been treated badly and will never return as a result. And we can think of bad service experiences in restaurants, hair salons, or service stations that certainly did nothing to cultivate customer retention or encourage the development of a long-term relationship. So small businesses don't always get it right—even though they are in a better position to do so.

When participants in focus groups talk about why they go back to a small business, they say things such as, "They know my name," "They know what I need even before I ask for it," "They make me feel as if they really want my business," "They treat me special." From the words people use to describe their interactions with small businesses, it is evident that there are positive feelings and emotions woven into their interactions with these companies. The main question that we will address in this chapter has two parts. The first deals with what a small firm has that a large firm may not have in terms of being able to cultivate genuine customer relationships. The second deals with what a large company can learn from a small business and whether it can implement some of the techniques used by small firms to manage relationships with their customers.

What Does the Customer Get? The Value of Dealing with a Small Firm

Earlier in this book I discussed the concept of value and the way in which customers assess the value they receive. Since price is only one component of the value proposition, and often a relatively unimportant one at that, we must consider the value a customer receives from a small business in light of the fact that the prices charged by smaller firms are often not competitive with those charged by larger companies. Many small firms, particularly in the retail sector, are higher priced than their larger competitors. Customers are often prepared to overlook the higher price and to keep going back. Why? Simply because value is delivered in different ways. It clearly doesn't only mean being able to obtain products and services at the lowest possible price.

Value is measured by the level of service, the expertise of the employees, how the customer is treated, and the way the customer feels in dealing with the small firm. Small businesses can customize their level of service, if not their products, to satisfy the needs and desires of individual customers. Small businesses do a better job of meeting their customers' higher-order needs and as a result retain their customers, even when bigger businesses are able to deliver better on the more functional aspects of the value proposition.

Small businesses, through their ability to get close to the customer, are able to satisfy customers and secure their loyalty. Very few small firms have frequent-buyer clubs or loyalty programs. The closeness between a small business and its customers is often a more genuine closeness, quite similar to the closeness people feel in strong personal relationships. Because of this, and the sincerity of the relationship, customers willingly return to the business without the loyalty programs or reward schemes. The intrinsic rewards that result from being treated well and feeling good about the interaction are more important to the consumer than the points and savings that are typical of the competitive market in other sectors.

When we look at value as what the customer gets as compared with what the customer gives, we still may be surprised that small businesses deliver value that many consumers find attractive. However, when we look at the drivers of satisfaction model and determine the customers' needs beyond the core product or service, we may better understand how small businesses can deliver better value for their customers than some larger operations.

For example, large supermarkets can provide greater selection, more services and products, and often lower prices than their smaller counterparts. However, some people prefer to shop at smaller, neighborhood grocery stores. The reason is often as simple as the way they feel when they walk through the door. Long-time customers like that the employees know their names and remember their preferences. The familiarity is often comforting to customers, and they will forfeit discounts and forgo selection in order to feel better about their shopping experience. Value is created by the atmosphere and the attention to the customer. When an employee remembers a customer's preferences, this makes the customer feel special, important to the business, and closer to the individual employee. This brings us back to the point made in Chapter 1 concerning whom the relationship is really with: the employee or the business. In the case of small businesses, this often overlaps since the owner or manager frequently works in the business and the smaller number of employees means that the customer is served by the same people time and again. As well, in the small firm employees are chosen, trained, and supervised directly by the owner. In addition, if a customer has a problem or complaint, he or she can often speak directly to the owner (if not, the employee can) rather than wait for the information to pass through several layers of management. This flatter management structure allows the customer to feel closer to the employees, the owners, and the business.

Why Doesn't Everyone Deal with Small Businesses?

If small businesses are so much warmer and more personable, give excellent service, and make people feel good, why doesn't everyone deal with small firms all the time? Because larger businesses may be better than small businesses at creating certain kinds of value. First, as we have already mentioned, larger retailers often have a better selection available. For many people this is important because they want to complete their shopping as quickly as possible without having to ask anybody for assistance. Secondly, many consumers like the convenience of larger companies because they often cater to more than one consumer need under one roof. For example, many people find it convenient and time-saving to be able to buy groceries, drop off film and dry cleaning, and rent a movie at one location.

For some consumers it is a matter of the type of relationship they want. Some customers do not want a particularly close relationship with a retail store and are satisfied shopping at a large retailer and maintaining what is essentially a functional interaction. However, the same customer may want a closer relationship with his or her financial services provider: It is often a matter of personal preference. Some customers are price shoppers. They will deal with Wal-Mart, rather than the neighborhood shoe store, because they are focused on buying at the lowest price. This is a form of value that Wal-Mart creates very well. Other customers want personalized service and advice and are prepared to pay more to buy at a smaller store.

Finally, sometimes it comes down to cost. While many of the consumers whom we have interviewed in focus groups and surveys say that they will pay more for products at a small business because of the way they feel doing business there, some customers may wish to do more business with small retailers but, within their budget, just not be able to. These customers either find other ways to satisfy their higher-order needs or these needs go unfulfilled.

How Do Small Firms Do It? The Underlying Factors

Let's take a closer look at how small firms create value for their customers. The following is an overview of the factors that we have identified in research that separate small businesses from their larger competitors. If these do represent the strategic competitive advantage of small businesses, then we ought to consider how larger firms might be able to borrow a leaf from the small companies' book. Can large companies adapt these small-firm qualities in developing relationships with their customers? I think they can.

Small firms have several advantages that make it possible for them to deliver better service and greater value than larger companies. Small firms are more innovative[1] mainly because they are not held back by rigid company policies and procedures. When an opportunity or idea presents itself, small firms can

[1] Anna Brady, "Small Is as Small Does," *Journal of Business Strategy* 16(2) (March/April 1995): 44–52.

often act more quickly because fewer people are involved in the decision-making process. They don't need to get approval from head office or even from the department manager. This innovation is tied to the entrepreneurial spirit and risk taking that give rise to the creation of many small businesses in the first place. Entrepreneurial activity, while encouraged in some large businesses, is not prevalent due to the structure and restrictions often thought to be necessary to run an efficient operation.

Related to innovation is the ability of small businesses to respond quickly to market and economic changes. The flexibility of small staff numbers, broadly defined job descriptions, and the open communications that exists in most small businesses allows them to respond to changes more quickly than some larger firms that are accountable to boards of directors and shareholders.

What They Talk About

Because there are fewer layers of management in small businesses, the customer often feels closer to the business and those who work there. This closeness is demonstrated through the conversations that the customers and business people carry on—not just the topics of conversation but also the tone and emotion. It is also demonstrated in the little things that the business people do for their customers and those the customers do for them. When a business delivers on the little things that are special for a customer, that customer feels that there is something special in the relationship. Recovery efforts and relationships can flourish when an employee is empowered to make decisions or can go directly to the owner or manager to get authorization.

When a genuine closeness and relationship exist, many customers of small businesses will do little things that show the staff that they care. Special occasions such as birthdays and Christmas are often remembered with small gifts and cards. This is important because it also gives staff positive feedback showing that their attention to detail and extra work are appreciated by customers.

Earlier in the book I talked about the relationships between customers and their hairdressers, dentists, physicians, and other "intimate" service providers. These relationships are comparable to those they form with small businesses; that is, they feel close to the employees with whom they deal most often and will return to them because they feel there is a certain closeness or, to use their terminology, a "comfort level." These relationships are special in that they move beyond the client–employee boundaries to something closer and more intimate. We only have to look at the types of conversations that many people have with their hairdressers and pharmacists to understand that customers feel close to these small business people.

Research by social psychologist Judith Beinstein has shown that topics such as personal and family matters, social problems, health problems, and vacations come up in conversations between customers and certain service providers.[2] Beinstein's research also shows that people who provide services such as hairdressing feel that it is important that they give their customers a chance to discuss subjects they may be unable to discuss with others and that when people feel good about the conversations they've had, they are more likely to return. Hairdressers often say that their clients talk to them about things that they cannot talk to anyone else about.[3] These types of conversations between customers and service providers show customers that there is a connection, or relationship, that makes them special. While not all small businesses allow for this type of interaction, nevertheless many small business employees get to know customers by name, and while they may not always serve the client, they know the client's preferences and will inform other employees about them. As well, in a small business employees have greater opportunity to discuss customers and their needs, so that most employees become aware over time of regular customers and the little things that are important to them.

They Know Me

Depending on the nature of the service, employees often become aware of the needs of members of the customer's family and even friends—remember Wilbur Johnson from Chapter 1. Like Wilbur, employees at a neighborhood grocery store will have watched families as they moved to the area, raised children, grew older and had grandchildren. This is especially true in rural settings, where storeowners live close to their customers and can anticipate their needs through changes in the family life cycle and structure and in employment status and income.

Employees in small firms are often cross functional in their approach to their jobs and therefore able to react to situations immediately without having to deal with company policies that may require a manager's approval. This facilitates a feeling of responsiveness which customers obviously appreciate. It also makes recovering from poor service experiences much easier because employees are able to demonstrate to the customer's satisfaction that they are action oriented and genuinely interested in solving the customer's problem.

---

[2] Judith Beinstein, "Conversations in Public Places," *Journal of Communication* (Winter 1975): 85–95.

[3] Grant McCracken, *Big Hair: A Journey into the Transformation of Self* (Toronto: Viking, 1995).

They Live Here Too

Many small businesses are viewed as an institution within their local community. Their support and commitment towards the local community have endeared many customers to them. They have become over time an integral part of the fabric of the neighborhood in which they operate or the segment of the market that they serve. Thus, they take on a very meaningful position in the lives of the people with whom they deal.

The influence of the small business owner/manager, who in most cases operates in an entrepreneurial environment, should not be underestimated. Individuals operating in this situation are able to demonstrate flexibility and quick decision making. Because the small business owner/manager actually works in the store, he or she can demonstrate genuine ownership. A hands-on management style is usually evident, and things get done. As a result, customers find this environment much more responsive and customer friendly because they get the feeling that they are being listened to. These managers know how to handle situations without having to consult company policies or seek permission from regional office.

Small businesses also often take on the personality of the people who own and manage them. Thus, a small firm develops a genuine personality of its own, one that is difficult to separate from the people who work there. In contrast to the cookie-cutter view and standardized profile of many multiple-unit large corporations, each component of which has to conform to the company's image, the small firm is personality-led. It becomes for the customer virtually indistinguishable from the people who own the company and who work there. They *are* the company to a much greater extent than is an employee of a bank or an airline.

Come on In

There is often an open door policy in a small firm, whether formally or informally, where both employees and customers feel they are able to communicate directly with the managers or owners of the organization when troubles arise or to obtain information. Such a feeling also sends the message to customers that "we are accessible." Even a customer who has never had any problems with the company has the sense that if troubles did arise, he or she would be able to ensure that the problem is rectified. In other words, customers have confidence that the company is ready, willing, and able to help when called upon. This reflects a commitment to the customer that is not always present in larger organizations, where procedures must be followed.

Less Red Tape

Generally, in smaller firms internal decision making is flexible, owing to a lack of bureaucracy in the organization. This may be related to the company's product and service offerings or to the processes and policies that they deliver to their customers. For example, a small firm is much more flexible than most larger organizations in changing store hours, for example, to accommodate customers, or in special ordering an item that the customer can't locate. For instance, if customers request a specific new product, the small business is often able to decide very quickly to offer the new product, whereas a larger organization will usually require the approval of a regional manager or head office.

Decision making in the small firm also provides faster response time in dealing with customer issues and complaints. As an added benefit, small businesses are able to track and monitor local trends and respond quickly to any changes that may occur in purchase patterns or competitive activity.

Decision making by the owner is also made with the best interest of the company in mind. In larger firms, product managers, for instance, may be apt to make a decision that will positively impact their specific product or division but may not be in the overall best interest of the organization. The "silo effect" is alive and well in many large companies. In small companies there are generally too few people involved for silos to develop. Employees in small companies tend to become multitalented and able to handle issues relating to a variety of areas of the company.

More Long-Termism

Small businesses generally focus more on longer-term profitability than do larger organizations. Larger, and particularly publicly traded, firms are continuously pressured to produce positive growth results on a quarterly basis. Small businesses, though created to generate a profit for the owner, do not operate under this pressure. They are able, therefore, to make decisions that may not result in immediate revenues but will in the long term generate even greater returns. In my experience, many small business owners seem to have an innate feel for what is in the long-term best interest of the company. They respond intuitively, without weighing the monetary value of the customer or whether there is a profit to be made on this transaction. This may be a function of the absence of sophisticated information systems in small companies, but most seem much less focused on whether or not each transaction or each customer is profitable and more focused on pleasing customers, knowing that this will deliver payback directly and indirectly well into the future.

The small business owner's attitude toward risk may be more flexible and tolerant than that of managers in larger organizations. The attitude is, if we don't try something new we'll never know if it would have worked. One result of this attitude and leadership is that employees are made to feel empowered in their decision making. They may be able to make decisions without fear of retribution if a wrong decision is made, provided it was made with the customer's satisfaction as the goal. This is dramatically different from bureaucratic organizations, where employees' main focus may be self-preservation or self-reward.

It is easier for staff in a small firm to be accountable for maintaining relationships with customers. For instance, if a regular customer has not visited the beauty salon during the past month, employees may begin to wonder why she has not been in recently. Is it because of a negative experience the last time she had her hair styled? Is she ill? Has there been illness in her family? Has she been on vacation? The employees will know that they have not seen her and will be able to take appropriate action, if necessary. They may, for example, assuming the relationship is a close one, telephone to see if there is anything they can do for the customer. The result is that the relationship is further cemented because the customer will know that the company truly cares.

Stew Leonard's, a family-owned and operated grocery store in Norwalk, Connecticut, is a good example of how a small business can keep in touch with its customers.[4] Every month, the store manager conducts an informal hour-long meeting with 12 of its customers where they are asked various questions about what improvements could be made to enhance the level of service within the store. The participants are paid a small amount of money for participating, and management receives great insights into how they can improve the customer's shopping experience. While the information the store receives is obviously critical to understanding how to better develop customer relationships, another benefit is that participants undoubtedly tell friends and family about having participated in the research. This sends the message to customers that their opinions are valued and that the store truly wants to develop a relationship with them.

Can We Bottle This?

In small firms, value is created for customers through close, personal contact with employees and management, and an emotional bond develops. It is obvious that larger firms can create value for the customer in many different ways and forms. One question these larger companies should address is the extent to which they are able to replicate the types of value created by smaller businesses. How-

[4]Michael Barrier, "A New Sense of Service," *Nation's Business* (June 1991), 16–24.

ever, it must be remembered that not all large businesses are able to do this, nor are larger businesses able to create the exact types of value created by smaller firms. Also, certain segments of customers do not want the personalized service created by the smaller businesses. Thus, while larger organizations should examine and learn from the ways in which small firms are able to create their own unique types of value for customers, there are limitations to how many of the small business strategies can be replicated in a larger business environment.

Overall, there is strong evidence to suggest that the advantages to be gained by small business are often the result of the management style of the owner/operator. His or her style directly impacts the organizational culture, which in turn directly influences the customer's experience of dealing with the company. The leadership demonstrated by the owner/manager is reflected in how the company operates and the face that it presents to its customers. Thus, we have genuine inseparability between the company and the people who work there. It is precisely this fact that contributes to the greater ease of establishing customer relationships in this context.

Small business operators are often perceived by their customers in both a business and a social context. For instance, the small business owner may attend the neighborhood church or coach Little League baseball. The interaction in the business environment between the small business operator and the customer may focus on everyday topics such as the weather, the car, the family, or the score of last night's baseball game. The customers may rarely discuss the actual purchase at hand. In other words, the interaction has been extended from a business context to a social context.

In a customer interaction with a small business, it is more likely that the customers understand that their business has an effect on the overall success of the firm. If they take that business elsewhere, the firm suffers. This results in feelings of *guilt* when, for whatever reason, they choose to place their business elsewhere. This is what is occurring with independent retail book outlets and the growth of online book retailers. While enjoying the variety and lower prices of the superstore, many avid readers feel pangs of guilt over the declining number of locally owned, independent bookstores.

Closeness in Small Business Relationships

While we often think of our relationships with family and friends as being closer than those we have with businesses, we can place both types of relationships on a continuum from very close and intimate to distant. An individual may feel closer to one sibling than another, or feel closer to parents and grandparents than to siblings. In the same way, a customer may feel closer to the deli where he or she buys a sandwich most days for lunch than to the service station where he or she buys gasoline once a week, particularly if the service station is equipped with a self-service, pay-at-the-pump system.

While the customer may appear to be loyal to a supermarket in the sense that he or she buys groceries there every week, that customer may not feel particularly close to the store or its staff, whereas the employees at the deli know him or her by name. Is this a function only of the number of times the customer visits the deli compared to the supermarket? Frequency of contact certainly does play a role, but the small deli has qualities that bring customers closer, such as its attention to quality, personalized, friendly service, and recognition of the customer's personal needs.

When customers shop at a large supermarket, it is less likely that they will form relationships with the staff members. Reasons for this include the style of service, which is almost completely self-service. It is possible to shop at a supermarket without speaking to an employee, except possibly for some small talk with the cashier at the checkout. Usually when conversation does take place it is to make a request for a product or point out an incorrect price on the scanner. This is quite different from the interaction that takes place between customers of a small grocery store and its employees. There, the same employees will serve the customer time after time and will get to know the customer well enough to engage in real conversation. Over a period of time, customers will often reveal more about their personal lives to employees of a small business because they feel that they have gotten to know these people. The sharing of personal information between customers and employees illustrates the closeness of the relationship just as it does between hairdressers and their clients.

Close relationships are acknowledged to be more solid and likely longer lasting. They are more likely to be formed where the customer comes into fairly frequent contact with the service provider, the service is of a personal or high-involvement nature, and a mutuality of interests and goals exists between the parties.

How Small Businesses Do It . . . or Don't

Small businesses seem to have a natural ability to get closer to their customers and build relationships with them. In fact, relationship building often occurs as a natural extension of the owner's and employees' personalities. As small business owners and their employees encounter the same customers over time, they get to know each other. The most important element in the process of building and maintaining relationships comes naturally to people as they conduct business—communication. It has long been recognized that communication is essential to strong and meaningful personal relationships. As relationships develop over time and people become closer, they understand the meaning in the things people do and say.[5] As customers and staff have more opportunities to interact, their conversations become more meaningful and a deeper understanding of each other develops. As a result, the parties feel closer and relationships form. In turn, employees and owners often know what customers want, even before they ask. For example, a neighborhood video store will set aside a movie for a customer, thinking that the customer would like it. The intuitive nature of such a relationship does not come into being spontaneously or haphazardly; it develops from the communication necessary to building the closeness in the relationship.

Not only is the level of communication important to the relationship between small businesses and their customers, but so too is the way people communicate. The tone of voice, the emotion in the conversations, the genuine interest in what customers have to say is seldom replicated in the interchanges between customers and staff at larger businesses.

While small firms generally do have closer relationships with their customers, there are some who just don't get it. Some small businesses never seem to get close to their customers or provide the kind of service that leads people to want to come back. In fact, some of them drive people in the opposite direction. Why does this happen? There may be several reasons, the most obvious being that they do not want to develop close personal relationships with customers. One reason for this may simply be in personality. Some small business owners are distant and do not much enjoy the relationships they have with their customers. Owners like this are likely to attract employees who feel the same, and the overall feeling within the business will be cold and distant.

Another reason for the lack of closeness between some small firms and their customers may be that the firms do not recognize the importance of excellent customer service. For a variety of reasons, some small business people do not focus on getting to know the customers and satisfying their needs. This often happens when small businesses operate as a monopoly, as can occur in rural areas where consumers have limited choice or in larger areas where there is only one supplier for a particular product or service.

Achieving customer satisfaction and developing customer relationships is not easy. Smaller firms may have an advantage in this respect, but there is certainly no guarantee that they will be successful.

Two That Do It Right

I would now like to introduce you to two small, family-owned businesses that are very similar in how they operate, though they are separated by the Atlantic

---

[5] Steve Duck, *Meaningful Relationships* (Thousand Oaks, Calif.: Sage, 1994).

Ocean. Neither of these companies has had the benefit of formal management training in marketing or customer service. Both firms have been in business for 50 years or more and enjoy the support of a loyal and devoted clientele, some of whom now shop for groceries and specialty foods where their parents and grandparents shopped before them. Both are run by the children and grandchildren of the founder, and both will tell you that they are doing nothing special. They are simply operating their businesses the way they always have.

Caviston's Food Emporium is a small family-owned and operated specialty grocer, fish, and poultry shop located in Glasthule, near Dublin, Ireland. As I got to know Peter Caviston and his family, it became apparent to me that his company's relationship with its customers is quite similar to the relationship a small grocery business near where I live has with its customers. This reinforced my view that the interaction between small businesses and their customers has many common features, regardless of where they operate.

Caviston's is a good example of how a small business can grow and prosper, even in times of rapid economic change, customer lifestyle changes, and increased competition. Cavistons began as a fishmonger's and has grown into a food emporium that sells cheeses, fish, poultry, deli items, prepared meals, baked goods and fine foods from around the world. Still, it has retained its high-quality service, friendly staff, and attention to customer needs. The owners' knowledge of fine food and its preparation have allowed them to better meet the needs of their customers. While customers can go to larger stores in the city to buy similar products, they continue to return to Cavistons because customer service is the focal point of the business.

Staff at Caviston's are noted for their friendly, responsive and personalized approach to serving customers. The sale of fish and other products is generally accompanied by a chat and advice on methods of preparation and serving. The expertise of the employees is important to the attraction and retention of customers. They depend on Caviston's for fresh products, quality, and a wide product range. This small business retains qualities of shopping associated with the past, when staff and owners were friendly and personal. Caviston's fits well with the community in which it operates. The staff and owners know what the customers want, and the customers know what to expect from them. This comes without the use of any form of advertising, although Caviston's is well known in its community for its sponsorship of rugby and an annual James Joyce festival and for in-store cooking demonstrations. Caviston's relies upon their reputation as a selling feature, as well as on their customers, who continue to offer positive word-of-mouth. As a testament to the quality of service offered, Caviston's was named Ireland's delicatessen of the year in 1994.

To better understand the attributes that Caviston's has used successfully to grow and succeed, a research team from University College Dublin conducted interviews with Caviston's customers. Certain commonalities are apparent in the findings. First, customers said that employees are helpful and approachable; they listen to customers and make them feel happy. Because of this, customers said that they are able to build a relationship with the employees. Customers also said that Caviston's has a very strong reputation and high credibility, the result of enhanced customer-oriented policies. Finally, customers said that Caviston's makes shopping an enjoyable and trouble-free experience.

With only the Atlantic Ocean keeping them apart, on the eastern edge of Canada, in a city known for its Irish roots, sits Belbin's Grocery of St. John's, another excellent example of a family-owned small business that has survived the test of time and competition only to become better known for its quality service and attention to customer care. Customers are treated with respect and are given top-quality service regardless of the amount of money they spend. Belbin's has been catering to a loyal base of regular customers for well over 50 years. Operating until their recent expansion from a very small retail store, Belbin's has specialized in the home delivery of groceries. While many of their regulars visit the store to buy their groceries, others take advantage of Belbin's delivery service—a service that has continued to thrive in an era where home delivery of many products fell out of fashion. These customers have typically telephoned in their grocery orders but now submit them by fax or through the Belbin's website.

Two aspects of Belbin's operation epitomize for me what their customers' relationships actually mean to the customers themselves. Robert Belbin, who now with his brother and cousin operate the company started by their grandfather, was describing to me one of his regular customers who has been buying her groceries from Belbin's for 40 years or more. Now widowed and living alone, she telephones weekly and orders a predictable selection of grocery items. These are picked from the shelves, boxed, and delivered in the Belbin's van. When he arrives at the customer's apartment, the Belbin's driver is typically invited to join the long-time customer for a cup of tea. He helps her unpack her groceries and spends a few minutes in conversation.

When I asked Robert Belbin if he makes any money on delivering groceries to this customer, his response was predictable. "I probably don't," he answered, "but I'm not going to stop. *We owe it to her.*" After years of doing business together, the customer knows that she can depend on Belbin's. What is really interesting is that Mr. Belbin does not feel he is doing anything extraordinary; rather, he is simply doing business. While the delivery of this customer's weekly order may not seem like good business from a financial perspective, the demonstrated importance of this one customer is a good indication of how Belbin's treats every customer and why the business has prospered through times of economic hardship and increased competition. The way that customers feel about dealing with Belbin's is a driving force behind the business and the reason for the long-term relationships and referrals that have resulted.

Belbin's also has customers that it serves on regular basis who require home delivery during business hours because they work full-time and value the delivery service offered by Belbin's. What separates Belbin's from other grocery stores is that they have been given the keys to the homes of several of their valued customers. These are kept securely in the safe in Robert Belbin's office, where delivery personnel, often the owners of the store, have access to them. During a delivery, the Belbin employee will not only take the purchased items inside the house, but will often place perishable items in the refrigerator and other items in cupboards so that the customers will not have to do this when they arrive home.

The high level of trust that Belbin's customers have developed towards the company has come from many years of treating their customers fairly and responsively. While some may argue that this situation is difficult to replicate, the Belbin's example shows us that these situations still exist. Indeed, the situation is not unlike what existed in rural communities not so long ago, where the local grocery store was a well-respected and integral part of the community.

How does an experience at Caviston's or Belbin's compare with the experience customers might have shopping at a larger grocery store or supermarket? It is safe to say that any customer will receive more personalized service and advice shopping at these smaller grocery stores, even if he or she does not shop there often. Customers who visit either of these stores for the first time experience friendly service and attention that long-time customers of larger retailers do not experience.

Often in smaller businesses employees will engage in conversation with customers even when they are not regulars. This is often attributed to the small staff numbers and the fact that many small business owners actually work at the business of serving customers. For the most part, these business owners are merely being friendly, and they hire employees who take the same approach to customer service and care. And they do care! The owners and employees of both Belbin's and Caviston's care about the way their customers feel and what they think of the business when they leave the store.

Threats to the Small Firm

Small companies will always exist and will presumably always be able to carry on business in the same personal way that has allowed many of them to build some of the most genuine of customer relationships. But, partly because of recent advances in technology, large companies are now able to offer their customers some of the same relationship-building tools and techniques that have until now been the stock in trade of the small company. Discussing the subject of customer relationship management, Stephen Hoare, writing in *The Times* of

London, observes that a customer can now expect to receive an e-mail message from an online bookstore containing the details of a new novel by her favorite author, will receive a message on her cellphone from the local movie theater advising of the availability of seats for a movie that evening, or will hear from her hairdresser with a message reminding her of the appointment at noon and offering to send a taxi.[6]

With the rapid advances being made in interactive technology, much larger companies are able to adopt technology and tactics for emulating the behavior of much smaller companies. To explore some of these advances, let's focus on what is happening in retailing, and in book retailing in particular.

In recent times, as a result of developments in technology, competition has been redefined for traditional booksellers, or at least its location. No longer are retail bookstores competing primarily with retailers in the same town or city. The major competition for most small independents is now on the Internet. But even the local competition has changed. In most cities in North America, the large superstores, with names like Barnes and Noble, Borders, and Chapters, have come to town and created a different way of buying books. But it doesn't stop there. Mass retailers such as Wal-Mart and Costco, who traditionally were not big in the book business are now accounting for a very large percentage of books sold.

The small neighborhood bookstore has offered a venue for people who like to spend time leisurely thumbing through books, consulting the knowledgeable staff, or chatting to other customers about the latest works by their favorite authors. While there are still some of these bookstores left, a dramatic shift towards superstores and Internet selling has occurred. It may be difficult to understand why people who obviously enjoy the experience of going to the small bookstores would suddenly give them up. Peter Desbarats, a Canadian journalism professor, talks about the guilt he felt after having bought several books from an Internet bookseller and a superstore when he realized that the neighborhood bookstore he had been going to for 12 years was closing.[7] Why *guilt*? Desbarats has a sense of having betrayed the relationship he had built with the two brothers who owned the bookstore. The telling line in his article is: "I dared not tell them that not only had I patronized one of the two local Chapters in suburban London but I had already bought several books from Chapters on the Internet."

More and more people are buying books from the Internet and the superstores. Why? Often the books are cheaper, and delivery is sometimes offered free. But

---

[6] Stephen Hoare, "Winning Our Hearts, Minds, Loyalty, and Hard-Earned Income," *Times* (London), 20 April 2000 (accessed from *The Times'* website: http://www.sundattimes.co.uk).

[7] Peter Desbarats, "Buy a Book On-line, Pay the Price in Time," *Globe and Mail* (Toronto), 3 June 1999, T1, T3.

these new competitors also create value in other ways. They have access to millions of titles, and the superstores have a depth of selection that most independents can only dream of. The superstores have also succeeded in many cases in creating a relaxed atmosphere and a sense of community. In Canada, the Chapters superstores include a Starbucks coffee shop. Books and coffee obviously make a successful combination, and the Starbucks, along with the armchairs and open fireplaces, serves to attempt at least to recreate the friendly, relaxed atmosphere of the local bookstore.

The online booksellers are attempting to create something approaching a genuine customer relationship. The functional advantages of the online booksellers are obvious—great variety, access to obscure titles, lower prices, and free delivery often offered as a special incentive. But the competitive advantages that they have created do not end there. The websites of Amazon.com, Barnesandnoble.com, and Chapters.ca are among the most user-friendly on the Internet. By being responsive, replying to orders immediately, keeping customers informed of the status of their orders, and allowing customers to track the shipment of their orders online, they are adding value. By being interactive, suggesting to a customer a certain title that he or she might like, and allowing readers to chat among themselves about the books they have read and read reviews contributed by other customers, online retailers are behaving very much like the employees of the neighborhood bookstore.

Some people are willing to abandon the relationship with the small local bookstore in order to save money and gain access to a much larger inventory. Or maybe they hope that they can have the best of both worlds if enough people continue to patronize the small bookstores. They can still go there to browse and engage in conversation, only to go home later and order their books from an online retailer; in other words, the small retailers can act in some respects as consultants to avid readers. Unfortunately, too many customers have had this same idea, and the small retailers cannot make money from the browsers who come and leave without buying anything. Some authors have actually forecast the disappearance of the neighborhood bookstore.[8]

What new value can small firms create in order to retain their customers who have been loyal for so many years? And what can they do to defend themselves against these new and different forms of competition? The challenge will be to see how small firms will sustain the relationships that they have built with their customers over the years, and whether those emotionally based relationships will be strong enough to withstand competition from new Internet-based businesses that can offer clear advantages in the creation of lower-order forms of value.

---

[8] Marina Strauss, "Small Book Stores Face Tragic Ending," *Globe and Mail* (Toronto), 19 June 1999, B1, B9.

That Small Business Feel

Some large organizations are doing extremely well in maintaining an atmosphere similar to a small business. One such example is Tim Hortons, a coffee and donuts chain that has over 1700 stores in Canada and 100 in the United States, making it one of North America's largest coffee and fresh baked goods franchise operations. Established in 1964, the company is named after Tim Horton, a well-known professional hockey player who was one of the company's founding partners.

Tim Hortons has gone to great lengths to position its stores as much more than simply a place to buy coffee and donuts. In many cities a visit to the neighborhood Tim Hortons is now an essential part of the daily lives of Canadians. This is evident from the long lines early in the morning of customers who must have their Tim Hortons coffee before heading to work. The company uses the slogan "Always Fresh" and places enormous emphasis on ensuring that all coffee and baked goods are as fresh as they can be.

However, it is more than high-quality products that has enabled Tim Hortons to grow and become such a central institution in the Canadian culture. As I have illustrated throughout this book, this company's success has at least as much to do with the relational bond that is established between the Tim Hortons brand and its customers. Some customers regularly tip Tim Hortons employees—not a common occurrence at most coffee shops.

How can an organization as large as Tim Hortons continue to offer such high quality service? For one, Tim Hortons has a commitment to making each store a friendly meeting place. This is achieved by hiring talented and qualified employees and offering them a reasonable salary and quality work environment, resulting in relatively low employee turnover. This in turn enables employees to have the time and opportunity to become acquainted with customers and come to know them on a first-name basis. The personalized service does not stop there. Because of the high level of customer loyalty and repeat visits, employees become very knowledgeable about the specific preferences of regular customers.

It is common in Tim Hortons shops for employees to recognize customers, not by name but by what they regularly purchase. Thus, as a regular customer approaches the counter to be served, he is likely to be greeted with "large double-double, right?" Such indications of recognition are welcomed by the customer with a smile and a feeling of satisfaction, knowing that the staff knows him well enough to remember what he usually orders (a large coffee, with double cream and double sugar!). This recognition of the customer is often taken even further by the staff having the coffee, including the correct amount of cream and sugar and the customer's favorite donut, ready to go at the usual time each day. Thus, customers are able to drop quickly in and pick up their snacks without having to be delayed. All this is done with a friendly smile and genuine concern for the customer.

In most large organizations you would not expect small business characteristics to be present at the local store level. But they are at Tim Hortons. One reason for this is that nearly all stores are locally owned and operated through franchise agreements. Thus, the owners and managers have a hands-on management style and are able to understand their customers' preferences. They are also committed to the enhancement of the local community: Tim Hortons is very supportive of local community events, sponsoring children's hockey and soccer teams and various charities. The children who participate in programs sponsored by Tim Hortons are affectionately known as the "Timbits," after the company's bite-sized donut holes.

As well, Tim Hortons supports The Tim Hortons Children's Foundation, which provide camp activities for children from underprivileged families. The children selected to attend the camps live in communities where Tim Hortons stores operate, and local churches, schools, and other organizations assist in the selection of children most deserving of attending the camps. To support this endeavor, once a year Tim Hortons hosts "Camp Day," when coffee sales from all of the company's stores are donated to the foundation. In 1999, a total of $2.7 million (Cdn) was raised.[9]

What is both impressive and intriguing is the very large percentage of Canadians who have established a relationship with Tim Hortons. A visit to one of the company's stores is a routine part of their daily activities. They are recognized by the staff with a smile and likely with a recall of what they regularly order. Many of them will sit in the store and drink their coffee and make conversation with other regulars who show up at the same time each day. Or they will "drive thru" on their way to work to pick up a cup of "Tim's," often foregoing the coffee that is available to them at no cost at the office. Tim Hortons is an international chain of independently franchised stores that has succeeded in establishing a brand relationship with its regular customers who would not think of going anywhere else.

To really understand why Tim Hortons has been successful, we need to consider how the company creates value for its customers and how, unlike many larger companies, it may be able to behave more like a collection of small firms. Tim Hortons has been able to create a sense of community for many of its regular customers. Interaction with staff and with other customers represents an occasion that has some meaning. It is a regular event in their daily lives. Although coffee is the company's main product, a trip to Tim Hortons is not about

[9] www.timhortons.com, accessed January 6, 2000.

coffee. It has simply become something that millions of Canadians and some Americans do every day.

The fact that Tim Hortons stores are everywhere—many Canadian cities have dozens of them, and many are now located in hospitals, airports, arenas, and other public buildings—creates convenience value, but it is something approaching community value that really attracts most people. Tim Hortons has become the equivalent of the old general store, where the townsfolk gathered around the wood stove or the cracker barrel, or the British pub where the locals collect to talk about the events of the day. The company's support for local charities and its children's camps simply reinforces that connection.

What Larger Firms Can Learn

By studying the relationships between small businesses and their customers, we can point to some definite things that larger firms can do to improve their customer relationships. It is evident from focus group research that the businesses to which people feel closest and most loyal are almost always small. Participants will say that they appreciate the way the staff calls them by name and remembers their preferences from one visit to the next. Very often the same people will say that they have no relationship with larger businesses because they feel they are just a number. This should tell us something about how customers prefer to be treated. Simple gestures like calling a customer by name are important to relationship building because they result in a more satisfied customer. But how can larger businesses know people's names and remember them from one visit to the next when they have so many customers? The use of detailed databases and tools to track customer preferences and habits is one way.

While database technology is already being used by many companies to increase customer contact and build relationships, it often results in less satisfied customers who feel that their privacy is being invaded by mail and phone calls that are perceived to be nothing more than solicitation for more business. This technology can, however, bring businesses closer to their customers by providing a wealth of knowledge about the history of the customer, spending habits, lifestyles, and relationship details. But having sophisticated databases is not always possible or necessary. As the Tim Hortons example illustrates, it is possible for a large company to successfully develop a genuine relationship with millions of anonymous customers.

Employees at larger organizations need to be encouraged to think at the community level, where decisions are made with the customer always first in mind. This is different from the corporate level of thinking. Consider the example of a vice-president of marketing of a large retail firm. This individual is responsible for the overall marketing activities of the firm, but how often does she visit stores and talk directly to the people who frequent them? In my experience, these tasks are left to less senior individuals in the firm. But if the VP is the individual who is ultimately responsible for these decisions, should she not be directly involved in the process, rather than relying on written reports submitted by junior managers or consultants? Only by taking this approach can the VP be confident that she fully understands customers and their issues.

A product manager who is launching a new service directed at young women aged 13 to 18 must begin to think and feel as a teenager does. The product manager must fully understand the buying habits of the target group, the issues teens are dealing with on a daily basis, what is important to them and what is not. An intimate knowledge of such information cannot be acquired by reading—it has to be experienced![10]

Larger firms need to have in place human resource policies that encourage employees to consider the impact that decisions will have on the overall success of their employer, rather than on a specific department or product line. However, policies alone won't eliminate the silo effect I spoke of earlier. Employers need to go to great lengths to hire and retain individuals who can see the broader picture, and they need to have ongoing training programs that encourages this broader thinking. Having multifunctional employees reduces the silo thinking and assists the firm in taking a longer-term approach to managing customer relationships.

Sponsorship also offers an opportunity for a large firm to position itself as being community-minded and integral to the success of the community in which it operates. For instance, Tim Hortons has achieved this through their sponsorship of youth sports programs. We will discuss in greater detail in Chapter 11 how companies can more effectively use sponsorships to drive customer closeness. This involves selecting sponsorships that will enhance the association between the company and the communities in which it operates.

Employees at large firms need to have the authority to make decisions when and where they are needed. Part of this involves having a decentralized management structure where delegation is expected. But this is not enough. Employees need to know that if they make a bad decision they will not be reprimanded, provided that they had the customer's best interests at heart. This is not to say that employees should not be held responsible, but rather that they need to feel that their every move is not being monitored. Such a situation can help in emulating the decision-making process that occurs in many small businesses.

The number of employees in a large firm can also influence the ability of a company to get to know its customers on a more personal basis. Companies that are very cost conscious and operate under a bare-bones structure often do not

---

[10] Cindy Waxer, "Paper-Doll Taps Youth Market with Know-How," *Globe and Mail* (Toronto), 20 April 2000.

have enough employees to enable them to take the time to talk to customers. All too often, employees are forced to move on to the next customer immediately after the sale has been made or the information provided. Large firms must establish a communications dialogue with their customers. Outgoing follow-up phone calls, birthday cards, and other similar means should be established with customers, as well as opportunities for incoming e-mail and 1-800 numbers. Customers need to feel that they have the means to contact the firm should the need arise, and that the firm can then deal with the issue, whatever it may be.

As we have seen, it is possible for larger corporations to adopt strategies used by small businesses that enable them to get closer to its customers. Used properly, these strategies can offer a competitive advantage. We will later turn our attention, in Chapter 9, to better understanding what types of relationships are most at risk and put strategies in place to deal with these.

8

Measuring the Equity in Customer Relationships

How Well Are We Doing?

In this chapter we discuss the need to measure how well a firm or organization is doing in the creation and management of customer relationships. A company cannot begin to improve on the relationships it has with customers until it knows the current health of those relationships: where they are strong and where they are weak; which customers have the strongest relationships and where relationships are at risk; which aspects of the relationships ought to be shored up; and what the customer finds appealing or unappealing.

To begin to understand how well the company is performing in the creation and establishment of genuine customer relationships, management must first subscribe to the view that relationships are both a necessary intermediate step to the establishment of long-term shareholder value and a result of the creation of customer satisfaction through offering superior value in many forms, including the highest possible level of service quality. Thus, to really understand how well the firm is performing in the area of customer relationships, we must also make sure that we have information on how well it is doing in offering customer value and service quality, as well as on the level of customer satisfaction being achieved.

Although a great deal of attention has been paid in recent years to the establishment of relationships with customers, considerably less effort has been devoted to the measurement of those relationships. Where measurement has been discussed, the focus has tended to be on the behavioral outcomes of relationships, rather than on the nature or health of the relationships themselves. Much of the work on relationship measurement has, in fact, reflected the rather narrow view of customer relationships that is fairly prevalent in marketing today, as we have discussed in earlier chapters. Many companies appear to be content defining a customer relationship merely as repeat buying behavior or customer retention, and they would tend to see patterns of customer behavior that involve the customer returning to purchase from the company over time as evidence of a relationship. As we have discussed, just as a behavioral definition of a customer relationship is inadequate, so too is any attempt to measure the strength of customer relationships that does not have a significant component devoted to the measurement of customer emotions.

By putting in place a research program that measures on a regular basis the strength or health of relationships that a firm has with its customers, management is demonstrating its commitment to assessing how well the firm is performing, not by the easily measured financial indicators that have formed part of corporate performance measurement for generations, but by the expanding group of intangibles that are increasingly being used by progressive corporations to gauge how well they are performing in meeting the long-term objectives of various stakeholder groups. We will begin this overview of the measurement of customer relationships by addressing the principal objective of management, namely the creation of shareholder value. We can thus gain a better perspective on what information management needs so it can be confident that it understands how well the company is performing in maintaining genuine relationships with its customers.

Shareholder Value

In recent years, considerable attention has been turned in corporate circles to the creation of *shareholder value*. This focus results from the realization that one of the most important responsibilities of management is the enhancement of shareholders' investment in the company. While there is good reason to advocate that the interests of other stakeholders—including employees, customers, and the broader community—should also be protected, the current focus of most large publicly traded companies is on the creation of shareholder value. But there is no generally accepted definition of what shareholder value involves. How exactly does management go about creating shareholder value?

Historically, shareholder value has been equated with current stock price. In many companies it still is. Management is perceived to be advancing the interests of shareholders if the stock price moves upward each quarter. Corporate performance and the compensation of CEOs are closely tied to such short-term financial measures as return on capital invested, earnings per share, and operating income.

There is growing disillusionment in some quarters with the nature of such corporate performance measures and the focus on historic, short-term, internal financial measures to guide investors and to assess shareholder value creation.

Some management thinkers, such as Henry Mintzberg[1] and Peter Drucker,[2] are openly critical of corporations that tie CEO compensation to short-term movements in the stock price and to corporate performance measures that are entirely financial and historic. They argue that achieving such objectives may not really add value for the shareholder over the long term.

A burgeoning movement has arisen in recent years, within and outside the accounting profession, focused on the development of additional measures of corporate performance and, by extension, shareholder value and on the acceptance in the accounting and investment communities of the legitimacy of non-financial, intangible measures as a basis for evaluating performance.

Historically, businesses have measured the things that can be easily and reliably measured or whose performance is automatically captured because they had to *for accounting purposes.* Companies measure sales because they have to issue invoices to customers and have to pay the tax department. They measure productivity per employee because it represents a basis for compensation and because increased productivity is a good thing. They measure things that are easily measured and are quantifiable in easily accepted units: dollars, minutes and seconds, number of defects, number of complaints, and so on. Missed in this process is the measurement of things that are relevant for the strategic management of customer relationships. The result is that most companies do not have available the information needed to assess how well they are doing in establishing and maintaining relationships with customers.

A focus on a "balanced scorecard" has emerged in the 1990s as stock exchanges, regulatory bodies, professional accounting organizations, some companies themselves, and various critics have come to the realization that historic, financial measures are an inadequate reflection of the actual performance of the corporation or of its ability to create *future* shareholder value for those investors whose time horizon extends beyond the next quarter.

At the senior management levels of some companies, attention has turned to the measurement and reporting of more intangible measures of corporate performance, things that are not reported in dollars or minutes and have typically not been measured in most organizations. These include customer satisfaction and retention, customer turnover, customer service standards, employee turnover, employee training, new product development, innovation, partnerships, and strategic alliances.[3] The movement toward the establishment of new corporate per-

---

[1] Henry Mintzberg, "How Fat Cats Can Slim Down," *Financial Times,* 29 October 1999, 13.

[2] Fred Andrews, "Drucker Disdains Corporate Myopia," *Globe and Mail Report on Business* (Toronto), 18 November 1999, B19.

[3] Carolyn Kay Brancato, *Institutional Investors and Corporate Governance* (Chicago: Irwin Professional Publishing, 1997), chap. 2.

formance measures is entirely consistent with a management emphasis on customer retention and relationships, which makes it all the more important that companies begin to measure these key corporate assets.

Short-term value creation is focused on managing the stock price so that sales and profit targets are met. Because stock price is so volatile, linked as it often is to the quarterly reporting of earnings, management in publicly traded companies is often encouraged to drive short-term revenues and profits through promotions that may, in fact, have the effect of diminishing long-term customer loyalty, and to cut costs, often by reducing staff and thereby impairing customer service. The effect, in the short term, is to achieve profitability and financial targets. But this does not mean achieving shareholder value, except possibly for those shareholders who wish to cash out on the back of a short-term jump in the stock price.

Real shareholder value is created by guaranteeing the long-term viability and growth of the company. Shareholder value creation, therefore, is intimately tied to customer loyalty, for it is this loyalty that will deliver the stream of earnings needed to drive sales growth. Customers deliver revenue, and they do so in perpetuity as long as they are satisfied. Long-term customer satisfaction drives customer relationships. Indeed, genuine customer relationships will never develop unless the customer is continually satisfied with the company and the way he or she is treated.

The links, then, are obvious. Management must pay attention to the creation of value for customers, which drives customer satisfaction, which leads to the creation of customer relationships, which leads to the retention of customers and their long-term patronage, which contributes to shareholder value. The starting point, therefore, in understanding genuine customer relationships and their impact on long-term profitability and shareholder value, is understanding how the firm is able to create value for its customers. It may be useful at this point to reiterate some of the observations made earlier about customer value.

Understanding Customer Value

It is important that marketing practitioners and others within the firm understand the connection between the various components of the chain that links customer value creation to shareholder value. Simply put, marketing is all about *creating value* for customers. Many companies today profess to be dedicated to value creation or adding value for their customers. The sad fact, however, is that few really understand their customers well enough to know exactly how they should go about creating or adding value in ways that customers will recognize and appreciate. Many firms fall into the trap of attempting to create value for customers, using as a definition management's own view of what the customer values. The result, while costing the company money to implement and deliver, leaves the customer cold because it simply does not represent a valued addition to the offer or, as it has come to be called in many firms, the *value proposition*.

This calls out for research directed at understanding value as defined by the customer. Customers see value in many places and many forms. It is not simply value for money. Value can be created and added for customers through many different actions and activities of the company. Value creation does not require product modification or price discounting. In fact, in many cases lower prices are counterproductive to creating a value proposition that customers will really find attractive. It makes a great deal more sense for companies to focus on creating value for customers through improving service delivery, increasing contributions to the community in which the customer lives, and making it easier for the customer to deal with them. Value relates to how the customer is served, how he or she is treated and made to feel.

Value can be added by making improvements in a company's service delivery processes and systems. Again, research is generally useful for determining where service quality meets customer expectations and where it is deficient. It is necessary to measure service quality at a series of different levels and not to focus only on the technical delivery of service. Although time and space do not permit a review of the details of service quality measurement, suffice it to say that the customer defines service as more than the functional provision of the product or service. It is important to examine the nature of the core service, the systems and processes that the firm has in place to support service delivery, the accuracy and timeliness of service delivery, and the interaction among the customer, the firm, and its employees and systems.

The value the firm creates for the customer contributes to the customer's level of satisfaction with the company, how it conducts its business, and what it has to offer. Again, there is more to customer satisfaction than meets the eye. Many firms take the pulse of customer satisfaction from time to time but measure the concept far too simplistically. We have to ask, satisfaction with what? It is, for example, entirely possible that customers may be quite satisfied with a company's core products or services, and even with support services such as delivery and billing, but so dissatisfied with the manner in which they are treated by staff that they will refuse to deal with the company ever again. Satisfaction is a function of the customer's interaction with the company on a number of different levels. All of these must be taken into account if we are to have an accurate picture of satisfaction and the factors that contribute to it.

Customer relationships are the result of long periods of customer satisfaction. If a customer is not satisfied with his or her dealings with a company, a close, positive, genuine relationship is highly unlikely (barring unusual circumstances) to develop. It takes a certain time for awareness to develop into familiarity and familiarity into a special relationship. Satisfaction is one of the conditions necessary for a genuine relationship to emerge. Companies need to know how far along they are in creating relationships with their customers. They need to know where relationships are strong and where they are at risk. They need to know the health of their customer relationships as compared with those of their competitors.

Longstanding customer relationships represent a company's most valuable assets, assets that will pay dividends well into the future. By knowing how much equity really resides in their customer relationships, a company can have a very good understanding of how these relationships will pay returns to shareholders in the future through their contribution to a stream of revenue on which the company can rely.

The measurement of concepts such as service quality, customer satisfaction, and customer relationship equity has to be tied directly to strategy. Many companies have established a corporate strategy of "relationship marketing" on the premise that they will achieve success through the creation and enhancement of customer relationships. We will set aside for the moment the question of whether many firms really understand the nature of customer relationships and what it takes to establish and sustain them. If a company subscribes to such a strategy, measuring its success in delivering on that strategy is imperative.

But this creates another problem, that of deciding how to measure performance against such an intangible objective. How do we know when a genuine relationship is in place? How do we know when it has been improved or when it is in danger of deteriorating? The very idea of measuring something as intangible as a relationship will immediately create skepticism in the minds of many managers. And yet much progress has been made in recent years in gaining acceptance for the idea that other intangible indicators of performance can and should be measured. More and more firms are measuring customer satisfaction and service quality. The measurement of customer relationships is but a small step farther along the path.

The Nature of Relationships

Customer relationships, like all human relationships, are formed over time. Both behavioral and psychological or attitudinal components or indicators must be present to indicate that a relationship exists. In other words, the customer must not only demonstrate loyalty in the form of repeat buying behavior and high share of wallet, but have an emotional commitment to the company as well. The emotive or attitudinal component is in fact the more important.

It is possible, as is evidenced in certain industries in which the repurchase cycle is very long, such as the funeral industry discussed in Chapter 1, for a strong emotive bond to exist between a company and its customers even in the absence of *buying* behavior. Of course, other forms of positive behavior may be taking place even though buying is not. For example, though a family may not buy more than one home from a real estate agent, this does not prevent them from recommending that agent to friends who are in the market for a new home. The longstanding relationship that exists may not manifest itself in the form of repeat buying, but that does not mean it is not a valuable relationship. The value to the firm, and the resultant contribution to shareholder value, come in the form of positive word of mouth that results in referral business.

Thus, marketing executives must have information not only on the observable, customer-contact forms of behavior, but also (and more important) on the state of the emotive connection with customers and insights into their nonobservable behavior toward the firm and its brands.

What is it about relationships that causes some to express confusion or blanch at the thought that they can be measured, let alone managed? To quote Brian Quinn, "A phenomenon to be understood or managed must first be delineated and measured."[4] Many organizations that purport to be practicing relationship marketing do not understand the essence of a relationship, particularly as the customer is likely to define it. Delineating a relationship means deconstructing it into its characteristics and essential components. A relationship is, above all, an emotional concept. It is impossible to conceive of a genuine relationship that is not characterized by emotions.

If the interaction between a company and the customer is not characterized by certain emotions, then no relationship exists. The customer's response in such cases is, "This is not a relationship; I rarely think of them; I never hear from them; they don't seem to care about me." Genuine relationships with businesses *do* exist, and they are, in this context as in all aspects of our lives, characterized by emotional bonds like trust, affinity, commitment, empathy, caring, and two-way communications.

The Relationship Continuum

I often ask seminar participants why a relationship is like beauty. Sometimes, a more cynical member will respond, "Because it is skin-deep." In some cases that may unfortunately be true, but the answer that I am looking for is that it exists in the eye of the beholder. In other words, no relationship exists unless the customer says it does. Also, like other related and similar concepts, relationships may be seen to exist on a continuum. Some relationships are perceived

---

[4] James Brian Quinn, *Intelligent Enterprise* (New York: Free Press, 1992), chap. 8.

to be (and may be rated by the customer to be) stronger than others, closer, longer-lasting, more likely to endure, and so on.

There is no denying that relationships are personal, emotional, and ephemeral constructs. They are difficult to define or describe. But the individual *knows* when he or she is in one. For example, when participants in a focus group are asked to describe their relationship with their electricity supplier, a quizzical look is likely to appear on their faces, and one participant may well say something like, or "I don't have any dealings with them; to me they're just a bill!"

Therefore, a relationship is in the same league as quality, service, value, and other marketing-related concepts that exist largely in the eye of the consumer. These concepts also share the characteristics of complex attitudinal concepts that clinical psychologists regularly measure so that they can assess the nature of attitudes toward certain objects, concepts, ideas, and behaviors.

Artificial Relationships

There are, of course, other forms of relationships that companies have with their customers. These are fleeting contacts that do not warrant the label "relationship." They include the meal at a roadside restaurant or in an airport cafeteria while on a business trip or vacation. The likelihood of ongoing contact or a genuine relationship developing is remote. Recently, many companies have established frequent-buyer programs or clubs to encourage repeat buying—the behavioral side of a relationship. These marketing tools might be labeled "artificial" or "spurious" relationships. They are predicated on creating an incentive to encourage customers to come back again and again, with the promise of a reward for their "loyalty." What distinguishes such a program from a genuine relationship is the possible absence of an emotional connection with the company. This is not to say that such an emotional connection cannot coexist with a frequency-marketing or club-card program—it is not at all unlikely, in fact, that membership in such a program may evolve into a genuine relationship. But such a program is not synonymous with and does not naturally lead to a genuine customer relationship.

Airline frequent-flyer programs and other such "loyalty" programs are designed to produce a behavioral result, namely, repeat buying and the related effect, increased "share of wallet." They are no more than a modern-day, database-driven equivalent of the trading stamp programs that reached their peak of popularity in the 1950s. In fact, interestingly, S&H Green Stamps have been relaunched in an electronic version to compete against such frequency marketing programs as Air Miles. But such programs must be seen for what they are, incentives to increase repeat buying, not evidence of genuine customer relationships.

Customer Relationships as Assets

Customer relationships have generally been accepted by progressive managers in most companies as assets that have to be managed strategically. Bill Birchard observes that "In the new economy, the most valuable assets have gone from solid to soft, from tangible to intangible. Instead of plant and equipment, companies today compete on ideas and relationships."[5] Betsey Nelson, FCO of Macromedia Inc., a Web software company, calculates value based on how close her company can get to its customers. She observes, "We're looking at the value over time of a relationship. . . . One thing that we know is that it's extremely valuable to us to own that customer relationship."[6]

Nelson goes on to observe that her interest is in the "core drivers of value." This may (or must) be examined at least at two levels. Nelson's focus is on the creation of value for shareholders, and in that context she is interested in what drives long-term customer value. But an incredibly important precursor to shareholder value is the creation of value for customers. Indeed, if a company is not successful in creating value for its customers, it can forget about achieving customer satisfaction or the long-term customer value that leads to a relationship and eventually to shareholder value.

Customer relationships may be viewed as long-term customer commitment or loyalty, which result from the fact that customers are satisfied not only by the company's products and services, but also by how they are treated by the company and its employees and are made to feel as a result of their contact and association with the company. Thus, relationships result from successively satisfying customers. Brian Quinn quotes the CEO of *Reader's Digest* as saying, "Our relationship with the reader is the key to the success of this entire company."[7] Jacques Nasser, President and CEO of the Ford Motor Company, speaking of the automotive business, recently observed that "This industry is being transformed from a nuts and bolts industry into a consumer one, and from a transaction industry into a relationship business."[8]

---

[5] Bill Birchard, "Intangible Assets + Hard Numbers = Soft Finance," *Fast Company* (October 1999), 316–36.

[6] Ibid.

[7] Quinn, *Intelligent Enterprise.*

[8] Tim Burt, "Ford Chief Takes a New Direction," *Financial Times,* 15 November 1999, 24.

Yet few companies measure the health of that relationship. Few companies know the cost of losing a customer or the payback from cultivating long-term, solid customer relationships.

Driving Customer Satisfaction

To understand how relationships are formed, we need insight into the factors that contribute to customer satisfaction. Many companies demonstrate a very narrow view of these factors, assuming that if they get the core product right and deliver it quickly and conveniently, the customer will be satisfied. My research over the past 30 years has convinced me that the drivers of customer satisfaction are much more complex than that. We have to appreciate that customer satisfaction is driven not only by functional aspects of product and customer service, but also by softer, "fuzzier" components that relate to how the customer is treated and made to feel.

Essentially, as many authors have recognized in recent years, customer satisfaction is all about value creation. We must therefore ask ourselves how we are creating value for the customer.

Brand Relationships

The importance of relationships with customers is not limited to those situations in which customers come into contact with a company and its employees. In fact, one of the most interesting and relevant applications of relationship thinking lies in the area of branding. Customers establish relationships with brands just as they do with companies and other organizations. Consumers develop brand loyalties, which are predicated on much more than repeat buying, and over time an emotional attachment to a brand emerges. Well-established names such as Kraft, Kellogg's, Volvo, Michelin, and Tide are examples of brands that have succeeded in creating such an emotional tie. Such brands add *meaning* to the lives of those who buy and use them. They become an important part of the lives of those consumers. By extension, consumers develop emotionally charged relationships with sports teams and rock bands. The unswerving loyalty of fans in the province of Quebec to the Montreal Canadiens is evidence of such a relationship, as is the extraordinary international popularity of European football clubs such as Juventus and Manchester United. These too are brands. As such, it is not sufficient for marketing executives to examine in their research such concepts as brand characteristics and brand personality; they must have insight into brand relationships. A wider discussion of brand relationships appears in Chapter 11.

Why Measurement Is Important

We have discussed four concepts that are integral to a complete understanding of the concept of customer relationships: value, satisfaction, relationships, and payback. Measurement focuses on the creation of shareholder value. It is important for management to understand from the customer's perspective how well the company is performing in each of these areas. If we do not measure such things, we cannot know how well we are doing in creating value for our customers and maintaining positive customer relationships.

Many managers probably believe measurement of such intangible concepts as customer value and relationships is impossible. It isn't! In fact, measurement is essential for feedback. If management does not measure such integral strategic elements, it cannot know what underlies customer relationships, how well the company is doing at creating those relationships, and how the company is benefitting from them. Only by measuring the health of the customer relationship can management understand how it can be strengthened.

I have always been intrigued by discussions I have had held over the years with senior managers of some large firms about their understanding of how to best manage customer relationships. In too many cases, the response is that this is done by capturing sales data at the checkout or analyzing the sales volume of individual customers. Some managers infer that customers who purchase more products and services must have a stronger relationship with the company. Why would they continue to purchase items if they did not have a relationship with the company? The problem is that this is an output-based view of relationships. *The behavior of the customer, as reflected in the number of products purchased, the frequency of purchases occasions, or the share of spending, is the* result *of the relationship, not the relationship itself.* If the relationship is strong, they will buy more, and more often. By focusing on a behavioral definition of a relationship, many managers ignore the essential attitudinal and emotional side.

In cases where the outcome is the focus, the idea of measuring relationships may still be accepted. The problem is that managers with this behavioral view do not understand that by focusing on behavioral outcome measures, they are measuring the wrong things (or at least not enough of the important things). They also do not demonstrate a fundamental understanding of the nature of a true relationship, one that is built on emotions. Measuring the strength or health of customer relationships is not the same as measuring customer satisfaction or service quality, both of which many companies do, and some do well. But measuring customer satisfaction and service quality is not enough.

Measuring customer satisfaction without measuring the factors that contribute to satisfaction produces a global number—"we're at 8.2, on average, on a 10-point scale"—but tells management little about what contributes to that score or what they can do to move the number to 8.5 within six months. We saw in Chapter 3 the tremendous payback that a company can enjoy by moving its customers toward total satisfaction—the ideal 10.

Measuring service quality is a move in the right direction in that it allows a company to delve more deeply into what contributes to customer satisfaction. Companies that do it well examine service quality along a series of service dimensions, looking at functional service delivery, timeliness, accuracy of fulfillment, responsiveness, and increasingly at the interaction between the customer and employees: how friendly are they? how knowledgeable, understanding, polite, and so on.

But measuring satisfaction and service quality, though it provides management with valuable information on how the company is performing in creating satisfied, loyal, and committed customers, gives management only some of the information it needs to create genuine long-term customer relationships. This is because, just as many factors other than service contribute to satisfaction, it takes more than excellent service delivery to create a relationship. The essential question that must be asked is, How good are we at creating value for our customers? This presumes that value may be created in many different ways, of which excellent service provision is but one.

We have all heard the old cliché that "you can't manage what you can't measure." Indeed, this is very applicable to the assessment of customer relationships. The key is not to understand that measurement is important but exactly what should be measured. One of the most troublesome issues facing management in implementing and managing a relationship-based approach to marketing is the lack of information available to them on the value of their customers. That is something an integrated program of measurement must address.

Creating Long-Term Customer Value (LTCV)

Most companies cannot even begin to calculate the value of customer relationships or the cost of losing a customer. Although a large percentage of companies will acknowledge the importance of customer relationships and their contribution to the creation of shareholder value, most have no idea what that contribution is or could be. It is critical that the importance of relationship building be demonstrated in measurable terms if management is to be persuaded of the payback to be realized from an investment in customer relationship building. A number of authors have recently begun to argue for the treatment of customer relationships as an investment[9] and for a clear demonstration of the link between relationship marketing and shareholder value.[10]

The building of customer relationships makes considerable sense only if one agrees with the impact of relationship building on the creation of long-term customer value (LTCV). Shareholder value in the future is dependent in large part on the loyal customers the company can rely upon to deliver the stream of earnings referred to previously. What then contributes to LTCV? It is more than the total amount that the customer can be expected to spend with the company over his or her purchasing lifetime. Though that is an important component, it represents quite a narrow view of customer value.

A customer who is truly loyal contributes *directly* to the stream of earnings flowing to the company in two ways. The first is through retention. If the customer is retained as a customer for many years, then the company or brand gains the benefits from that prolonged patronage, possibly over many years. This is the essence of the argument for creating customer loyalty. In its simplest manifestation, assuming a typical automobile buyer buys an average of 10 cars over a lifetime and spends an average of $25,000 each time, his or her lifetime value may be $250,000. Results of my research clearly demonstrates that a stronger, closer customer relationship very definitely leads to greater likelihood of customer retention—that the customer will be more loyal and will remain a customer much longer.[11]

LTCV is, therefore, much more than the simple forward projection of current spending levels. Ideally, we would like to be able to calculate the long-term profitability of a customer, but few firms capture the costs associated with serving a customer, and fewer still are able to associate specific costs with specific customers. In the absence of cost information, it makes sense to focus on the potential value of the customer in terms of the revenue that he or she can generate directly or influence.

But the second component of a customer's *direct* long-term value relates to the concept of *share of spend*. The customer who feels a certain closeness and a relationship to the company and the brand will not only remain a customer,

[9] Evert, Gummesson, *Total Relationship Marketing* (Oxford: Butterworth-Heinemann, 1999), chap. 6.

[10] Ian H. Gordon, *Relationship Marketing* (Toronto: John Wiley & Sons, 1998), chap. 3.

[11] James G. Barnes, "Exploring the Importance of Closeness in Customer Relationships" (Presented at the Relationship Marketing Conference of the American Marketing Association, *New and Evolving Paradigms: The Emerging Future of Marketing,* Dublin, Ireland, June 12–15, 1997); and id., "Closeness in Customer Relationships: Examining the Payback from Getting Closer to the Customer," in *Relationship Marketing: Gaining Competitive Advantage through Customer Satisfaction and Customer Retention,* ed. Thorsten Henning-Thurau and Ursula Hansen (Heidelberg and New York: Springer, 2000), 89–105.

but will give that company a greater share of total business in the category. This is the so-called share of wallet phenomenon. The research results presented later in this chapter also clearly demonstrate that bank customers, for example, will give their financial institutions a greater share of their total business if a strong relationship is in place. Thus, not only will the customer stay longer, but he or she will spend more, thereby adding to his or her LTCV.

There are other aspects, even more difficult to measure, of why long-term loyal customers are more valuable. These relate to the fact that loyal customers are likely to be prepared to pay higher prices once they get to know the company and its employees and are almost certainly less likely to quibble over price. They are easier to please and take far less time to court. They are also much more likely to be receptive to new products and services that the company introduces.

The financial, more direct aspects of LTCV can, in fact, be measured objectively using internal customer data. An examination of the customer records of many organizations will likely reveal that those customers who have been on the books for a long time are less likely to spread their business around and more likely to buy higher-priced products and services and give the company a bigger share of their total spending in the category. They come back to do business again and again and require little marketing effort or expense. They are obviously the company's most valuable assets.

What They Can Influence

Other aspects of the value of the loyal customer are more difficult to observe and measure but may in fact be greater contributors to long-term customer value: the related concepts of word of mouth and sphere of influence. Customers who have a solid, mutually beneficial relationship with a company, where they are treated well and made to feel important and valued, will delight in telling their friends, family, and associates. They will become advocates for the company and bring in untold volumes of business.

Simon Cooper, former CEO of Delta Hotels, would motivate his employees to provide exceptional service to their guests by telling them that every business guest at a Delta Hotel has a potential lifetime value of $300,000. Even the most road-weary business traveler would take many years to rack up this volume of business in room charges alone. But factor in the possibility that the customer concerned may influence the travel policy for his or her company or is a member of the national executive of a professional organization that has to decide where to hold its annual convention, and it is easy to see how one guest has the potential to influence much more than $300,000 in total future sales. This illustrates the dual concepts of referral business and sphere of influence. Yet few companies make any attempt to measure the extent to which their customers are prepared to engage in such referral behavior.

A customer's future intentions are related to the health of the relationship he or she has with the organization. Two primary aspects of future intentions are the likelihood of the organization being the customer's main supplier of products or services in the future and the likelihood of the customer recommending the organization to friends and family. These measures should be included in survey questionnaires to provide insights into future spending patterns and behavioral intentions.

Impediments to Estimating LTCV

Calculating the LTCV of a customer is not an easy prospect for most organizations. For some it is virtually impossible. The vast majority of organizations have no way of measuring the costs of serving a customer or capturing the direct costs involved in that service. This represents a barrier if we are interested in calculating the profitability of each customer. But many companies do not even have the ability to collect sales data, so they do not even know what volume of revenue is being brought in by each customer, let alone the profitability of that business. This is especially difficult in retail environments in which the customer is anonymous. This problem has prompted many retail organizations to establish frequent-buyer clubs so that most of the member's purchasing can be monitored by the use of the club card to record purchases. This is not the most accurate means of assessing the value of a customer, but it is a step in the right direction. There are clearly deficiencies in the information collected, just as there are in database approaches to estimating LTCV.

Firms that are in a position to track the sales of specific customers can develop fairly accurate estimates of the long-term value of individual customers. Where the company captures sales data on its customers, has some historic record of purchases made, and knows the approximate age of the customer, it can make certain assumptions about how long the customer is to remain a customer and how many others he or she is likely to influence. Armed with this information and preferably with additional data on the profitability of the customer, the company can estimate what the customer is likely to contribute directly and indirectly to the company's sales and profits in the future. As we will see later in this chapter, and as we saw when we looked at customer satisfaction in Chapter 3, these estimates are made even more accurate if the company also has information about how satisfied the customer is in his or her dealings with the company and the state of the relationship with the firm. My research results demonstrate convincingly that more satisfied customers and those whose relationships with the firm are close and healthy are significantly more likely to remain customers, to spend more, and to refer their friends and associates.

Companies that rely on automatic data capture at the point of sale, while they are able to capture sales made to individual customers, and even to make some estimate of the profitability of those sales, usually have no way of knowing what *share* of a customer's business they are enjoying. A bank, watching the customer's account balances and investments grow, may delude itself into thinking that it has a growing percentage of the customer's business, or even all of it, or even that it has a relationship with that customer. Not knowing all the details of the customer's life, the bank may in fact be enjoying a declining portion of the customer's rapidly expanding portfolio and of his or her family's business as the customer systematically places financial business with other institutions.

Measuring What Customers Value

One of the most important indicators of the performance of a company in creating and establishing a genuine relationship with its customers is its ability to deliver on various aspects of value for the customer. As we discussed in Chapter 4, it is important to realize that there are several different components of value, each of which contributes to the overall assessment of total value offered by the form to its customers. To illustrate this point, I will draw on the composite results of a number of projects that I have conducted for clients in the technology sector.

Using qualitative research methods, we have determined that customers and clients of firms in this sector generally identified seven different sources of value, labeled as follows: (1) price-based value; (2) access or convenience value; (3) service-based value; (4) community-based value; (5) enabling value; (6) surprise value; and (7) relationship value. Each of these components of the overall value offered is then described in a series of agree–disagree statements which allow us to measure the extent to which customers feel that the firm involved is successful at creating that form of value for its customers. In the same research, customers are asked to indicate how important it is to them that a company in this industry creates each form of value for its customers. For example, how important is it to you that Company X makes it easy for you to deal with them? The result of this component of a much larger customer relationship measurement project is that we develop two important indices relating to each of the components of value—how important each component is to the customers in a particular segment, and how well they believe the company is doing in creating that form of value.

Armed with this information, we can not only advise the firm on how well they are doing in creating each form of value, but we can also show how important each component is to each segment of the firm's target market. We can also use various multivariate data analysis techniques to show which components of value are more important than others in influencing customer satisfaction.

By producing results such as those presented earlier in Figure 4-4, we can indicate to a firm that they should concentrate their efforts on those components of value that are most important to customers. By focusing on those important value components where the company is underperforming, management can improve the offer that the company is placing in front of its customers, thereby improving its competitive position.

Measuring Customer Relationships

My understanding of customer relationships has come in part from many years of analyzing and interpreting data collected from hundreds of focus groups and customer surveys.

My view has been that most firms' interpretations of customer relationships are far too narrow. My focus has been to attempt to understand more about what constituted a genuine relationship, as defined by the customer. Because a relationship is essentially a psychological concept, I delved into the rich literature social psychology dealing with interpersonal relationships.[12] This literature revealed a vast resource of information on and insights into what constitutes a genuine relationship in any context. I have been applying the principles ever since.

One of the most obvious conclusions to be drawn from social psychology is that a relationship is a multidimensional construct and, if it is to be measured, has to be approached as a series of relevant dimensions. It is necessary to deconstruct a consumer's relationship with a company or a brand into a series of dimensions, including trust, reliability, responsiveness, communications, respect, affection, understanding, and other characteristics that one would associate with any kind of relationship. To measure customer relationships, we must measure of the dimensions of a relationship.

Unfortunately, many consultants and researchers measure only the behavioral or outcome aspects of customer relationships without paying any attention to the underlying emotive components that define a genuine relationship. Gordon Wyner of Mercer Management Consulting observes that, at a minimum, the measurement of customer relationships should address the following:[13]

---

[12] Daphne Sheaves and James G. Barnes, "The Fundamentals of Relationships," in *Advances in Services Marketing and Management,* vol. 5, ed. Teresa A. Swartz, David E. Bowen, and Stephen W. Brown (Greenwich, Conn.: JAI Press, 1996), 215–46.

[13] Gordon A. Wyner, "Customer Relationship Measurement," *Marketing Research* 11(2) (Summer 1999): 39–41.

- Who is the customer?
- How does the service provider make his presence known to the customer?
- How extensive is the customer's relationship?
- How long has the relationship lasted?
- Who else participates in the relationship?

While these are interesting questions, they do not get at the heart of what is a genuine relationship between customer and company. Wyner proposes measuring the ways in which the customer comes in contact with the service provider, media exposure to advertising messages, share of wallet and related measures, repeat purchases, portfolio purchases, customer satisfaction, duration of the relationship, and interaction with intermediaries. This list is inadequate as a measure of the strength or health of customer relationships because it pays virtually no attention to the softer side of the relationship: the most important emotional side.

Performance on Relationship Dimensions

Typically, to measure the central components of customer relationships I rely on a series of Likert-scaled agree–disagree statements that are generated from focus groups or depth interviews or constructed through reference to batteries of psychological scales used to measure various psychological constructs such as trust or mutuality of interest. Examples of such agree–disagree statements are presented in Figure 8-1.

In most relationship measurement projects, we will typically measure the customer's relationship with the client company on a series of 12 to 15 relationship dimensions. Those dimensions have been selected to be the most appropriate to the client's industry based on qualitative research with the client's customers and on our judgments concerning which relationship dimensions are likely to contribute to customer satisfaction and retention.

Depending on the scope of the project and on factors such as whether relationships with competitors are also being measured, a questionnaire will be devised which contains a series of three or four agree–disagree statements corresponding to each relationship dimension. The questionnaire is then administered in a customer survey, and summed scores can be calculated for each relationship dimension. Conclusions can then be drawn relating to the extent to which the customers trust the company, the extent to which they see the firm as reliable or responsive to their needs, caring, or sharing similar values.

- *"I get the feeling that _____ really cares about me."*
- *"_____ really understands my needs."*
- *"I am treated with respect by _____."*
- *"I often feel intimidated when dealing with _____."*
- *"I feel my business is safe with _____."*
- *"I deal with _____ because I want to, not because I have to."*
- *"Moving my business to another bank is just not worth the effort."*
- *"I can count on _____ to be there when I need them."*
- *"I never seem to be able to contact _____."*
- *"I feel comfortable dealing with _____."*
- *"_____ is an important part of the community where I live."*
- *"Dealing with _____ is like dealing with friends."*
- *"I really wouldn't deal with _____ if I didn't have to."*
- *"The employees at _____ really know their business."*
- *"_____ is a company that understands people like me."*

Figure 8-1 Examples of Agree–Disagree Statements to Measure Relationship Dimensions

Characteristics of the Relationship

In addition to focusing on the core dimensions of relationships, three other aspects of customer relationships have proven to be integral, not only to the understanding of genuine relationships, but to the measurement of the health of those relationships. These are relationship closeness, its emotional tone, and its strength.

Closeness appears to underlie many aspects of relationships. Social psychologists have developed approaches to the measurement of closeness in interpersonal relationships that can be appropriately applied to the measurement of customer relationships. Thus, any approach to assessing the health of a customer relationship should incorporate a measure of the closeness of the relationship.[14] A measure of the customer's satisfaction with the relationship is also appropriate, in keeping with the argument that these two constructs are interrelated, in that it is not possible for most customers to feel really satisfied with a relationship without feeling some relationship closeness.

[14] Barnes, "Exploring the Importance of Closeness"; and id., "Closeness in Customer Relationships."

Given that a relationship cannot be thought to exist without emotional content, it is appropriate also to focus on the emotional tone of the relationship to assess its closeness and therefore its likelihood of lasting. An *emotional tone* index can be developed, consisting of a number of positive and negative emotions or feelings, that involves respondents indicating the extent to which they experience each in their dealings with a particular company or brand.[15]

It is also important to consider the relative *strength* or *depth* of a customer relationship. Several approaches can be employed to identify this aspect, which indicates the likelihood of the relationship continuing. A measure of relationship strength might also incorporate the depth of customers' interactions with the company in question by including a measure of the *share of their category business* that they give to the company. Also, we can address the extent to which they feel strongly about the relationship by examining their perception of the *likelihood that they will still be dealing with the company in the future* and *whether they would recommend the company* to others. These three variables then represent indicators of the strength of the relationship that a customer has with a company or brand.

Creating a Customer Relationship Index

While no two customer relationship measurement projects are likely to be identical, there will be some similarity in approach taken. For example, in the approach that I outlined above, we are likely to have the following information collected from a company's customers, most likely through some form of survey research, administered over the telephone, through the mail, or through the company's website. We would collect information on the nature of the interaction between the customer and the company (the behavioral components, including frequency of contact, duration of the relationship, and share of wallet), the core relationship dimensions, the indicators of relationship strength (closeness, likelihood to continue and to refer), customer satisfaction, customer perception of value created on various value components, and the usual categorization variables that allow us to examine results by customer segment.

This research gives us a definite insight into the factors that contribute to the creation of genuine customer relationships, how a company is performing in terms of creating such relationships with its customers, where those relationships are weak and where they are strong, and what actions are likely to prove most

---

[15] James G. Barnes, "Closeness, Strength and Satisfaction: Examining the Nature of Relationships Between Providers of Financial Services and their Retail Customers," *Psychology and Marketing* 14 (December 1997): 765–90.

effective in improving relationships in the future. By using roughly the same approach each time, we can create a weighted composite index of the overall strength of the customer relationship. This index is then comparable across customer segments and allows the client to track its performance over time in improving its customer relationships.

The Payback from Solid Customer Relationships

For management to be convinced of the value of investing in the creation and maintenance of customer relationships, they must see that a payback will be realized from such an investment. It must be clear that launching a relationship management program that will move a customer along a relationship equity scale from a score of, say, 76 to a score of 85 will produce a certain payback for the company. An investment will be required from a company that strategically manages its customer relationships. That investment will come in the form of human resources, communications, and service improvement programs that are designed to create value for the customer, leading to greater satisfaction and greater likelihood of customer retention through relationship creation.

The payback from strong, close relationships comes from several sources, principally, but not exclusively: (1) the increased likelihood that the customer will continue to be a customer, (2) the length of time the customer is likely to remain a customer, (3) the greater percentage of his or her business that the customer will give the firm, and (4) the greater likelihood that the customer will recommend the company to friends and family members.

We can clearly demonstrate that stronger relationships, as reflected in greater closeness, higher positive emotional tone, and a higher overall score on the relationship equity index, will produce higher payback on each of these output or payback measures. It is the extent of this payback that is often surprising to clients.

For example, the data in Table 8-1, taken from the telecommunications, financial services, and retail grocery businesses, show that by creating closer customer relationships a company can achieve demonstrable payback in many forms. Clearly, those customers who consider their relationships with their telecommunications service provider, bank, or supermarket to be very close are significantly more likely to be satisfied in their dealings with those companies— the first step in the creation of long-term relationships. The closer relationships are also much stronger, indicating that they are much more likely to last.

Those customers who feel closest to the service providers in each of these industries are also significantly more likely to give that company more of their business. Those who feel less close are more likely to spread their business around. For example, in the banking business, those customers who feel very

Table 8-1 Exploring the Impact of Customer Closeness

Customers from three industries (telecommunications, banking, and retail grocery) were asked to indicate how close they felt toward their main service provider in each industry. The respondents were then divided into three groups, based upon their present level of closeness with their main telecommunications company, bank, or grocery retailer. The groups were as follows:

Group #	Description	Telcom	Banking	Grocery
Group #1	"Less than close" (rated their closeness as 1 to 5)	54.5%	32.7%	38.9%
Group #2	"Fairly close" (rated their closeness as 6 or 7)	23.8%	27.1%	25.3%
Group #3	"Very close" (rated their closeness as 8 to 10)	21.7%	40.2%	35.8%

Very significant differences were found in each industry, across the three closeness groups on all of the critical relationship and loyalty variables. Note that for the telecommunications industry, *share of business* is the percentage of customers who also buy their long distance telephone service from their local telephone service provider.

	Telcom	Banking	Grocery
*Relationship satisfaction***			
Group #1	7.2	6.7	7.0
Group #2	7.9	8.3	7.9
Group #3	9.1	9.1	9.1
*Relationship strength***			
Group #1	8.8	7.9	7.9
Group #2	9.1	9.0	8.7
Group #3	9.5	9.4	9.0
*Share of business**			
Group #1	83.9%	88.4%	76.5%
Group #2	92.4%	92.1%	79.3%
Group #3	92.9%	94.3%	82.6%
*Very likely to be with main telco/bank/ grocery store two years from now***			
Group #1	80.3%	64.0%	63.0%
Group #2	85.5%	83.2%	74.4%
Group #3	84.0%	94.3%	84.3%
*Very likely to recommend main telco/ bank/grocery store to others***			
Group #1	57.5%	36.0%	48.3%
Group #2	58.6%	71.7%	63.3%
Group #3	86.3%	83.6%	77.9%

** Significant differences exist at the 0.01 level.
*** Significant differences exist at the 0.001 level.

close to their main financial services provider give that company 94.3% of their banking business, while those who feel less close give only 88.4%.

In the areas of customer retention and referrals the numbers become even more impressive. Only 64.0% of bank customers who do not feel particularly close to their bank are confident that they will still be a customer in two years, as compared with 94.3% of those who feel very close. Similarly, 83.6% of those who feel very close say that they are very likely to recommend their bank to friends and family members. The percentage for those who do not feel particularly close is 36.0%, a number that should make bankers everywhere sit up and pay attention because it represents the future of the customer franchise.

By considering measures such as these, management can calculate the payback to be realized from increasing the closeness in customer relationships. Similar analyses may be performed by examining the emotional content of the relationship or focusing on an aggregate score for relationship equity. Using such input data as average weekly or annual spending and making reasonable assumptions about length of time as a customer and the number of others influenced through referral business it makes it possible to attribute a certain value to existing customer business and the stream of that business and referral business well into the future. Thus, it *is* possible to calculate the value of a long-term customer relationship and determine the loss to a business when a customer leaves to go elsewhere.

Tracking and Benchmarking Relationship Equity

Measuring the strength of customer relationships at a single point in time is not sufficient. The initial study benchmarks the starting point of the measurement exercise and will identify where the relationship is strongest and weakest and the customer segments that are most receptive to strengthening the relationship. The results will also point to areas where something has to be done to strengthen the relationship. Strategies must then be developed and implemented, typically in the form of the development of communications programs, improved systems and processes, and forward-thinking human resources policies.

This is not the end of the measurement exercise. It is the beginning. It is imperative that the measurement be repeated, perhaps quarterly or semiannually, to identify where weaknesses have been improved upon or, ideally, overcome. The benchmarking also enables management to understand how the company compares with companies in other industries and with competitors.

Measurement programs such as the one proposed here are capable of identifying the expected payback from implementing a customer relationship management strategy. Payback can be quantified in terms of improvements in customer satisfaction and strengthened customer relationships. It can be observed in the form of greater share of customer spending, increased loyalty and retention, and increased propensity to recommend the company to others.

Strategic Implications

Introducing a program to measure the health of customer relationships on a regular basis will provide very valuable information to guide management in implementing and managing of a customer relationship program. First, a measurement program such as has been described in this chapter will identify the overall health of the customer relationship and enable the company to track that critical measure over time to determine whether the relationship management program is successful in creating stronger, closer relationships with customers.

Secondly, the program will allow management to deconstruct the relationship into its component dimensions to determine where the relationship is strong and where it is weak. The examination of the relationship in terms of its various dimensions is also useful in determining which dimensions contribute most to the overall health of the relationship and customer satisfaction.

Typically, analysis of the data collected will reveal the overall position of the company on its "relationship equity index," which is composed of the various dimensions and indicators of the relationship. It will also reveal which dimensions of the relationship are most important in predicting and explaining the overall relationship index score. This then allows management to focus on those dimensions of the relationship that are most important to the target customer group and examine the company's relative performance on each of the dimensions.

It is not uncommon to find a company performing well on a number of dimensions of the relationship and less well on others. If the dimensional analysis reveals, for example, that the company is not performing well on dimensions such as responsiveness and communications, management should implement solutions that will bolster performance on those dimensions.

Analysis of the information obtained from a customer relationship measurement program will also allow management to determine how well the company is performing in building solid relationships with certain segments of customers. It is common, for example, to find that certain customer groups have stronger, closer relationships than others. This points out to management where relationships are weakest and where they are in danger of disintegrating. It reveals those segments of customers most likely to be "defectors" or "switchers" and those where the relationship is superficial or artificial. By focusing on those relationships that are most vulnerable, management can put in place programs to repair those relationships, assuming that appropriate long-term customer value can be generated by doing so.

Further analysis of relationship measurement data will reveal those segments of customers that have certain kinds of relationships with the company. For example, some customers may be quite satisfied with their dealings with the company, even though their relationship may not be particularly close. Often, in addition to asking customers to indicate how close their relationship is with a company, we ask them how close they would like their relationship to be. Generally, we find that approximately 30 to 40% of respondents will indicate that their relationship is just about right in terms of closeness; in other words, their current closeness and desired closeness are the same. Usually, 50 to 60% or more will indicate that they would want their relationship with the company to be closer, thus providing management with clear direction that it should get closer to its customers.

What is most interesting is that we consistently find approximately 10% of respondents who indicate that they would want their relationships to be *less close* than they are at present. These results remind me of a participant in a focus group that I was moderating many years ago who told the group that he had an "ideal" relationship with his bank, one that was, for him, totally satisfying. Asked to describe that relationship, he said, "It's simple; I don't call them and they don't call me." Clearly, customers who desire a more distant relationship have to be managed in a different way than those who want to be contacted on a regular basis.

By examining the state or health of customer relationships by customer segment, a company will be in a position to examine what actually constitutes value from the perspective of the members of each segment. The value to be derived from strengthening or making the relationship closer with particular segments will direct management toward the most profitable solution. For example, analysis of the results of a customer relationship measurement program may reveal that relationships with certain high-yield customers are less strong than they should be. By examining the details of that relationship and developing appropriate strategies to shore it up in those dimensions in which it is weakest, management can direct resources toward programs that will produce the greatest payback.

The approach to measuring the equity of customer relationships that has been described in this chapter has applications in a number of related areas. Although we have tended to describe the approach using large-scale service providers such as banks and supermarkets as examples, the same principles apply to brand relationships. The principles of relationship building are the same, whether we are talking about relations with retailers and other service providers or with national and international brands such as Nike, Michelin, and President's Choice. Similarly, the same approach can be used with other stakeholders of interest to management. Many companies are today directing attention to their relationships with employees, shareholders, suppliers, donors, and other important groups.

The principles inherent in our customer relationship measurement program are equally applicable in those and other contexts.

As more and more companies direct their attention to dealing with customers and others over the Internet, they are becoming increasingly concerned with what this technology-based interaction does to customer relationships. Banks, for example, should be particularly interested in knowing whether their customer relationships are strengthened or weakened when customers move from a branch and ATM-based approach to banking to one that involves banking on the Internet. Are large catalog retailers like Lands' End and J. Crew successful in establishing and maintaining relationships over the Internet? We will turn our attention to questions such as this in Chapter 10.

Direction for Management

The approach to the measurement of customer relationships that has been described in this chapter provides management with a clear direction for taking action to improve the state of customer relationships. It is a strategic approach, focused on understanding the higher-order needs of customers and creating satisfying, meaningful relationships with them as a means to ensure long-term corporate success. The results of this research are actionable because they produce for management a clear picture of the details of the company's relationship with its important segments of customers. Thus, different strategies can be developed for the management and cultivation of relationships with each segment.

Results are actionable also in that the relationship is broken down into its constituent parts and examined in terms of its emotional content. It is therefore possible to report to management that customers in a particularly critical segment are less trusting of the company, do not feel that the company is responsive enough, and say they rarely hear from the company. Results such as these have clear implications for management, not only in how the company conducts its marketing programs—*in fact, the implications may be less for the marketing department than for other departments of the company*—but particularly in areas such as employee training and staffing levels, customer contact strategy, marketing communications, service delivery systems, customer service levels, and even sponsorships and community relations.

This approach to the quantification of customer relationships allows management to tie together such critically important concepts as customer value creation, customer satisfaction, relationships, and shareholder value. It allows for the quantification of these complex concepts and brings them to an actionable level. It also permits the calculation of the payback to be obtained from an investment in the enhancement of customer relationships, thereby establishing a direct link with shareholder value creation. Such knowledge within a company certainly provides that firm with a strategic competitive advantage.[16]

[16] W. Glenn Rowe and James G. Barnes, "Relationship Marketing and Sustained Competitive Advantage," *Journal of Market Focused Management* 2 (1998): 281–97.

9

Identifying Relationships at Risk

When Relationships Turn Sour

We all know that relationships are transient things. Even the strongest personal relationships go through rocky periods, and sometimes people just drift apart. Relationships that have endured for many years often come for various reasons to an end, to be replaced with new ones which may grow into equally strong, close relationships that end up standing the test of time.

Parallels exist between our relationships with friends, family, neighbors, and work associates and those in a commercial context as the customers of various businesses and other organizations. Metaphors applied to personal relationships can be applied to our relationships as customers. As clients or customers of various organizations, we face the same challenges of relationship management and maintenance that we do in the interpersonal context. Events occur from time to time which cause us to "break up" with companies with which we may have been doing business for many years. Sometimes we are tempted to take some of our business from a company to which we have been loyal and give it to a new firm that has been courting us.

Psychologists Steve Duck and Julia Wood, writing about interpersonal relationships, comment on the impact that technological and social change has on the conduct of relationships: "[P]artners face new challenges in stabilizing, maintaining and conducting relationships in the face of ever-changing social conditions."[1] They could have been writing about the relationships between companies and their customers. These are generally less stable than our relationships with friends and neighbors, in that customers' relationships with busi-

---

[1] Steve Duck and Julia T. Wood, "For Better, for Worse, for Richer, for Poorer: The Rough and the Smooth of Relationships," in Steve Duck and Julia T. Wood, *Confronting Relationship Challenges* (Thousand Oaks, Calif.: Sage, 1995), 18.

nesses are less intensely felt, and need at least as much work on the part of the partners involved if they are going to succeed and endure.

From a business perspective, it is important that management realize that customer relationships are vulnerable and dynamic. Relationships change with each interaction. Each partner risks doing or saying something that will offend the other, bringing on a rocky period in the relationship. There may be a need to make up, or the customer may decide that he or she needs some space and will decide not to patronize that firm for a few weeks. As with interpersonal relationships, the offending partner may not even realize that he or she has offended the other or what has caused the rift. The company involved simply may not see or hear from the customer for some time, or in many cases may not even realize that there has been a disruption in what has been a positive relationship.

In this chapter we consider the vulnerability of customer relationships; the fact that they are constantly changing and that one of the parties to a relationship may decide to end it or change it in some way. Contrary to the popular view, breaking up, in the commercial context of a customer relationship, is not at all hard. Managers must be aware that some relationships with customers may be at risk. We need to be able to identify the telltale signs that relationships are in danger of disintegrating.

We will also address the fact that in certain situations it may be more difficult to establish genuine relationships in the first place. Some circumstances are simply not conducive to the establishment and maintenance of close, long-lasting relationships. As we observed earlier, some customers do not want such relationships. They just want to transact business, not get close or make friends. Management needs to understand such customers and be aware of those situations that are not likely to lead to long-lasting customer relationships.

Dealing with Relationships at Risk

By using techniques such as those discussed in Chapter 8, companies can identify where customer relationships are weak and where they are strong. By deconstructing relationships into their constituent components or dimensions, we can isolate those factors contributing to the disintegration of a once-strong customer relationship. Employing the methodology for relationship measurement presented in Chapter 8, we can dig more deeply into the factors that lead to relationship creation and maintenance. Once we examine the current health of customer relationships, we will likely conclude that these relationships grow weaker because the company fails to create those kinds of value that particular customers consider to be important, or fails to deliver on certain of the relationship dimensions that are critical to the creation of positive, genuine relationships.

Some customer segments will have closer or stronger relationships with companies than others. Those companies that understand and appreciate the value of genuine customer relationships will want to assess the health of their customer relationships from time to time. Typically, they will find not only that relationship strength will vary across segments of their market, but that certain segments will want different things from the relationship. Different components or dimensions of the relationship will be more important in driving overall satisfaction among different market segments. Only by analyzing how well the company is doing can we identify relationships that are underperforming, where the company is vulnerable to a weakening of relationships and where a real risk of customer defection exists.

Companies should periodically take the pulse of customer relationships so that they can determine how well they are performing in cultivating and maintaining genuine positive relationships over time. With that information, a company can address certain important questions:

1. How important is it to the company to salvage or strengthen the relationship with a particular segment of the customer group?

2. What will the payback be to the company if it succeeds in strengthening the relationship?

3. What will it cost the company to get to the point where the relationship is strong and is paying dividends?

4. What activities, programs, procedures, and tools are likely to be most useful in strengthening the relationship?

Once the company is able to identify which customer relationships are in need of shoring up, certain customer information should be available to allow questions such as these to be answered. Companies with good customer databases on purchase behavior and profitability can usually make an informed judgment on what the payback is likely to be, at least in terms of sales increases, if they are successful in moving the relationship equity index for segment A from, say, a 75 to an 85.

The information that the company needs relates to the state of the relationship as perceived by customers. Management in companies with well-developed information systems will also have access to automatically captured data dealing with various indicators that will provide clues concerning the current state of the relationship. These clues can be found in such variables as customer sales, visits, profitability, and complaints.

Whether the information comes from regular monitoring of the health of relationships through measurement of relationship equity, observation of indicators in customer databases, or both, management faces decisions about the improvement or strengthening of customer relationships. Can we turn things around and begin to repair the relationship with particular customers and segments? Which relationships should we attempt to salvage; to which should we turn our attention first? Which relationships should we allow to remain weak or even disappear completely? In short, where do we invest the effort in relationship building and maintenance?

Recognize Weakening Relationships

When a customer relationship begins to weaken or disintegrate, certain telltale signs that the customer may be poised to leave, or is at least starting to look for another company with which to do business, may be observed. If we have measured the health or strength of customer relationships using the kinds of measures that we have discussed—relationship dimensions, components of value delivered, relationship closeness, intention to refer, intention to remain a customer, and others—we will have a baseline against which to compare the current state of the relationship. Results of past measurements should, where possible, be stored in a customer data file, or at least captured and reported by customer segment. Through such analysis we can identify where relationships are weakest and where overall relationship equity may have slipped in the recent past.

One of the most obvious signs that a relationship is weakening is decreased customer spending; however, this could be related to many factors other than dissatisfaction with the firm's value proposition or enhanced competitive activity. As lifestyles and life cycle stages change, so too do customer needs and preferences. A parent who has been spending several hundred dollars a year on children's footwear will begin to spend less as the children become independent.

Incomes increase or decrease over time, and changes in income levels and employment status can also have profound effects on spending. A family faced with an individual losing his or her job will be inclined to decrease spending on nonessential items such as eating out, vacation travel, and high-priced clothing. As a result, the behavioral side of the relationship between companies that provide such items and these customers will often be strained, but there may be little that the retailer or service provider can do. In situations such as this, the emotional side of the relationship may be as strong as ever, despite the decline in spending levels.

In other circumstances, however, a reduced level of spending on the part of a regular customer may send up a red flag for a company that is committed to maintaining solid customer relationships. Thus, an effective information system will produce on a regular basis information that highlights, for example, those regular customers who are considered valuable but whose spending is down by, say, 20% from the same period last year. Often such a decline in spending will reflect a weakening of the customer relationship and indicate that the customer is spreading his or her business around among a larger number of suppliers. Thus, our share of wallet may have slipped. This indicates a lower level of loyalty and of relationship equity, and may mark the beginning of a more rapid deterioration in the relationship in the future.

Numerous signs of disintegration often appear if the customer relationship is at risk because of customer dissatisfaction. A reduced level or rate of sales, along with an increased number of complaints and/or infrequent contact with the customer, should signal to the company that the customer's behavior is probably a result of more than the usual changes in life cycle and lifestyle. In smaller firms, employees can often notice changes in shopping or purchasing patterns. One will observe to another, "We haven't seen Mrs. Jones in here in a while." Larger firms must rely on databases to indicate when purchasing levels have dropped off or when once-regular patterns of shopping or buying behavior become irregular. A gap of several months in a relationship that was once marked by weekly visits is a sure sign that something is up that warrants management's attention. The challenge then is to initiate contact or communication that will reveal more about the customer's feelings towards the company and the relationship. Unless such contact is made, the relationship may deteriorate further. Meanwhile, the customer is in the process of establishing a relationship with other firms.

Another obvious sign that customer relationships are at risk is an increase in the number of complaints received. Complaints are a signal to the company that the customer requires something other than what he or she is receiving. When they are accompanied by decreased spending and less frequent contact, it is safe to assume that relationships are weakening. The conventional wisdom today in progressive companies is that a customer complaint represents an opportunity to set things right. Unless customers are encouraged to complain, management is often unaware that there are difficulties in the relationship.[2] Complaints that are resolved quickly and to the customer's satisfaction often result in higher levels of customer loyalty and relationships that are potentially stronger than they were before the problem that led to the complaint.[3]

These indicators of possible customer relationship deterioration have parallels in interpersonal relationship. Complaints and less-frequent contact are indicators, in both cases, that relationships are becoming less strong. In a business setting, the result from the company's perspective is that the customer will buy less from

---

[2] Kurt Jeschke, Henning S. Schulze, and Jack Bauersachs, "Internal Marketing and its Consequences for Complaint Handling Effectiveness," in *Relationship Marketing: Gaining Competitive Advantage Through Customer Satisfaction and Customer Retention*, ed. Thorsten Hennig-Thurau and Ursula Hansen (Heidelberg: Springer, 2000), 193–216.

[3] Valarie Zeithaml and Mary Jo Bitner, *Services Marketing: Integrating Customer Service across the Firm*, 2d ed. (New York: McGraw-Hill, 2000).

the firm in the short run. But the long-term implications are much more important. In the interpersonal context a partner who is growing weary of or dissatisfied with the relationship is likely to contribute less time, energy, and effort to making the relationship work. The challenge facing the company when it encounters evidence of slippage in the strength of customer relationship is how to restore that strength. Before that, however, determining which relationships merit attention and action may be necessary.

Which Relationships Do We Keep?

When a relationship begins to weaken, one's first instinct may be to try to regain the customer's business and rebuild the relationship. This makes perfect sense if the relationship is worth fighting for. There are, however, customers that a company may not want to retain. Companies must carefully analyze the value of the relationship, both in the present and for the future, and determine whether it may be better to let it decline further or even disappear.

Relationships that we want to restore are those that have been strong and close but for some reason have begun to disintegrate. They may be with customers who are valuable not only because of what they buy but because of the referrals they make, or who boost staff morale because of their positive interactions and feedback, or who enhance the image of the business because of their activities and role in the community.

A relationship may not be worth saving for several reasons, the most obvious being that it is not economically viable. When customers cost more to serve than they bring into the business, it may be better to allow the relationship to die, unless the customer can be encouraged to spend more in the future. This is presuming that we do not consider the softer reasons for retaining the customer sufficient to make investing in relationship restoration worthwhile.

However, a company should consider many factors before making a decision based on the value of the relationship. First, a customer's current buying and spending patterns may or may not be indicative of his or her future behavior. Consider the 20-year-old college student who is paying for college with summer earnings and student loans and is using basic services at his or her bank. This customer represents a potentially profitable customer for the future once he or she graduates, gets a job, buys a home, begins to make investments, and requires many more products and services. However, many financial institutions invest very little in serving such customers and building relationships with them because in the short term they may not contribute much to the firm's bottom line.

Another factor is what I term "historic customer value." This is something I encounter particularly in small firms that cannot afford the luxury of sophisticated databases that would allow them to calculate the value of a customer. They are likely to work hard to keep a customer who has been doing business with them for years, simply because that customer has contributed to the growth and success of the company and the firm feels an obligation to keep the relationship going.

Deciding what relationships merit salvaging assumes that the company will take a hard-nosed view of the situation, predicated on a reasoned assessment of whether the relationship is worth saving. "Worth" here is usually defined as monetary worth—are we making any money on this customer? Management needs the right information to make such an assessment.

Most businesses have a great deal of information about their customers. Credit applications, purchase records, payment records, complaints, and inquiries are valuable sources of information that can be used to serve the customer more effectively and help identify, through changing behavior patterns, when a relationship is at risk. The key is ensuring that this type of information is current and accessible. With the increased use of technology for database management, it is easier for businesses to develop and maintain detailed customer information. Without this information, it is difficult to determine whether and why buying patterns have changed, or which relationships we should try to save.

When Are Customer Relationships Most Vulnerable?

Management should be aware of the times and occasions when customer relationships are most vulnerable, when there is a genuine risk to the service provider that the customer will jump ship and take up with a competitor. The factor that characterizes most of the examples that follow is that *change* is taking place. That is when the danger is very real that the relationship will fall apart. Consequently, it is necessary that management manage the transition from one stage of the relationship to the other.

When Employees Are Promoted or Transferred or Resign or Retire

Established relationships with companies are at risk when an employee who has been dealing with a particular group of customers is no longer available to deal with those customers. This is one of the inherent dangers in a company's decision to transfer an employee to another department, office, or branch. That employee's regular customers may start looking around for options, including dealing with another company. The same situation presents itself when an employee resigns to go to work with a competitor, decides to retire from the firm, or takes a temporary leave of absence.

The firm is vulnerable at these times, especially when the customer's relationship with the individual employee is stronger than it is with the firm. This is most likely to be the case where the employee is important in the provision of the service. For example, where there is frequent contact between employees and customers and the employee plays more than an incidental role in service provision, the customer is likely to be receptive to leaving when the employee leaves. A supermarket cashier is unlikely to take many customers when he or she leaves to go work for the rival supermarket several blocks away, but a skilled auto mechanic or a popular hair stylist will very likely take customers when he or she establishes a new business or moves to a competing firm.

The customer relationship is also susceptible to breakup when the service provided by the employee who is leaving is an especially personal one, such as physiotherapy or hairdressing. These employees often take some of their customers with them. This is also a risky situation for the company if the product or service being sold is a commodity in the mind of the customer. The customer is likely to feel that it really doesn't matter which firm he or she buys from and may be receptive to switching his or her business to the employee's new company.

When the Customer Relocates

A very large percentage of households in North America relocate to new homes each year, many to new cities and towns many miles away. When a customer moves, his or her life is disrupted, and many existing relationships end and new ones begin. While it is simply impossible to retain relationships with some service providers, most especially those where physical presence of the customer or of some major possession is required, it is possible for other service providers to transfer the relationship with the customer to the new location. Customers have to end established relationships with physicians, dentists, mechanics, lawn care services, and home cleaners when they move to new cities. Many large national or regional organizations that operate in multiple locations, however, can be successful in transferring the customer's business and the relationship to the new location. This is the case with banks and other financial services providers, which, even if they do not have a branch in the new location, can handle the customer's business today electronically through telephone and the Internet.

Some years ago, when a customer moved to a new city or town, his or her business disappeared as well. Today, much of that business can be retained and the relationship protected if the company is able to transfer the relationship to another branch office closer to the customer's new location, or if the relationship can be managed at a distance through technology. This is a good example of where technology can be used effectively to continue a relationship. For example, in banking, the concept of locating a customer's accounts at a particular branch is archaic, particularly in a time when many customers never visit that branch and know none its employees. In the future, accounts will no longer be "domiciled" at a particular branch location. Instead, the account will be with the bank, not the branch. While it will then be easier to follow the customer wherever he or she moves, the challenge for the bank will be to ensure that the relationship is with the bank and not with the staff of a particular branch.

At the Time of Store or Branch Closure

A company's relationship with its customers is also placed at risk when it decides to close stores, branches, or offices. The company must have in place a strategy to migrate the customer's relationship to the new location. Again, this is less likely to be a problem when the customer's interaction with the company is via technology or other distance systems and processes. For example, most customers are quite ambivalent when an insurance company relocates its local branch office. They may not even realize the move has taken place. Similarly, the clients of a call center do not really care where the center is located. But when a retail chain closes one of its stores and reopens in a new location, or when a bank closes a branch, customers have an opportunity to find a new company with which to deal. The relationship is vulnerable until the customer is safely relocated to the new location. Consider, for example, the situation created when a supermarket chain closed one of its neighborhood stores, and the problems it had in migrating customer relationships to a new superstore that it opened less than a mile away.

The chain, which we'll call Supermart, is a major Canadian food retailer and real estate developer. It was November, and Supermart had spent many months of political wrangling to obtain planning permission to build a new shopping center and superstore on a vacant site in the east end of a major city. Supermart had operated a small neighborhood supermarket at the eastern end of Victoria Avenue since the 1970s. In late 1998, the store had competition from several major competitors within one or two miles of its east end location, an area which had experienced rapid population growth in recent years and which was thought by many to be "over-stored" in terms of supermarket capacity.

A large tract of land less half a mile from the Supermart store had recently been rezoned and became available for commercial use; nearby residents had lobbied vociferously for it to be converted to parkland. Eventually, after more than two years of political infighting at the municipal government level, Supermart was given planning permission to convert the property into a combined commercial and residential development, with a major shopping center and residential building lots. Within days of approval being received, construction began, and the shopping center, containing a Supermart superstore, medical clinics, a bank, dry cleaners, and other small retailers, was to be open for business on Saturday, November 21.

Of course, it had always been Supermart's plan to close the small Victoria Avenue store once the new store was ready for business. One week before the new store was to open its doors, the following notice was posted on the doors of the Victoria Avenue store:

THIS STORE WILL CLOSE ITS DOORS
AT 6 PM, FRIDAY, NOVEMBER 20, 1998

During the week that followed, inventory was systematically moved from the old store to the new location, so that by Wednesday—three days before the store was to close—shoppers were greeted with half-empty shelves, an absence of staple products such as potatoes, and only two open checkout lines. Regular shoppers, many of whom had been shopping at the Victoria Avenue location for almost 30 years, were forced to go across the street to Supermart's major competitor to buy many items which were not available at "their" supermarket.

At 6:00 PM on Friday, November 20, the small Victoria Avenue store closed its doors for the last time. At 7:00 AM on Saturday, November 21, the much larger Supermart in the new shopping center opened amid much fanfare.

Long-time shoppers at the old store were dismayed. Apart from the rather terse notice posted at the door of the old store, they had received no other communications from Supermart about the closure of "their" store and opening of the new one. With such a selection of supermarkets to choose from, including a new competing superstore approximately two miles away, many loyal Supermart customers decided to shop around. One observed that she felt as if a good friend had moved to a new home and organized a housewarming party to which she had not been invited.

When We Don't Treat Them Fairly

Customer relationships are in for rocky times when customers feel that they are not being treated fairly. These situations occur more often than businesses realize. Customers have a fundamental need for justice—to be treated fairly.[4] Customers are ready to end a relationship as soon as they get the feeling that someone else is receiving better treatment, especially if they cannot see why.

---

[4]Benjamin Schneider and David E. Bowen, "Understanding Customer Delight and Outrage," *Sloan Management Review* (Fall 1999), 35–45.

In an earlier chapter we talked about customers of an oil company who were given a considerable discount simply because they threatened to move their business to a competitor. Customers of long standing who had not complained were dismayed to learn that others were given the discount when they were not. I have observed the same situation in the long-distance telephone business, where "switchers" are offered impressive monetary incentives to return to their former long distance supplier. Customers who have never left feel slighted when obviously unfaithful customers are rewarded for their disloyalty.

This represents a dilemma for businesses, one that is not easily monitored. The customer perceives the unfair treatment, but as with so many customer reactions, it is perceptual and difficult for a company to detect unless the customer complains. In my experience, the negative feelings are more pronounced the longer the customer has been in the relationship or the more loyal the customer perceives himself or herself to have been. In a sense, the hurt is deeper the more the customer feels that a genuine relationship has existed. The reaction often heard in research with disaffected customers is, "How could they treat me like that, after all the business I've given them over the years?" This is also why many companies will confirm that a large percentage of their complaints from customers begin something like, "My family and I have been customers of your company for well over 30 years, and . . ."

When the Customer Becomes Less Valuable

This is a difficult situation. From time to time, companies assess the relationships they have with specific customers, or more likely with segments of customers, and decide that the relationships are not profitable and should be altered or ended. The most evident problems in this situation have to do with the adequacy of the information on which the company is basing the decision and the process to follow. Typically, someone on the finance side of the business will decide that the company is not making any money on this customer or group of customers. A proposal is presented to devote fewer resources to serving these customers or to get out of that business entirely. Banks and other companies face this situation when they decide to close branches, provide fewer services to certain customers, charge them for services that the bank had previously provided at no charge.

First, the company must be confident that the data upon which the decision is being made are not only accurate but complete. In light of our discussion earlier of the difficulties associated with calculating long-term customer value, the company should be sure that terminating a relationship with an apparently less than valuable customer does not jeopardize relationships with other, more valuable customers with whom that customer is associated. Consider the dangers inherent in making such decisions based solely on financial data that obviously do not tell the full story.

Secondly, businesses must also consider the negative fallout that often occurs as a result of making decisions to terminate or dramatically alter relationships with certain customers. Banks regularly meet with public and political criticism when they close branches in rural communities and inner-city neighborhoods. The perceived message is that these customers are no longer important to the banks, which are widely viewed as providing a public service. The situation is made no less palatable when the banks report record profits each year. Similar situations arise when a company implements a program to alter the way it delivers its services to certain customers. When deliveries are no longer free, or when the performance of the service is now delegated to the customer to perform, the reaction is often negative.

When It's Time to Fire the Client

Related to the examples above is the situation when a company decides that it can no longer continue a relationship with a customer or client, even though that relationship may be a profitable one. Some businesses are beginning to face up to the fact that they don't want all the customers and that some customers may be costing the company more in intangibles than management may be realizing. Increasingly, particularly in professional services firms, management is coming to the decision that they can no longer keep a client who causes problems with employee morale. Companies are no longer prepared to allow their employees to be abused by clients or to allow employees' lives, both professional and personal, to be ruined by overly demanding and unprofessional clients. The owner of a public relations company in California took the unusual step recently of firing a client because of numerous episodes that told her that the client was only interested in ordering her staff around like servants. "This isn't working out" for several reasons, she told him. "But most of all, you're a jerk."[5] Ending this kind of unproductive relationship does wonders for employee morale and productivity and probably frees up time to work for clients who are a lot more satisfying and fun to work with.

Threats to Strong Relationships

In many situations, as outlined below, establishing and maintaining close, strong relationships with customers presents companies with a difficult challenge. Man-

---

[5] Sue Shellenbarger, "Clients Are No Longer King," *The Globe and Mail* (Toronto), 10 March 2000, B9.

agers must make well-developed strategic decisions in attempting to create an environment conducive to the formation of genuine customer relationships.

Technology-Based Relationships

We will turn our attention in Chapter 10 to the very current issue of establishing and maintaining relationships with customers on the Internet. This challenge is but one example of the growing problems created by the trend toward dealing more and more with customers via technology. By definition, technology-based relationships involve less contact with company employees, either face to face or over the telephone, and more interaction with technology in the form of IVR telephone systems, debit cards, automated banking machines, interactive kiosks, and the company website. Much of the service that at one time was provided by employees is now obtained by the customer himself or herself through interaction with the company's technology.

Technology-based relationships are difficult to establish and maintain, as we will see when we discuss the Internet. Research suggests that customers tend to perceive less value in services that are delivered by technology, possibly because of the obvious absence of human input—input that is generally associated with some expenditure of effort.[6]

The result of creating arm's-length access to service through technology is that customer relationships begin to erode because customers no longer have direct contact with the firm or its employees. No longer do they meet tellers in the branch or talk with order-takers for the catalog company. For new customers, no opportunity exists in the face of the new channels for genuine, emotive relationships to be established. The relationship between a customer and a bank or telephone company is entirely convenience based, with little or no affective content. Customers see the existence of the new systems as enabling them to take control of service delivery, facilitating access and making it much more convenient to obtain routine services. But many resent the fact that such systems result in an erosion of the relationships that existed in the past. They long for a closer relationship and someone to turn to when they need them. The result is increased cynicism and a propensity to switch service providers. The challenge companies face when they launch such systems is how to foster closer customer relationships in the face of the technology and preserve the genuineness characteristic of more personal customer relations, as embodied best in small business settings. Management must ensure that customers enjoy the convenience,

[6] James G. Barnes, Peter A. Dunne, and William J. Glynn, "Self-Service and Technology: Unanticipated and Unintended Effects on Customer Relationships," in *Handbook of Services Marketing and Management,* ed. Teresa A. Swartz and Dawn Iacobucci (Thousand Oaks, Calif.: Sage, 2000), 89–102.

and the company the productivity, that many of the advanced technologies provide.

Anonymous Customers

Christopher Lovelock makes a valuable distinction between "membership" and "anonymous" customers.[7] "Membership" customers leave a trail behind when they buy something from a company or otherwise interact; anonymous customers are like ships in the night. We don't know who the anonymous customers are—they don't have an account with us and aren't members of our frequent-shopper club. Today most businesses have some method for tracking their interaction with many if not all of their customers. Historically, banks, telephone companies, credit card companies, and electrical utilities have been able to "know" all of their customers because the nature of their business was such that all customers had accounts. While we can debate just how well these companies know their customers, there is no denying that they at least know who they are.

Contrast this with the situation for many other businesses, many of whose customers typically pay cash or interact with the company very indirectly. This is the case with public transit systems, movie theaters, newspapers, and many personal service companies, such as dry cleaners and shoe repair shops. It is also the case for very large manufacturing companies that sell their products through retailers and rarely have an opportunity to interact directly with the people who buy, use, or consume their products. In these situations, building customer relationships is difficult, but not impossible.

When a customer is anonymous, a company is unable to undertake activity to strengthen the relationship. Many retailers have addressed this issue through the creation of frequent-shopper clubs, which are intended not only to offer incentives to customers to continue and increase their patronage, but also to provide the company with a database of information on the customer and his or her characteristics and behavior. Transportation companies sell their customers season passes and thereby create customer lists; sports teams and entertainment venues do the same. Consumer products companies such as Kraft, Kellogg, and Nike attempt to solidify customer (or, more accurately, consumer) relationships with their brands by personalizing the contact through their websites and various customer clubs. We will revisit the subject of brand relationships in Chapter 11.

---

[7] Christopher H. Lovelock, *Services Marketing,* 3d ed. (Upper Saddle River, N.J.: Prentice-Hall, 1996), 39–41.

Long-Distance and No-Contact Relationships

Absence does not always make the heart grow fonder. Companies that attempt to carry on meaningful relationships with their customers at a distance face a considerable challenge. Some fundamental elements are missing, notably regular contact and communications. Increasingly, many companies are doing business around the world, making contact with customers who will never visit their offices or stores and never make face-to-face or even voice contact with their employees. Of course, catalog retailers have been carrying on business like this for years. Other companies are so successful at the delivery of their core product that there is no functional reason to make contact with the customer. This is characteristic of what I have labeled "taken-for-granted" services, such as those provided by public utilities, where a customer's biggest complaint may be, "I never hear from them."

Taken-for-Granted Relationships

I have long been intrigued by the relationship challenges faced by companies and organizations that provide their customers with what I term taken-for-granted (TFG) services: those that are delivered to the consumer continuously, usually via technology, without the customer having to initiate the repeat purchase. Examples include utilities such as cable television, electricity, telephone service, gas, water, and home-heating oil. Whether the service is used continuously or occasionally, it is always readily available to the consumer. For some of these services, such as cable television, the customer pays the same each month for the service regardless of how much he or she actually uses it.

A more recent example is Internet service. Customers expect to be able to go online whenever they wish without having to request the service each time. As people become more dependent on technology to deliver service constantly and with consistent quality, more services are becoming taken for granted. Many aspects of personal banking and shopping are becoming taken for granted as more people use telephones and the Internet to carry out tasks such as bill payments, account transfers, and loan applications.

Why do I refer to these services as "taken-for-granted"? Quite simply, most customers rarely if ever think of them. We don't walk into a room and, before switching on the light, contemplate whether or not to buy electricity. Most of us do not give insurance a second thought, never thinking that at all times our home and auto insurance policies are working for us, protecting us, and we are in fact paying for that protection. Most consumers think about such services only when they have to renew or pay for them or when a problem occurs, such as when the electricity company experiences a power failure, the ISP's server crashes and we can't access the Internet, or we have an accident and have to file a claim with our insurance company. Companies in TFG service sectors do themselves no favors by not making contact with their customers, thereby further enhancing the distance between them and reinforcing the common feeling among customers that there is no relationship.

In addition to the fact that TFG services are continuously available even though they may be used only occasionally and do not require that the customer initiate repeat purchases, these services may be delivered through a contractual relationship and are often associated with utility companies that operate in a monopoly environment. The delivery of the service often involves little human contact and is more likely to involve technology. Low failure rates also characterize TFG services, and when failure to deliver the service does occur, great dissatisfaction results because customers have become accustomed to the service being available when they require it.

Taken-for-granted services are also characterized by a low involvement level on the part of the customer. That is, he or she does very little information seeking or comparing of alternatives when searching for a supplier. One reason for this in many situations is absence of competition. As well, customers view all suppliers as basically the same in quality of service and the manner in which it is delivered. As a result, TFG services are viewed as commodities and are difficult to differentiate in the marketplace. Customers make their purchase decisions based on price and pay little attention to the support services and technologies used by the firm. It doesn't help that many suppliers of these services also tend to view themselves as commodities, competing for market share on the basis of price and doing little to differentiate themselves from their competition in terms of support services, technical performance, how they make their customers feel, and how they interact with customers.

It is the core service that is taken for granted. While TFG services share three of the characteristics of services in general—intangibility, perishability, and ownership—they are distinct in that they are homogenous rather than heterogeneous and are separable from a human supplier. They are homogenous in that they provide the same core service to all customers. Unlike other services, which are inseparable from the person who delivers them, TFG services are delivered anonymously, unobtrusively, and usually without human contact.

One question often raised is whether TFG services providers need to develop relationships with customers and, if they do, how they can go about building these relationships. Those interactions with customers that do occur usually have a negative tone because they usually result from failure by the service provider to provide the service or problems with billing or support services. Both the service provider and the customer can feel taken for granted and are inclined to view each other negatively because of the codependence. Customers often feel trapped in TFG situations because of the lack of alternatives and as a result are poised to switch to the competition as soon as it becomes available. This readiness to switch should prompt TFG service providers to examine the relationships they have with their customers. Even if competition is limited and apparently will continue to remain so in the future, an organization should look at the longterm—building relationships with customers does not happen overnight.

One challenge in this situation is that the consumer really has no reason to want a relationship with the supplier. From the customer's point of view, as long as the product or service is delivered at a reasonable price and the service is reliable and consistent, a relationship would not provide anything extra.[8] For an organization that delivers taken-for-granted services, however, there are many reasons to develop strong customer relationships. Even when companies operate in monopolistic (or near-monopolistic) situations, there is a threat of competition. Given the new technologies that have emerged in recent years and the potential for even more, no industry or organization is immune to competition. Deregulation of the long-distance telephone market produced threats for organizations that once held monopolies on the service. As a result, telecommunications companies have had to turn almost exclusively to price competition and diversify their operations to become less dependent on the long-distance telephone business.

Some Just Don't Want a Relationship

We observed earlier in this book that not all customers want to establish close, genuine relationships with companies. We saw in Chapter 8 the evidence of a "closeness gap" indicating that as many as 10% of customers actually want a *less close* relationship with service providers in certain industries. Linda Price and Eric Arnould have shown in their research in various service industries that a fairly large percentage of customers do not consider their relationship with hands-on service providers to be particularly close and certainly aren't interested in such relationships becoming friendships.[9]

Susan Fournier and her colleagues raise the specter that maybe all customers don't want to have relationships with companies[10]—a thought that seems to have escaped the attention of many firms that relentlessly pursue the establishment of what they term relationships, oblivious to the fact that they are not genuine

---

[8] Donald P. Barnes, and James G. Barnes, "The Special Case of Marketing Taken-For-Granted Services" (paper presented at ASAC Conference, 1995, Windsor, Ontario).

[9] Linda L. Price and Eric J. Arnould, "Commercial Friendships: Service Provider-Client Relationships in Context," *Journal of Marketing* 63(4) (1999): 38–56.

[10] Susan Fournier, Susan Dobscha, and David Glen Mick, "Preventing the Premature Death of Relationship Marketing," *Harvard Business Review* 76 (January–February 1998), 44.

relationships in the customers' eyes. Other authors suggest that where customers do not really want to get very close to a company, the company should examine what value or benefits the customers perceive they are getting now or could potentially get from such a closer association.[11]

The conclusion is often that the company has not done a very good job of demonstrating that additional value can be created for the customer by "getting closer." The challenge is to create more "relational benefits," as customers are generally already aware of the functional and process benefits that the company can offer. In fact, the fact that these customers are not interested in deepening the relationship suggests that they are aware of and satisfied with the benefits created at this more functional level. The challenge to the company is to raise the bar and to make the softer, relational benefits more relevant for the customer.

Keep an Eye on Them

The message from this chapter is clear. Customer relationships have to be managed. They don't go on and on, generating the stream of earnings that is so important to the enhancement of shareholder value, without a lot of work on the part of the company involved. For the relationship to be kept a strong, stable one, it must be monitored. Management must keep a watchful eye on the state of its relationships with its customers, with segments of its customer base, and with important individual customers. This means monitoring the health of the relationship, using tools such as those described in Chapter 8. But it also means that the company must be vigilant of those situations that expose the relationship to disruption. A company that is serious about establishing and maintaining customer relationships will have strategies in place to manage the transition of relationships whenever change is taking place.

Companies that do a good job of managing relationships with their customers will also be aware that they can't have strong, positive relationships with all of their customers, and that in fact they shouldn't. Relationships are difficult to establish in some situations, and effective strategies are demanded here because there are considerable barriers to be overcome. Relationship making is difficult work; companies must rise to these challenges if they are to reap the long-term benefits.

[11] Thorsten Hennig-Thurau, Kevin P. Gwinner, and Dwayne D. Gremler, "Why Customers Build Relationships with Companies—and Why Not," in Thorsten Hennig-Thurau and Ursula Hansen, eds, *Relationship Marketing,* ed. Hennig-Thurau and Hansen, 369–91.

10

Establishing Customer Relationships on the Internet

The Internet Revolution

No innovation of recent times has had such a profound impact on customer behavior and how business is conducted as the Internet. The use of the Web has already radically changed customer expectations about convenience, speed, price, service, and comparability.[1] Just as supermarkets changed grocery shopping and large malls provided customers with more convenience and selection under one roof than they could imagine, the Internet presents a completely new way of doing business in the 21st century.

More and more customers are using the Internet to make purchases, but this is not the only impact the Web is having on consumer behavior. Consumers are going to the Web to find information on products, services, costs, and features before they go to buy. This is increasingly the case for car buyers and purchasers of other major items who are researching retail prices and comparing products online before they go to the dealer. Colleagues of mine who are in health care tell me that patients are showing up for appointments at physicians' offices armed with the latest information on their illnesses, downloaded from the websites of Johns Hopkins or the Mayo Clinic. Consumers are equipped with more information than ever as a result of the abundance of free, quality information available on the Internet. It is expected that even those businesses who do not have a Web presence (if there any such businesses in a few years) will be affected by their customers' use of the Web and will have to adjust their business practices to suit today's informed consumer. To deal with such radical changes, business will have to rethink the need to develop stronger relationships with

---

[1] G. Hamel and Jeff Sampler, "The e-Corporation," *Fortune,* 7 December 1998, 80–92.

their customers through the creation of an e-commerce strategy that is grounded in the fundamentals of customer relationships.

But the very idea of having a relationship with a person or business over the Internet seems at first to defy everything we know about relationships. How can we be close to someone if we are in a different city or on the other side of the world and only have contact via technology? How can we share the emotions that are so important to relationship building? The notion that we can build trust and loyalty through a medium so new and diverse as the Internet may be puzzling to many; however, every day more and more companies and individuals are succeeding in doing just that.

Many businesses are increasing their presence online and doing a greater portion of their business over the Internet than we thought would ever happen. Many other businesses exist only on the Internet: the so-called pure-plays. They are truly global in nature; customers may have no idea where they are physically located, but it doesn't matter. Many of these Internet-focused companies, especially the Internet consulting companies, claim to be able to strengthen customer relationships, largely through outbound communications and the use of sophisticated CRM software. However, as we will see, this will not necessarily lead to the creation of a genuine customer relationship.

It may be impossible not to get caught up in the hype of the Internet and the expectations many investors have for it. Consider the press coverage of the IPOs of many Internet startups. Many go public with a market capitalization of hundreds of millions of dollars on minimal sales and no hope of being able to break even for several years. However, it might be useful to step back from the excitement and consider that the Internet is just one more way of reaching customers. Although it holds considerable promise to force companies to change the way they do business, it still must be governed by the principles that guide the establishment and maintenance of customer relationships in conventional contexts. The underpinnings of genuine relationships must be present if companies operating on the Internet are to be successful.

The issue is one of creating as solid and close a relationship with customers online as many companies have with their customers offline. But the prevailing image of Internet usage has been "surfing," the implication being that the medium is best used for moving quickly from site to site in search of information or the best deal. The challenge for a company doing business online or who wish to reach particular groups of customers is to stop them from surfing and encourage them to bookmark the company's site and use it on a regular basis— in short, to establish some form of a relationship that sees the customer coming back again and again. Sound familiar? It's no different on the Web. The principles of relationship building are the same; only the venue is different. We must still create value for customers, do what's necessary to achieve long-term customer satisfaction, and give them reasons to do business with us on a regular or even exclusive basis.

In this chapter we will examine the similarities and differences between establishing customer relationships through traditional business channels and establishing them through the Internet. We will look at current research in this area and determine where some of the pitfalls lie. We will consider how we can create value for our customers and get closer to them by utilizing the Internet effectively. We should keep in mind that we are at the very early stages of the development of the medium. There is a great deal to learn, and there are numerous predictions that many businesses will fail to develop the clientele they need to sustain a presence online. In fact, Forrester Research recently predicted that most companies that operate exclusively on the Internet will be out of business within a year.

Who's Using It? Who's Not?

I won't bore you with statistics about how many households are connected to the Internet, or how many people have access to the Internet from home or work. The numbers, by the time you read this, would be horribly out of date. The pace at which the Internet innovation has diffused through society has been impressive indeed. In most developed countries, we are close to seeing a majority of residents and virtually all schoolchildren being regular users. As always when one examines customer behavior, some very interesting patterns in usage across user groups are evident. Recent research conducted by the Bristol Group in the United States and Canada found that almost 58% of adults surveyed were users of the Internet. Predictably, the highest level of Internet usage (73%) was among those aged 18 to 24, while the lowest (36%) was among those aged 55 and older. The pattern of Internet buying across the age groups was, however, surprising. The *lowest* percentage of Internet buyers was found among the youngest Internet users. Only 25% of those aged 18 to 24 had purchased anything online in the preceding 12 months. Conversely, the highest rate of Internet buying (43%) was among those aged 45 to 54. Even 29% of those aged 55 and older had bought online.

These results confirm recent research that we carried out with Canadian university students where we found that, despite the fact that virtually all of them were regular users of the Internet, only 17% had ever bought anything online. Their reasons for not buying online included being reluctant to provide credit card numbers or not having a credit card in the first place.

An interesting corroborative research result was reported by PhoCusWright, a Connecticut research firm, who indicated that 76% of airline travelers who had access to the Internet said they wouldn't buy online, primarily because of lack of personal contact. This is especially important in vacation travel, where most vacationers are likely interested in advice from a real person who has been there or who can provide informed opinion on what's available at various des-

Table 10-1 Internet Usage by Age Group

Age Group	Using the Internet	Bought Online Past 12 Months
18–24	73%	25%
25–34	62	39
35–44	55	34
45–54	55	43
55+	36	29

Source: Bristol Group.

tinations.[2] Increasingly, companies that do business on the Internet are realizing that they must emulate the offline environment as much as possible; they can't simply rely on the technology to deliver an online service. If they do focus on the technology, they are providing only half of the value that the customer needs and wants. They may be able to deliver on the functional, but they are missing out on the emotional.

McKinsey Consulting has undertaken a segmentation of online consumers that provides a valuable understanding of the various types of customers to whom online marketers might direct their offers. McKinsey and Media Metrix analyzed online behavior using a sample of active online consumers from the Media Metrix panel of 50,000 Internet users.[3] They divided the Internet market into six active segments, labeled Simplifiers, Surfers, Bargainers, Connectors, Routiners, and Sportsters. The characteristics of these segments, including the percentage of the total base of Internet users accounted for by each, are presented in Table 10-2.

The *Simplifiers* spend little time online but account for half of all online transactions. They have specific objectives in mind, and they want to accomplish them quickly and easily. They are experienced Internet users, and they want Internet marketers to make it easy for them. They want "end-to-end" convenience: ease of access and use, readily available and reliable information, and easy returns.

The *Surfers* are a fairly small segment but account for 32% of time spent online. They move about the Net quickly, spending little time on each site. They require novelty and variety to get them back. The challenge is getting them to put down roots.

[2] Paul Grimes, "On-line Industry Tries to Compensate for Lack of Human Contact," *Globe and Mail* (Toronto), 29 January 2000, T4.
[3] McKinsey Marketing Practice, "All Visitors Are Not Created Equal," April 2000 (accessed at www.mckinsey.com).

Table 10-2 Online Consumer Segments

Segment	Percent of Internet Users	Hours Active/ Month	Unique Domains Accessed/ Month	Pages Accessed/ Month	Percent Buying
Simplifiers	29	7.1	62	1021	87
Surfers	8	30.2	224	4852	71
Bargainers	8	8.3	43	1295	64
Connectors	36	5.7	54	791	42
Routiners	15	8.2	32	624	50
Sportsters	4	7.1	47	1023	51
Average		9.8	74	1398	61

Source: McKinsey Marketing Practice, "All Visitors Are Not Created Equal," April 2000 (www.mckinsey.com).

The *Bargainers* are on the Internet for one purpose: to obtain the best deal available. While they are a small percentage of Internet users, they account for 52% of visits to eBay and are heavy users of priceline.com, uBid.com, and Quote.com. They are classic price shoppers who are looking for the best prices and are turned on by the "excitement" of the search.

The *Connectors* are newcomers to the Internet. They are just learning to use the medium and are trying to figure out what's online for them and how they can derive value. They use the Internet to connect with other people through chat lines and sending e-greeting cards. The Connectors need reassurance when using the Internet, and established offline brands are able to provide this. The owners of major brands have an advantage, therefore, in attracting this segment to their online sites. They can lead the novice Internet user online by delivering an integrated strategy that provides a lifeline to this segment.

The *Routiners* are creatures of habit. They visit the fewest websites and spend more time at each one. Over 80% of their time online is spent with their top 10 sites, mostly news and financial services.

The *Sportsters* are similar to the Routiners in that they too are not particularly adventuresome. They spend even less time online but visit more sites, choosing to concentrate on sports and entertainment sites.

Research results such as these begin to shed light on the fact that Internet users demonstrate a diversity of behavior that is typical of virtually any market. Trying to treat all segments alike is a recipe for disaster. As McKinsey concludes, "Given that Internet profitability is so dependent on customer repeat purchases and higher average transaction size, winning a loyal customer base in one of these segments is more likely to be profitable than skimming all of the segments."[4]

[4] Ibid.

Technology-Based Relationships

Technology allows people and organizations to communicate more easily with others all over the world, and in "real time." Regis McKenna uses this term to refer to the way in which many of us now receive information—as it happens.[5] We experience real time when we watch live TV coverage of an event, withdraw cash from an ATM, or join a chat room on the Internet. We use technology to stay closer to our friends and family who live thousands of miles away by sending pictures of a newborn child via e-mail shortly after the birth. New technologies and communications have allowed doctors in one part of the world to guide a physician through delicate surgery being performed in a remote region thousands of miles away.

Technology is all-pervasive in our lives. Automobiles have onboard GPS systems that beam signals off satellites to let us know when service is needed or to guide us through the traffic maze of a strange city. Airlines are introducing online reservations systems allow customers not only to purchase tickets online but also to print their boarding passes and luggage tags on their home or office printers, thereby allowing them to bypass the increasingly long lines at airports, drop their tagged baggage on a conveyor belt, and go straight to the gate. Online booksellers now routinely e-mail regular customers when a book that they think they will like is added to inventory. Anxious investors can receive e-mail messages from their brokers on their cellular phones, advising on the latest movements in their portfolios, regardless of where they are located.

Much of the same technology that has allowed lives to be saved and grandparents to see their newborn grandchild halfway around the world has been used to change the way businesses deliver services and products and the way people shop. While the technology allows many customers to access products and services that they could not obtain in their local area a few years ago, it has also helped to isolate some companies from their customers.

Many consumers find technology-based relationships cold and impersonal. In many cases, these feelings are not far removed from those experienced in taken-for-granted services, which we discussed in Chapter 9. Consumers do not feel close to the supplier and often feel that they are not getting the service they are paying for. Some customers may actually resent having to deal with the technology and avoid it where possible. While it may be more convenient for many of us to use ATMs, card-equipped gas pumps, and self-ticketing machines at airports, some individuals prefer to deal directly with employees. They receive a certain comfort level from dealing with a real live person.

Let's reconsider for a moment the implications of implementing technology in an effort to add value for consumers. Customers generally appreciate the

---

[5] Regis McKenna, *Real Time* (Boston: Harvard Business School Press, 1997).

convenience value that is created by the introduction of many new technologies. But there is an important shortcoming: by allowing the customer to deal with us entirely through technology, we are removing human contact, the opportunity for conversation and the opportunity to "read" a situation. To quote a passenger at Newark International Airport who just used a ticket kiosk to check in and obtain a boarding pass, "They're quicker even than when there are no lines. I don't have to talk to anyone."[6] Precisely! The passenger has summarized both the advantages and the shortcomings of technology-based service delivery. The same is true of the Internet.

Let's consider the banking industry, which has in the past 20 years undergone dramatic changes to the way it does business. ATMs, introduced to most banking customers in the 1980s, made it possible for many to go months without ever entering a branch. This was a wonderful use of technology since customers could perform routine banking transactions at any time and from any number of locations. The banks no longer needed as many staff to serve customers on the front line and could concentrate on serving those customers who were most profitable. Some customers, of course, resisted and even resented the technology and wanted to continue to visit their branch every week to do business and be served by real people. For those customers, banks continued to employ front line employees. With the introduction of telephone banking and, more recently, Internet banking, customers did not need to leave their homes to carry out a variety of transactions. The banking industry was more profitable than ever and many customers were getting what they wanted from their banks—efficient service at their convenience. Many customers considered this a step in the right direction for an industry that had been characterized by inconvenient hours of operation and long waiting lines.

In recent years, however, many of the same technologies that allowed banks to give their customers improved service have allowed customers to become more informed about their choices of banking services available and made it easier for them to purchase products from any number of suppliers. Customers can now apply for loans and other credit products on the Internet with traditional banks that have online services and with other financial services companies such as WingspanBank.com and ING Bank that offer services only on the Internet, unencumbered by the costly branch networks of the conventional banks. Until the advent of Internet-based banking, the process that most customers followed in applying for a mortgage involved in-branch appointments with a small number of banks.[7] The Internet has given power and freedom to customers and broadened their choices to global proportions. Location is no longer as important, and the restrictions of geography no longer allow banks and other businesses to

---

[6] David Leonhardt, "The 'Airport Experience': There Is Hope," *International Herald Tribune,* 9 May 2000, 1, 12.

[7] Hamel and Sampler, "The e-Corporation."

capture people who have no options and to mistake that "relationship" for loyalty. In the few years during which the Internet has moved into the mainstream, it has revolutionized an old industry and introduced new players who have no history in the industry but who definitely represent the future.

Persuading customers to move their business or their contact with a company online creates considerable challenges. It certainly points out the weakness in a strategy that *encourages* customers to reduce their direct contact with a company in favor of moving their business to the Internet. Such a strategy encourages customers to shop around and exposes them to competition that they have never met before. We see this again in financial services, where recent research by the Bristol Group indicates that 25% of Americans and 38% of Canadians say that they will do most of their banking on the Internet in the future.

Such results are not surprising, and many business people, including many bankers, would express satisfaction at them. They reflect a growing acceptance of the use of Internet-based banking, which is, after all, cheaper for the banks to deliver than traditional service, which involves the costly employment of branch staff and upkeep of buildings. Encouraging the migration of customer relationships to the Internet is a great example of short-term thinking. Research shows that once Americans move to Internet banking, they give less than half of their banking business to their main bank, which they gave 80% of their business to before moving online.[8] By moving their customers to the Internet, thereby saving on costs and making banking more "convenient," banks are exposing them to the competition, often with no compensating strategy to retain the relationship. The technology becomes a two-edged sword.

Why the Internet Is Different

If we think back to the principles that we have been discussing, it should be obvious that the fundamentals of relationship building are the same, regardless of the context. We create value for customers, thereby increasing satisfaction, leading to retention and relationship building. One way in which value is created is by delivering superior customer service. Many companies are currently learning their way around the Internet. They are struggling to understand how to deliver service online. The result, not surprisingly, is that customer service is certainly no better on the Internet, but it is probably no worse than in many other situations. We all have stories to tell of terrible service experiences which occurred in our interactions with many different types of companies in many

[8]Bristol Group, "E-Business at the Speed of Like," March 2000 (accessed at www.bristolgroup.com).

different situations. There is no reason to expect that customer service will be any better online. Companies will simply make mistakes dealing with customers. It's as simple as that.

Several years ago I read of a research study that showed that a very large percentage of telephone messages left for the sales departments of Canadian industrial firms were never returned. Presumably these calls were from customers or prospective customers who wanted to buy something. This finding is astounding, but not surprising. The same thing is happening online. Virtually any regular Internet user can regale you with stories of e-mail messages that are not returned, 1-800 help lines that lead to impenetrable voice mail systems, and "contact us" buttons that lead nowhere. The result is frustration for the visitor to a company's site and a tendency to abandon efforts to deal with the company.

I would suggest that delivering excellent customer service on the Internet is even more important than it is offline. The customer or prospective customer is operating on his or her own. When logged on to a company's website, the customer is in charge of delivering his or her own service. We are not there to help. We can't read the situation, can't anticipate a need for information, and can't sense frustration. The easiest thing for the customer to do, when he or she senses difficulty, is to walk away, so to speak. The company must realize this and take steps, as we will discuss later in this chapter, to ensure that customers are assisted along the way and experience the quality of service that will keep them coming back.

Where the Internet Creates Value

We spoke in Chapters 3 and 4 about how value can be created at each of the five levels of the drivers of customer satisfaction model. The proliferation of technology-based, self-service systems such as the Internet and the associated increase in e-commerce activities are supposedly improving the quality of customer service. Some customers value highly the option of accessing bank services or buying lawn furniture or searching for quotes on car insurance from their homes at midnight. However, it must be remembered that the Internet (like most forms of technology) creates value primarily at the lower three levels of the drivers of customer satisfaction model. This is because many companies who have taken their business online have focused on offering low prices, efficient service delivery, access to large inventories, and convenience.

The Internet does enable customers to access the core product service that they need: the financial transaction, the airline reservation, the lawn furniture, or the latest Shania Twain CD. It also delivers support services by enabling customers to access information or effect transfers of funds or purchase products. The Internet also generally enables service to be carried out in an efficient and timely fashion, leading to the conclusion that the service is technically accurate. In short, as the Internet is presently being used by most companies, it creates value in the form of access and convenience. Where the focus is on offering the lowest price available, clearly the attempt is to create value for money.

But the Internet may eliminate, or make very difficult, interaction with employees of the firm, and seems to allow for little attention to how the customer is made to *feel* by the interaction. Relatively few companies attempt to create genuine customer relationships online. In fact, at this early stage of utilization of the Internet to establish bonds with customers, many companies are likely to create primarily negative emotions, rather than positive ones. As a result, organizations that have established close, strong relationships with their online customers are few and far between.

Many reviews of "excellent" websites evaluate the Web presence of various companies almost exclusively on their *functionality*. This says it all. But being functional is not enough. *Relationships are not functional; they are emotional.* Much of what drives customer satisfaction has little or nothing to do with the functional aspects of what we are selling. To be successful on the Internet, companies have to get beyond being functionally acceptable.

The feelings associated with a person-to-person exchange have an overriding influence on all other elements of the interaction. How the customer is treated by or interacts with representatives of an organization is critical to effective customer management. The increasing use of the Internet, however, means that the social component of customer interaction is being systematically displaced. And an overwhelming number of online companies seem not to recognize the importance of these emotions in the interaction. Companies operating online generally perceive that the Internet addresses the accuracy and efficiency of service delivery. But many ignore the considerable value added by contact with employees. In the astounding world that has been created on the Internet, companies need to compensate for the loss of human contact through the creative design of their websites and the provision of parallel and back-up systems.

The Challenge Ahead

As mentioned above, the Internet has been synonymous with surfing, as many customers have become adept at flitting from one website to another with great facility and little loyalty. The average Internet user, according to the McKinsey study referred to earlier in this chapter, accesses almost 1400 pages per month, with surfers accessing 4852 (see Table 10-2). In addition, there is considerable evidence that customers engage in a great deal of window shopping on the Internet, browsing through online storefronts and placing items in shopping baskets, but never checking out. Various research reports estimate *that as many as two-thirds of customers who place items in their shopping baskets at e-retailing sites do not check out.* They abandon their carts in the middle of the virtual aisles. Imagine the confusion if the same percentage of shoppers left their carts in front of the checkouts at your neighborhood supermarket and simply walked away. Why does this happen? The first plausible explanation is that many sites are so difficult to navigate or make it so difficult for customers to complete the transaction that they abandon the effort in frustration. The second is that the virtual shopping trip takes place in the privacy of one's own home, which makes it far easier to walk away from the purchase without any fear of embarrassment.

One challenge, therefore, is to get more people to buy online, to overcome the reluctance to complete the purchase. Visiting the site is not enough. Companies need to be able to persuade visitors to put down roots. Online relationships are built on more than click-through rates and page impressions. The concept of "driving eyeballs" to a website is the modern equivalent of a conventional retailer encouraging drive-by traffic. The online relationship does not differ from the customer relationships described throughout this book in being centered on feelings and emotions. The difficulty lies in transferring those feelings into an online environment.

Research by the Bristol Group reveals some interesting facts about the nature of online relationships. Internet users who purchased clothing, books, and CDs online were asked to compare their relationships with the online retailers with their relationships with conventional retailers of the same products. Interestingly, satisfaction levels with their dealings with both types of retailers were virtually the same, but the online relationships were much less close and much less likely to last into the future, supporting the view that online relationships are still quite transitory. The fact that satisfaction levels were found to be identical online and offline confirms the observation made earlier that customers value the creation of different types of value in the two situations. While they value the convenience, access, and efficiency offered by the online e-retailer, they place greater value on the interpersonal, emotive aspects of the offline relationship.

Table 10-3 Online Satisfaction and Relationship

	Internet Customers	Offline Customers
Satisfaction (10-point scale)	8.0	8.1
Closeness (10-point scale)	4.9	5.9
Very likely to recommend	48%	56%
Very likely to still be a customer in two years	43%	62%

Source: Bristol Group.

Creating Relationships on the Internet

Numerous companies purport to be able to assist clients to develop relationships over the Internet, such as agency.com, Scient, BroadVision, NUA, Matchlogic, and Vignette. Suth companies do have the capabilities to develop stronger relationships with customers, but in most cases their definition of a stronger relationship is based on repeat site visits, more page impressions, higher spend, and so on. These are all behaviorally based indicators of the success of the site and only tangentially related to relationship building. As I have suggested throughout this book, while these types of behavior *may* indicate a strong emotion-based relationship, they do not necessarily lead to such an outcome.

It may seem that with customers having unlimited choices and information on the Internet, building relationships may not be possible or worthwhile. After all, the competition is only a click or two away. While building relationships on the Web will require some new processes and skills, it is necessary to ensure that customers are satisfied, and the creation of value is a crucial contributor to this. Let's examine 10 ways that a company can contribute to developing genuine customer relationships online.

1. Deliver Great Service

Customer service and the satisfaction that results are critical for the development of online relationships. We have known for some time that delivering excellent service and ensuring customer satisfaction are critical to improved relationships and retention in any situation. As the Internet becomes an accepted, essential part of interacting with customers and others, businesses are fighting to attract and retain customers. And many of the same things that lead to satisfaction in traditional business apply to Internet relationships. While the essential components of service excellence, value, interactions, and after-sales service may be

```
1. Deliver great service.
2. Gain the trust of customers.
3. Understand the online customer.
4. Communicate.
5. Customize and personalize.
6. Be responsive.
7. Create a sense of community.
8. Integrate.
9. Create involvement.
10. Offer them an option.
```

Figure 10-1 Steps to Creating Genuine Online Relationships

the same, the delivery and communication of these are very different in an Internet environment.

In many organizations the development of customer relationships and service quality initiatives in response to the Inernet remains slow. For instance, relationships established prior to the implementation of technology begin to erode because online customers no longer have direct contact with the firm or its employees. When relationships are already on shaky ground on the Internet, companies cannot afford to place them in even greater jeopardy by delivering shoddy service. Yet that seems to be precisely what is happening.

Ellen Neuborne of *Business Week* bemoans the fact that customer service online actually slipped in the first few months of 2000, coming off the extremely busy Christmas e-retailing season.[9] When we talk about online customer service, we are dealing with the same things that make for good service offline: e-mail confirmation of orders, availability of inventory, letting the customer know up front that an item is out of stock, advising of shipping charges *before* the customer starts to check out, and so on. Neuborne observes that few retailers seem to take customer service seriously, even though it should be possible for them to get the service function technically correct and thus gain a competitive advantage over conventional retailers.

2. Gain Their Trust

Many of the people who are now using the Internet are new to the medium and are not particularly comfortable with using it. The relatively small percentage of Internet users who have made online purchases shows that some still are reluctant to provide credit card information. In the Bristol Group research referred to earlier, only 22% of Americans and 17% of Canadians agreed that "I feel comfortable giving personal information over the Internet." In addition to concerns about the security of providing credit card and other financial information, many simply are worried about the lack of privacy on the Internet.

To reassure customers that the information they provide will not be misused and that their privacy will be respected, some companies now provide guarantees on their sites confirming their adherence to a code of conduct relating to the security of information. Amazon.com places its privacy guidelines on its site and provides a customer's bill of rights, both intended to send the message that the site is secure. Amazon.com also guarantees that if a customer's privacy is ever abused, they will take full responsibility for any credit card losses that may result.

[9] Ellen Neuborne, "It's the Service, Stupid," *Business Week E-Biz,* 3 April 2000, EB 18.

3. Understand the Customer

One of the most important rules that e-retailers and others who have established a presence on the Internet must remember is that they are still dealing with customers. What satisfies customers in an offline environment will satisfy them on the Web. Too often, companies seem to become enamored of the Internet and its technical capabilities and forget that they are dealing with the same people they dealt with offline. They delegate responsibility for development and management of their websites to technical staff whose focus is on the technology and not on the customer. The result is often that the customer is forgotten. The best advice is to go back to the basics of customer value creation and customer satisfaction. Think like the customer.

Companies operating on the Internet must understand consumer psychology. A website must not only be technically beautiful to behold, but also be easy to use. The site should reduce customer frustration and provide positive reinforcement for the customer's decision to deal with the company.

Scott Kirsner of *Net Company* accurately observes that "you are not the customer." He quotes Phil Terry, CEO of Creative Good, a New York e-commerce consulting firm: "The people who shop on the Web are different from the people who create Web sites. Web developers know the difference between Java and JavaScript, and they like downloading plug-ins. Customers come to a site and say, 'When do I get my plane ticket?'" [10]

4. Communicate

We observed earlier that communication is one of the essential features of a relationship. It is impossible to conceive of a relationship flourishing without regular communication between the parties involved. This is no less true on the Internet. With the customer in charge of the interaction, it is up to the company to ensure that appropriate two-way communication takes place. The communication must allow for the customer to contact the company easily, and outbound communication to the customer must be genuine.

Communication through the Internet has to involve more than e-mailing customers with offers or technology-based artificial reminders based on the customer's past behavior. These are the equivalent of junk mail and are treated as such. Be careful not to rely only on technology to manage communications with online customers. Consider the Amazon.com site. Once you have purchased a book online, Amazon.com "remembers" what book you purchased and rec-

---

[10] Scott Kirsner, "Four Rules for Great Expectations," *Net Company*, no. 1 (Fall 1999), 19 (accessed at www.fastcompany.com/nc/001/019.html).

ommends similar books that you might also be interested in purchasing. Through sophisticated collaborative-filtering software, the site also tells you what other books were purchased by customers who have purchased the same book as you. By taking this approach, Amazon.com is able to get to know you and your likes and dislikes in reading material.

However, this approach is not always effective in impressing the customer. A colleague of mine recently purchased his first book from Amazon.com. It was a fairly obscure book on the social and cultural significance of bread in various cultures. My friend bought it only because it would be of value in a consulting assignment he was working on at the time. He really has no serious interest in bread and will most likely never purchase another book on the subject. But now, every time he logs on to the Amazon.com site, it recommends other books on the subject that he might find enjoyable—books on baking healthy bread, on the nutritional value of ethnic breads, and on choosing a breadmaking machine. He finds this frustrating, and while it may not be catastrophic, it is an annoyance brought about by attempts at "relationship" building through personalized communications.

That is not to say that occasional outbound communication with a customer via e-mail is not effective. It can be if the communication appears genuine and offers the customer news or information that is of value. If it is based on data mining and comes across as a blatant sales effort, then it will be rejected. Like any communication, it must be sincere and designed to meet certain needs of the customer. Otherwise it is intrusive. Customers or prospective customers will see occasional newsletters, information about upcoming events, special offers, personalized news or links to relevant sites, advance notice of new products, or articles that may be of interest to them as recognizing that they are important and demonstrating an interest in them.

Making it easy for the customer to contact your company is also an essential communications aspect of managing a website. I suspect that failing to allow customers to make easy contact and failing to respond to contacts made are among the leading causes of frustration with online companies. Most companies that are serious about communicating with their online customers and prospective customers will provide their e-mail address on their website, often behind a "contact us" button to be clicked. Far too many, although apparently well intentioned, then make it difficult for the customer to actually make contact, or complicate the contact unnecessarily.

Many use the opportunity to collect information about the customer. Before allowing the customer to send an e-mail message, they ask a series of questions so that they can place the customer in a database, presumably for later contact. The result often is that customers, faced with the daunting task of answering often inane questions about where they learned of the company and which products they are interested in, will abandon the effort to contact the company. They resent the intrusion into their privacy and are loath to divulge personal information just to get a question answered. The result is possibly a lost customer. Certainly such activity nips many relationships in the bud.

Others make it technically impossible to send an e-mail message. I tried recently to make e-mail contact with Mercedes-Benz USA. Before accepting an e-mail message, this company requires that the visitor to its site complete a lengthy questionnaire. While it is possible to avoid completing much of the questionnaire, certain fields, including name, address, and post code are mandatory. However, the site accepts only U.S. zip codes. Visitors who live in other countries—like me—need not try to make contact.

Most companies that are serious about communication will provide visitors to their sites with a number of options for making contact. Not all customers want to send an e-mail message and wait for a response. Some companies provide online chat rooms where customers can exchange messages with employees of the company in real time. Many companies provide a toll-free telephone number so that visitors to the site can talk with employees. But providing visitors with these options is not enough if the options don't work. We'll talk about situations where they don't when we address the issue of responsiveness below.

5. Customize and Personalize

The challenge for management when using the Internet as a service delivery channel is to design measures of personalization into the contact. Making the contact as personal as possible is one route to establishing ongoing contact and the beginnings of a relationship. Many Web-based companies allow visitors to their site to customize their Web pages with information of particular interest and relevance to them. Thus, we have myYahoo!, mySchwab, and mySAP. This represents an effective way of building a connection between the customer and the company.

Companies like Furniture.com take the personalization experience a step further by providing access to the company's 20 design consultants by phone, e-mail, or live chat. Consultants like Diane McGowan aren't paid on commission, but they do identify customers who need help and then offer assistance. She monitors the Furniture.com site and often asks visitors if she can be of assistance. She can provide detailed information about products the visitor is interested in and can even send out swatches of material with personalized handwritten notes.[11] This level of personal service, coupled with a corporate

---

[11] Scott Kirsner, "The Customer Experience," *Net Company*, no. 1 (Fall 1999), 12 (accessed at www.fastcompany.com/nc/001/012.html).

obsession with quality and creating the right experience for the customer, contributes to high levels of repeat business and customer loyalty.

6. Be Responsive

Not responding to e-mail from customers sends the message that they are not important enough for you to get back to them. There is no faster way to end a relationship. In a study of 325 British websites, only 62% responded to a simple e-mail query. The remaining 38% did not respond at all![12] We have all met similar treatment. Companies encourage customers to "contact us," and then we never hear from them, or it takes them days to get back with a simple answer. Think about the frustration this creates for customers and the lost opportunity it represents for the companies involved.

Many companies get themselves into trouble by not having the resources or the systems to allow them to handle volumes of e-mail messages. The same applies to companies that make it impossible for customers to reach them through more conventional means. We have all tried to contact companies that encourage us to call on their 1-800 line, only to find that it is impossible to get through to a human being. I called one recently, having obtained the company's toll-free number from its website. After pressing an interminable series of numbers ("if X, press 1; if Y, press 2; etc"), I reached a point where I was advised to "send an e-mail message to the following address . . ."!

If companies want to be serious about their involvement on the Internet, they must provide the parallel systems needed to allow customers to make contact. They must install the resources and systems to allow them to handle the volume of contacts speedily and efficiently, and they must put in place policies and processes to ensure that messages are answered promptly. If you ignore customers, they will have gone elsewhere by the time you eventually respond.

7. Create a Sense of Community

Many companies that have been very adept at creating a "community" in an online environment. A community in a traditional sense is generally a group of individuals who live in close proximity to one another or have something in common. A collection of relationships is a necessary condition and might just be an excellent definition of a community.

---

[12]Rod Brooks, "Customer Relationships in the Digital World," *Marketing Magic,* 28 March 2000 (accessed at www.tka.co.uk/magic/archive/featur19.htm).

If you go to any of the more popular search engines and type in the words "online community," you will find many thousand, if not several million, websites. As you work your way through this list, you will find many companies that claim to have the ability to develop "online communities." But look beyond the hype and you will see that their definition of an online community is based on the number of visits to a site, the number of messages left in a discussion group, and so on, all of which are behavioral measures.

However, a true online community must be capable of fostering the emotional linkage between the brand, the community, and the consumer. To do this, you must get your customers communicating with you and with each other. There must be a sharing of ideas on topics that are of interest. You must get to a point where customers want to assist other customers in solving their problems. Companies must put strategies in place that will enable a bond to form. Jupiter Communications suggests employing e-mail and chat rooms, offering personalized websites, and offering organizational calendars to assist customers in planning their schedules.[13]

An excellent example of an Internet community is provided by eBay, which positions itself as "the world's largest personal online trading community."[14] On average, eBay receives 1.5 billion pages views a month! Visitors to the eBay site are able to auction items on eBay, and potential buyers will bid on the items, with the highest bidder purchasing the item. This may at first seem like a commodization of products, with price being the key differentiating feature, but eBay has added peripheral services for a human component to the interaction. Customer sales representatives are available 24 hours a day, 7 days a week, to assist with any customer problems. Feedback forms are also available so that buyers and sellers can leave notes on individuals with whom they have transacted.

MyFamily.com is another example of a startup Internet company that is attempting to establish itself as an online community. MyFamily.com has positioned itself as "the leading service offering families a rich communication experience for keeping in touch and strengthening the family. MyFamily.com bridges gaps in time and distance through free, private Web sites where families can hold family chats, create online family photo albums, and maintain a calendar of family events."[15]

8. Integrate

One of the recent Internet buzzwords is "clicks and mortar" strategy. This builds on the traditional "bricks and mortar" view, according to which retailers and

---

[13] Jupiter Communications, "Next Generation Community: From Retention to Revenue," (available at www.nua.je/surveys).

[14] eBay at website (www.ebay.com).

[15] MyFamily.com website (www.myfamily.com).

others have traditionally built their branches in close proximity to where customers live, work, and shop. This is the reason we have seen the growth of satellite bank branches in nontraditional places such as grocery stores in recent years. The clicks and mortar strategy highlights the need for an integrated strategy that combines traditional distribution with the Internet. Companies that are able to combine a traditional offline presence with an effective online offering may be at a competitive advantage in the future.[16] The major catalog retailers, such as Lands' End and L.L. Bean, with their established distribution and fulfillment systems, are one example. These companies know how to manage relationships over long distances and have perfected the provision of customer service without ever meeting most customers face to face.

Organizations must offer multiple channels for customer interaction and communication. Websites are an obvious component of this interaction, but communication channels may also include catalogs, kiosks, traditional retail stores, and television in the near future. An integrated strategy will be the key to survival because customers want and demand flexibility in shopping venues. Some companies are taking advantage of integration by welding an Internet strategy onto an established network of retail stores. Major retailers like Wal-Mart and Sears took their time refining their Internet strategies and now are poised to take advantage of the synergies that the Web affords. Some major retailers, including The Gap and Chapters, now include computer terminals in their stores so customers can order online. Points on frequent shopper programs are earned both in-store and online. Customers are offered the option to have their online purchases delivered to their homes or to a nearby store. Unsuitable products can be returned to a store. The guiding principles are flexibility and convenience through integration.

Websites must be integrated with other business processes. For instance, at e-commerce sites, customers should be able to interact directly with the company. If they run into trouble, customers should have the option of placing a telephone call to a customer service representative without having to start over. To take this even further, the option of placing an Internet telephone call should be made available. This way, the customer and the company representative can work through the problem together. Also, companies must be quick to respond to e-mail messages sent by frustrated customers; otherwise the frustration compounds itself.

9. Create Involvement

To borrow a phrase we used earlier, to be successful on the Web, companies are going to have to create as positive an *experience* as possible for their customers.

---

[16] "The Real Internet Revolution," *The Economist,* 21 August 1999, 53–54.

Creating a negative experience will lead to customers not coming back. They can defect far more easily in an online environment, where convenience is not even an advantage as it can be for offline retailers. Successful Internet sellers like Dell Computer have realized that owning the customer experience and ensuring that it is as positive as possible will guarantee repeat business, positive word of mouth, and other benefits of a solid customer relationship. Richard Owen, VP of Dell online, describes the customer experience as "the sum total of the interactions that a customer has with a company: products, people and processes. It goes from the moment when customers see an ad to the moment when they accept delivery of a product—and beyond. Sure, we want people to think that our computers are great. But what matters is the totality of customers' experiences with us: talking with our call center representatives, visiting our Web site, buying a PC, owning a PC. The customer experience reflects all of those interactions."[17]

The Internet affords a company the opportunity to create customer involvement. For example, FedEx makes it possible for me to track my shipments online. I take great comfort from knowing where my package is at all times on its route to Australia. I am fascinated as I watch it make its way to a Canadian sorting point and on to Denver, Honolulu, and eventually to a FedEx depot in Sydney. I'm involved with its progress all the way. It causes me to visit the FedEx site several times and addresses a number of emotions, including peace of mind at knowing when the package arrives at its destination and is signed for by Jack or Mary at the front desk—an actual name for verification!

Lawrence Holt of Quidnuc, a British consulting firm, says that Web-savvy customers are part of a do-it-yourself group who thrill at being able to check the status of their orders at all times. Kenneth Stickevers, VP of Gateway.com, indicates that the ability to check on the progress of their orders attracts visitors to the Gateway site. He observes, "A person will check on the status of an order five times over the two-week period it takes for the computer to arrive as opposed to one phone call during the same period before the Web."[18]

10. Offer Them an Option

Not everyone wants to use the Internet or even has access to it. The fundamental premise of market segmentation is that all customers cannot be treated alike. This must be considered when determining the value created by the Internet and

---

[17] Kirsner, "The Customer Experience."

[18] Stephen C. Miller, "Anybody in There? Sites Strain to Build in Customer Service," *New York Times,* 22 September 1999 (accessed at www.nytimes.com/library/tech/99/09/biztech/technology/22stev.html).

technology in general. Thus, when implementing e-commerce applications, firms should develop alternative and parallel systems to deliver the emotional content that characterizes genuine customer relationships. This is where the "clicks and mortar" companies may be at a competitive advantage, allowing customers to continue to purchase products and services online or offline, as they choose. Ideally, the best strategy is to integrate the two, providing customers with the option of using either or a combination.

Such a flexible system would allow customers to access either the technology-based or the more conventional, personal delivery option, while also allowing utilization of *both* new and traditional channels. Without opportunities for personal contact and the resultant affective component, organizations leave themselves vulnerable to being taken for granted by consumers and to becoming a commodity. This has been seen historically in the case of utility services such as electricity and telephone services and increasingly in the technology-based delivery of financial services. The banking industry is in danger of becoming a commodity by going online. Ernst & Young LLP state that "financial products are almost ideally suited to commodization, and examples of the commodization trend abound."[19] The examples they give include reduced margins on mortgage products and the difficulty experienced by customers in distinguishing among mutual funds because of the overabundance of information. Companies that put all of their eggs in the Internet basket run the risk of not being able to develop an effective differentiation strategy.

Building a Closer Internet Relationship

Too many senior managers of companies that I have spoken with over the last two or three years believe that if they simply create a functional e-commerce website, customers will come to spend their money. They say things like, "We need to get closer to our customers" and think that a website will solve the problem because it will make it easier for the customer to view the products they sell. In the same breath, they say, "It'll be cheaper than mass-producing and mailing out catalogs." Clearly these individuals do not have a clear understanding of what closeness means, especially in an Internet context.

Placing emphasis on the functionality of a Web site and expecting it to deliver a close, genuine customer relationship is misguided. This is like a restaurant owner concluding that location is the sole factor to consider in deciding to open a new restaurant. While location is important, it is certainly not the only strategic

---

[19] Ernst & Young, "E-commerce: 1999 Special Report on Technology in Financial Services, 18 (accessed www.eyi.com).

factor to differentiate the restaurant from the competition. Customers must understand what value they will receive by dealing with a particular company. As we discussed in Chapter 4, the form of value derived from the interaction may come from a number of different areas. Customers must first feel that value is being created from the interaction before they can begin to feel close to a company. Companies that are establishing a presence on the Internet must ask the same kinds of questions that any company must ask in any context when setting up a customer relationship strategy.

In an international research study of customers' usage of and attitudes toward the Internet, the Bristol Group asked over 1600 respondents in Canada and the United States whether those who had dealt with companies online felt any closer to them as a result.[20] Only slightly more than one-quarter said they did. This is an important finding because it demonstrates that simply building a website is not sufficient. Indeed, we may infer that the online presence has the potential to affect the relationship negatively. To overcome this feeling, customers must be made to feel that the online interaction resembles a personal interaction. Companies must design aspects into their Internet strategies that will encourage the development of long-lasting closer customer relationships characterized by high levels of emotional content.

The challenge for companies migrating to the Internet is to preserve the relationship they have enjoyed with customers in the offline setting while achieving the benefits from dealing with customers online. This integrated strategy will form the business model of the future.[21] Banks and other companies that now deal with customers both online and offline need to know whether they have succeeded in maintaining a positive, strong customer relationship as customers move to dealing with them online. They need to consider just how well they are doing in creating a close, genuine relationship in the online setting.

Just How Good Is Your Site?

All companies that have established a presence on the Internet should assess just how well they are doing in establishing and maintaining customer relationships. To what extent are visitors to the site getting the information they need? Are they satisfied with the usability of the site? And to what extent is the site contributing to a closer relationship between the company and its customers? These important questions must be addressed if the Internet is to be an important

[20] Bristol Group, "E-Business at the Speed of Like."
[21] "The Real Internet Revolution."

tool in contributing to the creation of relationships with customers—not delivering those relationships single-handedly, but being a factor in their creation rather than an impediment.

Many companies focus on the functionality or usability of their websites. Reports abound of customers simply giving up on their attempts to do business with companies online—39% of shoppers fail to buy because sites were too difficult to navigate; 56% of attempts to search for information fail; 62% of customers had an "I give up" experience within the past 60 days.[22] The obvious conclusion is that many companies make it very difficult for visitors to use their sites in a satisfying way, obtain the information they need, and conclude business. Many firms, as a result, are now turning their attention to making their sites much more user-friendly, designing or redesigning them with the customer in mind.

But this is not enough. If the Internet is to become a tool that contributes to the creation and maintenance of genuine relationships with customers, then companies must pay greater attention to what their Web presence is doing to relationships. To determine just how effective a website is and the extent to which it is contributing to genuine relationship creation, we must examine its impact on customers at more than the functional level. A website has to be more than functionally effective; it has to contribute to the creation of positive emotional reaction in customers. It must deliver the right experience, show customers that the company is paying attention and cares about their business, and make them feel good about their dealings with the firm. In short, it must support the company's efforts to deliver value at a series of levels.

Kelly Mooney of Resource Marketing of Columbus, Ohio, has developed an Internet-shopping audit tool, the E-Commerce Analyst Watch, that examines 50 attributes of websites and groups them into nine areas of evaluation, including customer service, gift giving, special promotions, and postpurchase follow-through. The objective is to create the most satisfying experience possible for customers, an experience that will cause them to come back again and again. Mooney's advice to online retailers in particular includes:

- Don't simply place the pages of your catalog on the website and think you are suddenly a competitive player in the cyberworld.

- Satisfy the customer at every turn; make it a seamless experience.

- Own the customer experience; make the site easy, intuitive, and accessible; personalization is critical.

---

[22]Robert Hercz, "Making It Click," *Canadian Business,* 10 January 2000, 19–21.

- Avoid creating barriers to the easy and successful use of the site.

- Earn the trust of customers by letting them reveal their information at their own pace and offering them advice at each step of the way.[23]

This is solid advice for companies embarking on the Web journey. It is also critical that companies use their Web presence to create value for visitors and customers at each level of the drivers of customer satisfaction model. Figure 10-2 presents examples of the types of criteria that may be applied at each level to assess the extent to which a company's website is effective in creating genuine customer relationships.

The Internet performs best in presenting a core product or service. In fact, many firms have limited their involvement on the Web to providing the most basic of service or information—the equivalent of putting the corporate brochure up on the website. Without differentiating the offer from competing sites, the firm is essentially commoditizing its offer and competing largely on price, which is the principal appeal of many sites.

The provision of support processes and services is the focus of most website evaluations that address the issue of functionality. How easy is it to navigate the site and conclude business? At this level, the emphasis is on the technical aspects of site design: speed of the site, ability to navigate efficiently, availability of desired information, and ease of loading graphics.

The technical performance of the site is evaluated on the basis of whether the visitor was able to obtain what he or she wanted, in a timely manner, and in a form that was acceptable. Is it possible to complete the transaction, obtain the information, and actually have the product delivered when needed?

A firm's website can also facilitate the interaction with the company and its employees. The ability to send an e-mail message (and get a prompt response), make contact through a 1-800 number or by live chat, and create a more personal contact between the customer and the company are all part of the delivery of service at this level.

Of course, the customer's emotional response to the company is evoked at each of these levels. The most common negative emotion that seems to be associated with the use of websites is frustration. We have many statistics reporting the abandonment of efforts to do business. A company that is serious about doing business online must address reducing such negative emotions where possible and replacing them with emotions such as delight. Much can be done at this ultimate level to ensure that the emotions engendered are conducive to the building of genuine customer relationships. Otherwise visitors to Web sites cannot be expected to return to put down roots.

---

[23] Anna Muoio, "The Experienced Customer," *Net Company,* no. 1 (Fall 1999), 24 (accessed at www.fastcompany.com/nc/001/024.html).

```
┌─────────────────────────────────────────────┐
│ Core Product or Service                      │
│   online purchasing                          │
│   offering lowest prices                     │
│   providing wide selection                   │
│   access to required information             │
│   visual presentation of products           │
│   options re service delivery                │
│ Process and Support Systems                  │
│   delivery and billing                       │
│   credit options                             │
│   statements re security information         │
│   1-800 help line available                  │
│   e-mail access                              │
│   speed and navigability of site             │
│   appropriate links                          │
│ Technical Performance                        │
│   accuracy of information                    │
│   ability to connect to links                │
│   items in stock                             │
│   efficient delivery                         │
│   on-time delivery                           │
│ Interaction with Company and Staff           │
│   timely response to e-mail                  │
│   toll-free access to help desk              │
│   live chat to employees                     │
│   provision of regular communication         │
│ Emotional Elements                           │
│   interactivity                              │
│   ability to involve others                  │
│   involvement in tracking order              │
│   chat rooms                                 │
│   customization                              │
│   personalization                           │
│   recognition of repeat visitors             │
│   creation of online community               │
└─────────────────────────────────────────────┘
```

Figure 10-2 Website Evaluation to Drive Relationship Building

Winning in the Online World

While the Internet has spread rapidly through society and is now used by a large and rapidly growing percentage of people, some will resist its use and some will never go online. We have examined in this chapter some of the ways that companies can go beyond the view of the Internet as technology and use it to build genuine customer relationships.

Who will be the winners in creating those genuine relationships? I believe some firms have a head start and a natural advantage. Catalog companies and multilevel retailers such as L.L. Bean, Lands' End, J. Crew, and Eddie Bauer already know how to deal with their customers via technology and have a distinct advantage in managing relationships online. So too do traditional major retailers whose established brand names will inspire confidence and will carry considerable weight in enabling them to make the transition. Companies such as Sears, Wal-Mart, Nordstrom, and The Gap have added the Web to the array of channels through which they can deliver products and services to their customers. Finally, those pure-play Internet companies that do not have a physical presence may have a more difficult task establishing credibility with online customers. Some, such as eBay, Amazon.com, eToys, and Garden.com will succeed largely because they do it right and have first-mover advantage. There is not a lot of room in the online category. Being third-best means not being in the business.

But even the best make mistakes. I have never understood why a company would bother to tell visitors to its site when it was last updated. I'm not likely to be impressed with a line at the bottom of the screen advising me that the site was last updated March 27, 1998. What kind of message does that send about the company and the importance it places on the Internet? Yet others do similar, if slightly less obvious, things to get in the way of customer satisfaction and the possibility of generating repeat visits. E-mail messages generate no response. Catalogs ordered online never arrive. A "things to come" section never delivers on its promise. Confirmations of orders received are so late that the items have already arrived.

All of these examples are merely Internet manifestations of mistakes that companies routinely make in the offline world. This should tell us something about how interaction with customers should be managed online. The principles are precisely the same. The Internet is a new medium, and many customers are not yet completely familiar with its use. They need your help. They get frustrated more easily because of their unfamiliarity with the technology. All the more reason for companies to pay attention to how their presence on the Internet makes the customer feel and to take appropriate steps to create the most positive experience possible.

Customers may see the increased use of the Internet as enabling them to take control of service delivery, facilitating access and making it much more convenient to obtain routine services. But many resent the fact that such systems result in an erosion of the relationships that existed in the past. The challenge companies face when they launch such systems is to foster closer customer relationships in the face of the technology.

The introduction of the Internet as a means to deliver certain components of service should be taken as a part of a long-term corporate strategy. The focus should be on using the technology to create mass customization—to allow greater efficiency, consistency, and value while allowing the customer a sense of recognition and individuality. This should be combined with attempts to segment customer groups, allowing them the choice of how or when or whether to use the technology.

The emphasis has to be on integrating the use of the Internet into all other aspects of how a company interacts with its customers. As many organizations intentionally migrate their customers online, established relationships are at risk. Steps must be taken to protect them and to use appropriate strategies to maintain and strengthen existing relationships. It is imperative that a company's Internet strategy result in the creation of value for customers and other visitors to the website. Without this essential building block of a relationship, there is little hope that genuine customer relationships will result.

11

Extending the Concept of Relationships

A Slightly Different View

Relationships are fundamental to the long-term success of the firm. It has been a consistent theme of this book that the existence of strong, genuine customer relationships offers companies a mechanism for developing and sustaining a competitive advantage. But the concept of customer relationships is not limited to those situations where companies meet their customers, either in person or via technology. Companies that are focused entirely on developing conventional customer relationships and that fail to work on developing relationships with other stakeholders and in other contexts place themselves at a competitive risk.

In this chapter we begin to extend the concept of customer relationships in several directions. Throughout this book, we have tended to discuss customer relationships largely in the context of companies and other organizations that interact with their customers directly, through interpersonal contact between the customer and the employees of the company. Those commercial relationships are the most like the personal relationships in our lives. In Chapter 10 we raised the issue of the impact on customer relationships of the fact that organizations are increasingly interacting with customers through technology. Now we will examine another kind of customer relationship, that between the customer and the brand. Branding is already an important concept that has captured the attention of senior managers. It will become increasingly important as more and more companies embark upon branding strategies that are ultimately intended to create a bond between the customer and the brand. Unless these strategies are grounded in the kind of thinking that leads to the establishment of customer relationships, they will not succeed. The most successful brands are those that have a strong, meaningful relationship with their customers and with the public at large.

Secondly, we will extend the concept of customer relationships into an exciting new direction by applying our view of relationships to the connections that customers feel toward various events, personalities, and what marketers term "properties." Sponsorship is big business. Many large corporations make million-dollar decisions every year on where to spend their sponsorship budgets: which events to sponsor, which athletes or rock stars to associate with, which well-known person to engage as spokesperson for a company or brand. Individual consumers have emotional connections with major sports, events, properties, and famous personalities. The challenge is to maximize the *fit* between the company's brand and the possible options for sponsorship or association. The key to doing this is to ensure that the customer has a compatible relationship with the brand and the selected property.

In Chapter 12 we will examine a natural extension of the concept of relationships, from the customer to other stakeholder groups that are fundamentally important to the success of the organization. While customers must be the focal point, firms also must have solid relationships at many levels and with many stakeholders.

In essence, solid relationships must exist with all stakeholders and in all contexts in which your business operates. As we extend the concept even further, we should keep in mind the principles of relationship building stressed throughout this book. It should be obvious why developing solid relationships with customers is important, even though in the future we may interact with them less and less. In fact, in situations where we rarely interact directly with customers, the development and maintenance of genuine relationships are likely *even more important* because of the challenges and inherent vulnerability of that customer business.

It should also be obvious that the fundamental nature and dimensions of relationships are the same regardless of the context in which the concept is applied. The essence of the approach to relationship development and maintenance is the same whether we are talking about a relationship in a face-to-face professional or personal service context, a retail relationship, a brand relationship, or relationships with employees, suppliers, shareholders, or others. One of the key points that we have emphasized is that all relationships are emotionally based. Trust, commitment, empathy, and the other critical emotional elements must be present.

Everyone's into Branding

Branding has become quite fashionable. Branding consultants abound, and the dot.coms are spending millions of dollars to establish their brands by advertising in the most visible places. The objective is to register their brands in the minds of customers and visitors to websites. But do any of them stop to ask what a brand is? New brands are launched every day. New companies are established every day, and new products put on the market. Each of them has a name, but do they have *brands*? A colleague of mine recently surprised a new technology client by observing, "At the moment, you have a name; it will take some time before you have a brand." I couldn't agree more. It takes time to become a brand.

A brand is more than a name or a logo in the same way that a relationship is more than an interaction. In fact, the concepts of brand and relationship parallel each other in the sense that emotional underpinnings are associated with both. A brand is more than corporate identification or the name of the firm. It's not design or packaging; it's an emotional connection between a company and its customers and the public. It's not what we sell; it's who we are, what we stand for, and what we mean to people. Regis McKenna says a brand is a relationship that customers know and value. It is "an active experience."[1]

As we'll discuss later, customers do establish genuine relationships with brands. Brands come to mean something special to people; they are important parts of their lives. Most consumers would likely consider the idea that they could get "close" to a brand of spaghetti sauce or shampoo a sign of weakness. Yet we all have brands that we go back to again and again, that we have been using for many years and that define who we are. Our friends and family could not imagine us using any other cologne, driving any other car, or wearing any other brand of running shoe.

Conceptualizing a Brand

There is no doubt that consumers develop close attachments to brands, both corporate and product. In research studies, they will describe their favorite products and services, and favorite companies to deal with, in increasingly complex and emotive terms. To consumers, the brands with which they have developed close relationships are no longer inanimate objects or companies. They take on progressively greater degrees of animate or even human characteristics as the relationship deepens. We can conceptualize a brand as moving through four stages on its journey from being merely a name to being a genuine relationship partner. In many ways, this way of looking at brands also parallels the way that brands have been viewed in marketing circles over the years and the way that marketers have measured the success of their branding efforts.

The goal of the initial branding activity after a brand is launched is to generate *brand awareness*. After all, it's difficult to develop a relationship if consumers have never heard of the brand. Many companies still measure the effectiveness

[1] Regis McKenna, *Real Time* (Boston: Harvard Business School Press, 1997), 100–01.

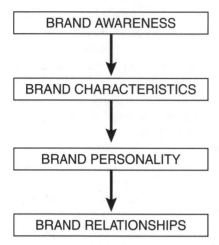

Figure 11-1 Progression of the Concept of a Brand

of their advertising in part on the degree of brand awareness that has been generated—they focus on measures such as aided and unaided brand recall. The first step on the road to developing a brand relationship is to make sure that customers in the target segment are aware of the brand. This explains why large volumes of advertising dollars are lavished on the launch of new brands.

A brand must then be imbued with certain *characteristics*. It must become known for something, associated with something. The question at this point is, "What is it like?" What adjectives will people use to describe the brand to others? Is it modern or old-fashioned, young or old, masculine or feminine, soft or hard, progressive or slow to change? Focusing on such questions allows us to identify the characteristics of the brand as seen by customers. It relates to the positioning of the brand as defined by the company that owns it. Much research is devoted to determining how brands are positioned against their competitors on what are determined to be salient brand characteristics.

The next stage in the progression toward brand relationships is to begin to imbue the brand with human characteristics as we consider the *brand personality*. This is a necessary step if we accept that consumers develop relationships with brands. Developing such a relationship with what is after all an inanimate object, or even worse a concept, is easier if the consumer can think of the brand as having similar characteristics to a person with whom he or she might establish a close relationship. In fact, we tend to develop relationships with brands that share many of the personality traits of people with whom we would associate.

This concept of brand personality is what motivates focus group moderators to ask the well-worn question, "If Budweiser were a person, what sort of person would he be?" Having asked that question dozens of times over many years, I can attest to the value of the responses. Participants in qualitative research often go on for 30 minutes or more describing in vivid detail the kind of people who would be represented by a particular brand. They are describing not only what kind of people they are in demographic terms (age, employment, marital status, kids at home), but a great deal about their lifestyles (where they vacation, what kind of car they drive, what TV programs they watch, what books they read) and their personalities (are they friendly, sullen, outgoing, shy, kind, caring, open, retiring?). By extension, these research participants are presenting a detailed picture of the personality of the brand, which can then be used to position the brand against the competition and to validate the positioning strategy of the marketing department.

The final stage of the evolution of the brand from mere name to the epitome of success is the achievement of a *brand relationship*. At this point the customer has achieved a closeness with the brand that is every bit as important as that with a retailer or the corner dry cleaner. The brand becomes important in the life of the consumer.

Earning Your Stripes

The status of an established brand, one with which many consumers have developed lasting relationships, is earned, not bought. The cultivation of brand relationships takes a lot of work and investment in quality, as with other customer relationships that we have been discussing. A brand relationship cannot be bought by spending vast amounts of money on advertising to support a brand launch. Most of the world's leading brands have been around for many years, delivering consistent product and service quality to their customers. The exception to this is those companies that seem to have burst full-blown onto the brand scene, coming out of nowhere to become well-established leaders in their respective sectors, most of which did not exist or were underdeveloped 10 or 15 years ago. These are firms like Microsoft, Starbucks, Intel, and Amazon.com that have first-mover advantage in new sectors. Because of their position as market leader, their brands take on a cachet worthy of firms that have spent decades cultivating their brand relationships.

Over time, as brands become established and develop relationships with their customers, they acquire *brand equity*. We tend to think of equity as a financial concept that has historically been associated with tangible assets. Brand equity is the accumulated value that the brand has assembled by virtue of the loyalty of its customers. The concept of equity is appropriate because the loyalty of one's customers represents one of the firm's most valuable assets. The equity in a brand resides not in the brand itself but in its relationships with its customers. It is the depth and strength of customers' relationships with a brand that create the value of that brand, its ability to sustain customer loyalty and a strong flow of revenues into the future.

Companies must realize that there is equity in established brands. That equity is the sum total of the positive aspects of brand relationships with customers, less the negative aspects of those relationships. In other words, established brands have certain positive aspects and certain negative ones. This is a fact that must be assessed when a company considers changing a brand name or dropping a brand from its product line. Recent decisions by Procter & Gamble and Unilever to reduce the number of brands in their product lines raise issues such as these. How do we decide which brands to drop? The answer: we drop those brands that have the least brand equity—where brand relationships are weakest.

When companies merge, management often wishes to change the name and create a completely new entity. This has happened recently with the demutualization of life insurance companies and the privatization of utilities that were formerly government owned and operated. Thus, when pharmaceutical companies Ciba and Sandoz merge, the result is Novartis. Mutual Life of Canada becomes Clarica upon demutualization. Telecom Eireann becomes *eircom* when its shares are floated. The challenge in all of these cases relates to the impact on brand relationships of a change of brand or the establishment of a new brand. What do names like Novartis and Clarica mean to people? Perhaps they mean something to the senior managers who participated in the branding decision, but little to customers and the public until the brand becomes well established. The issue then is whether the equity that was resident in the former brand has been lost and whether the new brand is now facing building brand relationships and equity from scratch. There are no brand relationships with the new brand unless the company is successful in migrating those relationships with the former brand to the new brand.

In the case of Telecom Eireann, the company was faced in mid-1999 with the challenge of giving a fresh face to the company when it became investor-owned. In moving the corporation from the government-owned telephone utility of Ireland to a publicly-traded competitive company, management had to transfer the positive emotional equity in the Telecom Eireann brand to the new *eircom* brand, while leaving behind the baggage associated with its public utility days. The new company was to be seen as progressive, professional, and friendly. The first challenge was to create widespread brand awareness of *eircom,* and then to employ strategies that would successfully establish positive relationships between the new brand and the Irish people.

Many brands started life as mere names or words that at the time probably held little meaning for customers—brands such as Xerox, Intel, and Nike come to mind. Yet over time these have become some of the world's most successful and valued brands.

The Meaning in Brands

Brands become valuable to customers and to their owners only when they become meaningful. Like other relationships, they take on meaning over time. We speak of meaningful relationships as those that endure and that hold a central place in our lives. The same may be said of brands. Those that are most important to us add some meaning to our daily lives. Some brands become part of us. But only a very few brands take on such status in the lives of most consumers, and some consumers seem more likely to develop brand relationships than are others.

Susan Fournier of the Harvard Business School correctly claims that customers do not buy particular brands over and over again simply because they like them or because the products or services perform well. "They are involved in relationships with a collectivity of brands so as to benefit from the meanings they add into their lives. Some of these meanings are functional and utilitarian; others are more psychosocial and emotional. All, however, are purposive and ego centered and therefore of great significance to the persons engaging them."[2]

But how is meaning created? How do some brands come to occupy such a central place in our lives? Brands take on more meaning as we increase our experience with them. Meaning cannot easily be created through advertising and other forms of communication, which are more effective at creating brand awareness. As consumers share experiences with brands, the brands come to represent something, to stand for something. The mention of the brand evokes images in the mind of the customer. The brand with which the customer has a meaningful relationship takes on a salience and a centrality in the customer's life. A solid emotional connection develops. The brand becomes a loyal and trusted friend, one the customer can rely upon to perform as expected every time.

As such, then, brands with which the customer can identify, those that are closely identified with his or her persona, create considerable value for the customer. That value is created at the highest emotional level and has its roots in the memory and personality of the individual consumer. Certain brands are "right" for the customer, and most successful brands have succeeded in creating an emotional connection. Kraft is such a brand; its range of branded products occupies a central place in the lives and homes of many consumers. The emotional connection with Kraft for some customers may go back to their childhood, when Kraft was associated with peanut butter sandwiches and toasting marsh-

---

[2] Susan Fournier, "Consumer and Their Brands: Developing Relationship Theory in Consumer Research," *Journal of Consumer Research* 28 (March 1998): 361.

mallows over a campfire with Mom and Dad. Brand meaning is shared memories and shared values.

What Makes a Brand Great?

There are a lot of misconceptions about what a brand is. Some people consider it to be a particular product, others the name of a company. Each may be accurate, depending on the context in which the name of the product or firm is used. One definition of a genuine brand is that it "is a 'way of life.' It's not just about a word, it's about passion, commitment, and a unique promise that gets fulfilled every day."[3] Not a bad description of the emotion present in a real brand. Certainly sounds like a relationship.

Scott Bedbury, Starbucks' Senior Vice President of Marketing, offers an interesting point of view, given the strength of the Starbucks brand and the fact that he was involved with introducing Nike's "Just Do It" campaign in the late 1980s and early 1990s. One of Bedbury's suggestions is that great brands must have a long-term focus, implying that brands must be prepared to invest the resources necessary to build the brand.[4] Such a strategy would enable the brand to "travel world-wide, transcend cultural barriers, speak to multiple consumer segments simultaneously, create economies of scale, and let you operate at the higher end of the positioning spectrum—where you can earn solid margins over the long-term."[5]

Bedbury also suggests that a great brand knows what it represents to the consumer. But the viewpoint of senior executives has no bearing on what the brand represents in the minds of consumers. Only by spending the resources necessary to ask consumers continuously what the brand represents to them and what their relationships are with the brand can management understand what the brand represents. Another of Bedbury's brand principles is that "a great brand is a story that's never completely told. [It] is a metaphorical story that's evolving all the time. This connects with something very deep—a fundamental human appreciation of mythology." He also states that "stories create connections for people [and] create the emotional context people need to locate themselves in a larger experience."[6]

Brand equity is a concept that is frequently used to describe brands, though it is often misunderstood. It has been described as "the totality of the brand's

---

[3] Duane Knapp, *The Brand Mindset* (New York: McGraw-Hill, 2000), xvi.

[4] Alan Webber, "What Great Brands Do," *Fast Company* (August-September 1997): 96–100.

[5] Ibid.

[6] Ibid.

perception, including the relative quality of products and services, financial performance, customer loyalty, satisfaction, and overall esteem toward the brand. It's all about how consumers, customers, employees, and all stakeholders *feel* about a brand."[7] Together, the definitions of brands and brand equity highlight the emotional connection that can reside in a brand. Indeed, it is the existence of an emotional connection that makes a brand; otherwise, it is only a product or company name.

And how does a company go about becoming a brand? Jack Myers, a consultant with Myers Consulting Group in New York, suggests that four elements must be present in a brand: differentiation, relevance, effective communication, and consistently fulfilling the promise.[8] He states: "In these complicated, chaotic and changing times, we turn to our familiar and trusted brands as a lighthouse to guide us and provide us with certainty and comfort."[9] The existence of trust and promise is what creates a brand. For instance, consumers know what to expect when they purchase a can of Coke, attend Disney World, or take the family to McDonald's for Saturday lunch.

Great brands rely on what they mean to people to ensure their success. They create value by creating meaning. When brands reach the status where customers have genuine relationships with them, there is little need to stress value for money; the brand's loyal customers take that for granted. Purchasing a brand like Heinz when buying ketchup is second nature for many consumers. They don't wait until Heinz ketchup goes on sale. Great brands with solid customer relationships sell a much higher percentage of their total volume at full price than do lesser brands that must compete on price. Brands like Chanel and Gucci are rarely if ever discounted. Solid brand relationships are not based on price competition; they are grounded in emotion and values that mean something to the customer.

Where Brands Are Relevant

Building relationships with brands is becoming increasingly important as customers have less direct contact with the employees of the firms they do business with. The notion of a brand relationship is most easily appreciated and understood in the context of what most of us think of when we hear the word "brand," namely the major consumer brands that surround us in our everyday lives. We encounter world brands like Coca-Cola, Xerox, Mars, Yoplait, Kraft, and Ford

---

[7] Knapp, *The Brand Mindset*, 3.

[8] Brenda Dalglish, "Canada Lacks Brand Power, U.S. Consultant Says," *Globe and Mail* (Toronto), 18 November 1998, B29.

[9] Ibid.

at every turn. Other brands have thrust themselves on the world stage and become famous and extremely well entrenched in a relatively short time—Nike, Starbucks, and Amazon.com. What makes these brands rather than mere names? At what stage in its acceptance and diffusion into the marketplace does a company or product's name deserve to be called a real brand? I believe it is when the mention of the brand can truly be said to convey a sense of meaning; when customers and noncustomers attach a certain importance to the role of the brand in their lives; when the brand can be truly said to *stand for something*.

To achieve success, companies like those above, most of which are manufacturers of what are generally termed fast-moving consumer goods, had to develop a brand image that spoke to customers, that conveyed the message that this product is right for you. The vagaries of distribution channels have meant that most of us would contentedly go through life without ever meeting someone from Kellogg's, speaking with a representative of Folgers, or coming face to face with a ketchup maker from Heinz. Yet we knew these brands, and they have occupied an important place in the homes and lives of many of us. These packaged goods brands developed the first brand relationships. They had to because it was retailers who controlled distribution and actually met the consumer. These manufacturers' brands developed a truly long-distance relationship.

Until very recently, manufacturers of consumer products had very little contact with the consumers of their products. Contact was largely through advertising, packaging, and in-store displays. The distribution channels used to get the products to consumers were not controlled by the manufacturers. Essentially, they had delegated contact with their end consumers to retailers, who consummated the customer interaction. They built the reputation of their brands on the basis of the quality of their products and the emotional messages conveyed through advertising.

Now technology has changed all of that. Today, brand relationships that were for the most part noncontact relationships are suddenly becoming more like conventional customer relationships, characterized by direct contact with the customer. Through the application of technology, brands such as Heinz, Del Monte, Crest, Nestlé, Campbell, and Ivory are in a better position than ever before to establish and maintain genuine relationships with customers. They are now able to reach around the retailers to "touch" their consumers directly through their websites, call centers, e-mail, recipe clubs, kids' clubs, and newsletters. Manufacturing firms that rarely if ever made contact with end consumers are now reinventing themselves as relationship marketers. Those who have predicted the end of brand loyalty are dead wrong. Major consumer packaged goods brands are alive and well, and their customer relationships will only strengthen in the future.

The idea of brand relationships is becoming very pertinent in other contexts. Think about the companies that are operating in what we have termed "taken-for-granted" service situations. These are increasingly having little if any contact with their customers. They have the same problem the consumer products manufacturers faced: they rarely if ever meet the customer. These companies, because the opportunity to establish customer-employee relationships is no longer available, must borrow a leaf from the book of the brand relationship experts at Nike, Coca-Cola, and Michelin.

So too must companies that deal with their customers primarily or exclusively via technology. Many firms are systematically eliminating human contact from their dealings with customers. Done in the name of productivity and efficiency, this has the potential to cause irreparable damage to customer relationships. When all of the gasoline companies have installed self-serve pumps that allow me to swipe my VISA card and pump my own gas and leave without ever speaking with an employee, what incentive do I have to go back again and again to a Shell station? None, unless the company has succeeded in establishing a relationship between me and their brand. They have to give me a reason, and that reason may well be embodied in how I feel toward the brand.

Consumers are now buying a wide variety of products and services over the Internet. As electronic commerce becomes more widely accepted, customers will have less face-to-face contact with service providers and are less likely to deal with a company at an interpersonal level. In such situations, the customer will have much more of a relationship with the company's brand than with employees of the organization. The customer, while a regular user of the company's products or services, may in fact not only never meet or even talk with employees of the organization, but may know little if anything about the company or where it is located. To that customer, the brand is just a brand. The challenge here is how to build and maintain strong, close relationships with customers who are never seen, who have a world of choice, and who may feel little loyalty to any one firm. In this situation, the concept of brand building takes on a whole new meaning.

Three categories of companies have been very successful in creating strong brand relationships with their customers—*brand* relationships because customers are unlikely to establish relationships with employees of the firm, either because they never meet them or because they deal with many different locations of the firm. Companies like AT&T, Allstate, State Farm, and VISA deal in intangible products, where the offerings of one company are often indistinguishable from those of another. These companies, however, have succeeded in developing a reputation for service, quality, and innovation that leads consumers to trust them and feel that they can rely upon them.

Major retailers have also succeeded in building strong brand relationships that ensure that customers will get the same *feel* regardless of which store they visit. Companies like IKEA, The Gap, Starbucks, The Body Shop, Tim Hortons, and Tesco have succeeded in creating meaning for their customers by offering a consistent quality experience. Others, like L.L. Bean, Lands' End, and Amazon.com, do the same over great distances and in a virtual store environment.

Finally, other major service companies create a brand experience that develops for many into a lasting relationship. They do so by making the experience memorable. Such an experience is not the exclusive preserve of entertainment and hospitality companies like Four Seasons, Disney, and Seabourn Cruises. A company like Kinko's has proven that a service as mundane as photocopying can be turned into a brand that stands for something by offering efficient, friendly service with amazing consistency.

Expectations of Brands

Brand relationships are personal and contextual. Some consumers will develop stronger brand relationships than others, but this is no different than customer relationships in other contexts, where, as we observed earlier, not all consumers want a close relationship. But for some consumers brands occupy a central part in their lives. The brands that they use and rely upon are an essential component of what defines them as individuals. Which brands a customer will develop a close relationship with will depend on the categories of products and services that are important to that customer. A golfer may develop a strong relationship to brands like Callaway or Titleist, yet these brands may not be even at the awareness stage with a nongolfer. While I may know of or even admire a well-established brand like Harley-Davidson, I have nothing approaching a relationship with the brand because motorcycles mean little to me. To a young family, a brand like Johnson & Johnson may achieve relationship status, but the strength of that relationship may diminish as the children grow up.

A true brand relationship is specific to the individual and is based upon his or her experiences over time. Brand relationships are not developed solely or maybe even largely by effective marketing programs, or at least marketing in the traditional sense. While advertising, price incentives, and new product features will stimulate interest and trial, a relationship will develop only if something clicks between the customer and the brand. The brand must live up to the promises made in its advertising, and it must be right for the customer. What the brand stands for must mirror the values of the customer, thus, the Body Shop will succeed in developing a solid relationship with some customers, while Revlon will succeed with others. The relationship is based on experience with the product. While advertising can create awareness and implant the characteristics and even the personality of the brand, these are primarily descriptors. The brand relationship comes to exist only after the customer is satisfied with how the brand is performing and with how he or she is made to feel by association with it.

Consumers expect the owners or makers of brands to live up to their end of the relationship as well. In keeping with our observation earlier that genuine relationships are two-way, customers expect consistency of behavior and quality. As relationships develop and strengthen, consumers view their brands as essential components of their lives. They trust them and rely on them, and the brands become part of them as individuals. They feel an affection for their favorite brands that is as strong as an interpersonal relationship. They feel let down and hurt if a favorite brand is discontinued or if the formulation is changed so that it's "not like it used to be." The companies that manufacture branded products run the same risk that services companies encounter when they make changes in how they operate or how they deliver service. Thus, brand repositioning, repackaging, and reformulation are all strategic decisions that are fraught with risk in that they tend to be disruptive of established brand relationships.

Creating Meaning and Emotion Around Great Brands

Consider the example of the Kraft brand. Kraft has reinvented itself from a traditional manufacturing company to a firm that values the relationships that customers have with the Kraft brand. In Canada, the company recently redesigned the package of its flagship product, Kraft Dinner, to make it appear more up to date and mainsteam. Kraft Dinner (known outside Canada as Kraft Macaroni and Cheese) is the most frequently purchased grocery item in Canada, with over 90 million boxes sold annually. At the same time, the company launched an advertising campaign that focused on the emotional aspects of the product to "awaken warm and fuzzy memories so consumers who stopped buying it will try it again."[10] It is the deep emotional connection that consumers have with the Kraft brand that the company is tapping.

One of the world's most recognizable sports teams is Manchester United, the legendary English soccer team that is consistently at or near the top of the Premiership standings. Recently they have taken a strategy of transferring the positive equity in the Manchester United brand through other ventures by opening a number of retail outlets in other countries, including Ireland, the Middle East, and Southeast Asia. The club's managing director of merchandising states, "The most important part of having a retail site is that it allows us to present

---

[10] John Heinzl, "Kraft Dinner Serves up a New Look," *Globe and Mail* (Toronto), 13 January 1999, B29.

the Manchester United experience [and] we are trying to give the fans an opportunity to get closer to the club."[11] Sounds like a relationship to me.

In the same vein, Nike has been of the world's most successful brands at creating an emotional link with its customers. What is most amazing is that they have done this in a product category—footwear—that has the potential to be treated as a commodity item. However, Nike has been anything but a commodity in its short life of 30 years. The "swoosh" signature is recognized the world over, and their advertising budget is an ad agency's dream, with annual spending of hundreds of millions of dollars.[12]

Nike has developed a unique communications strategy, and, from the company's beginnings, they have always chosen sports celebrities as endorsers of the company's products. Over the years these have included Dennis Rodman, Charles Barkley, John McEnroe, Michael Jordan, and most recently Tiger Woods. During his time as a Nike endorser, each was at the top of his game and each conveyed the image of excellence, coolness, and perfection. Scott Bedbury suggests that while customers are unlikely to assess the features of a particular type of insole, they will certainly consider the last-second winning shot by Michael Jordan that lifts them to an emotional charged state. "A brand reaches out with that kind of powerful connecting experience. It's an emotional connection point that transcends the product. And transcending the product is the brand."[13] It is this emotional connection that Nike has been able to leverage so successfully.

Let's look at another recent example. MVP.com is a recently launched e-commerce web site that sells sports-related equipment. What differentiates MVP.com from other e-commerce sites is that it is partially owned by Wayne Gretzky, John Elway, and Michael Jordan. Between the three, they have played professionally for 49 years, have won 12 championships, and own 9 championship and 15 regular season MVP titles.[14] These individuals are clearly deserving of the title MVP! The strategy that MVP.com has employed highlights the equity that exists in these *brands* who are sports personalities and celebrities. By intimately involving these three individuals (Elway is Chairman of the Board), MVP.com has received a tremendous amount of media coverage that would not have come their way otherwise. While this is important, it is not the critical factor. What these three individuals offer is very positive brand equity. The MVP.com strategy is to leverage this equity by transferring it from the

[11] Rob Griffin, "Manchester United Expands into Ireland," *Sunday Post,* 31 October 1999, 2.

[12] Greg Goldin, "When Brand Is Grand," *World Business* (November/December 1996), 18–23.

[13] Webber, "What Great Brands Do," 98.

[14] MVP.com website (www.mvp.com), accessed March 14, 2000.

brands, in this case the sports personalities, to the new brand, the MVP.com website. There is a "fit" between the two.

Building the Brand through Sponsorships

One of the most effective means of building a relationship between a brand and its customers or the general public is to engage in appropriate sponsorships and associate with the right people. Companies associate with certain "properties" as sponsors so that they can, in some way, derive benefit for their brands. Except in the most philanthropic situations, companies expect some tangible payback from their association with sporting events, arts exhibits, performances, and community activities. Otherwise why would they lend their names? All decisions relating to sponsorships and associations must therefore be approached strategically. Is the property or association under consideration "right" for the company. How can a company decide among an array of opportunities that are presented each year? The decision must be based on fit.

Most large corporations have an imposing list of properties to choose from when it comes to sponsorship. Some of these are national in scope and may include lending the company name to a golf tournament or even a pro tour, being a lead sponsor of the television coverage of a major event such as the Super Bowl, or sponsoring of a national high school science competition. Companies are often asked to consider attaching their names to sports stadiums, theaters, arts centers, or buildings on university campuses. Many more opportunities present themselves at the regional or local level, where there are always colleges, symphony orchestras, and seniors clubs worthy of support. Most corporations will agree that the demands upon their sponsorship budgets far exceed the money available.

While companies often associate with events and organizations as corporate sponsors, there are other situations where the principles of sponsorship also apply. This is most obvious where a company is sponsoring the participation of an individual or team in an event, such as when VISA sponsors the Canadian bobsled team or when a company sponsors a national tour by a rock band or a concert pianist. The same principles apply when a company is selecting a spokesperson for its brand or a "personality" to appear in its advertising.

In all of these cases, the sponsoring company is interested in establishing an *association* with an individual, an organization, a property, or an event, so that the company will derive some benefit. The benefit is difficult to quantify and is almost certainly subject to opinion. To apply the perspective of this book, the company is entering into a relationship with a property, event, or individual to enhance its own reputation and image, thereby improving its relationship it with its customers and the public. Will the association enhance the brand? Will a transference of emotional equity occurs from the property or individual being sponsored to the sponsoring company or brand? If not, the sponsorship money is not being well spent.

The sponsorship budget should be viewed as an investment by the company in strengthening the equity in the brand. If the sponsorship is perceived by the target audience—customers for the most part—to be inappropriate or even offensive, the potential to do damage to the brand is quite high. Yet in a very large percentage of companies with whom I have discussed the subject in recent years, when sponsorship is mentioned eyes roll and there is general snickering or laughter. That is because in many companies the decisions relating to sponsorship are anything but strategic. Examples abound of companies lavishing millions of dollars of sponsorship money on golf tournaments, opera festivals, or rugby teams because the CEO loves golf, opera, or rugby.

One could argue that it is the CEO's prerogative to determine where sponsorship dollars should be spent. I disagree. Sponsorship is as important a marketing decision as is advertising. It is a valuable tool in building and strengthening relationships between a company's target customers and its brands.

Forms of Sponsorship and Association

Sponsorships can build the emotional connection between customers and brands by transferring emotional equity from the property or celebrity to the sponsoring brand. Some forms of sponsorship are plainly commercial in nature, such as Air Canada's sponsorship of Grand Prix racing or Bell Canada's sponsorship of the Canadian Open golf tournament. Others are more philanthropic, such as a company's sponsorship of a symphony orchestra or children's choir, or quite socially oriented, such as corporate contributions to hospital foundations and universities. Companies are increasingly treating decisions relating to sponsorship strategically and are even engaging in "strategic philanthropy," indicating that they are looking for a return on their sponsorship investments even where those are not blatantly commercial, as in contributions to universities and children's hospitals.[15]

Closely related to sponsorship decisions are decisions dealing with company associations. A firm should approach strategically decisions relating to persons and organizations with which they want to be associated. This situation arises when companies are selecting individual performers, artists, or athletes whose careers or performances they might sponsor, personalities whom they might select as endorsers or spokespersons for their products or brands, and other

---

[15] Thomas A. Hemphill, "Corporate Governance, Strategic Philanthropy, and Public Policy," *Business Horizons* (May-June 1999): 57–62.

companies with whom they might associate in co-branding or shared loyalty marketing programs—for example, when an airline is deciding which hotel chains and rental car companies it wishes to partner with in its frequent-flier program.

The principles outlined in this section deal with the issue of matching the company's brand with the right individual, team, organization, or company to provide the best fit, which will enhance the relationship between the brand and its target customers and market segments.

What Did We Get Out of That?

Traditionally, companies have assessed the effectiveness of sponsorship decisions through measures such as awareness and recall of the event and attendance. Measures in place to assess the payback from sponsorships are generally rough and not focused on the relationships that the sponsorship or association is intended to strengthen. Whether the event pulled an audience 10% higher than last year's is irrelevant in terms of whether the sponsoring company derived any real benefit. Whether customers and others think better of the company and its brand for having been associated with the event is the main issue to be addressed. The measures many companies use to assess the payback from sponsorships, if they use any measures at all, are reminiscent of the early tools associated with the assessment of advertising effectiveness. It is surprising that sponsorship evaluation has not progressed much beyond that stage. Knowing how many people turned out for an event, or how many watched it on television, or how many bought our soft drink at intermission is an inadequate basis for deciding whether the sponsorship money was well spent.

Sponsorship means more than offering customers a good time by bringing them an event or an experience. By sponsoring a property such as a rock concert, an arts festival, or a tennis tournament, a brand must try to leverage the equity resident in the property in a way that will enhance the consumers' relationship with the company and its brands. Therefore, the emotional equity resident in the sponsored property not only has to be positive, it has to be appropriate.

As we have established, consumers clearly have established relationships with and emotional attachments to major companies and brands. It should also be clear that consumers can have a similar relationship or attachment to various properties, events, and personalities—which, one could argue, are themselves just another form of brand. Duane Knapp opens his book *The Brand Mindset* with a quote from Martha Stewart: "I am a brand."[16] Companies, as they make strategic sponsorship decisions, must harness the equity in the relationship that

---

[16] Knapp, *The Brand Mindset*, 1.

customers and others have with the event or property being sponsored and transfer it to the brand. Put another way, the company must make sure that the relationships that customers have with the sponsored properties and the sponsoring brand are compatible and mutually reinforcing.

Some sponsorship opportunities are more meaningful to certain segments than others. The key for the sponsoring company is to sponsor those properties and events that have the most meaning for their target segments and will result in the greatest transference of emotional equity. The right sponsorships can further strengthen an already-strong customer relationship with the sponsoring company.

Sponsorship also allows a company to establish stronger relationships with those customers whose relationships are less stable, if those sponsorship activities are relevant and meaningful to that segment. In such a case, a "meaning transfer" occurs, whereby the meaning and emotional equity attributed by the customer to sponsorship properties move from the property to the brand. To complete the process, consumers acquire the meaning in the property or event though consuming the sponsor's products and services or simply by feeling an association with the brand.

Strategic Sponsoring

A strategic approach must be taken to match sponsorship properties with brands. Companies and their brand strategists must develop an approach to strategic sponsorship and association that includes definition of sponsorship objectives and outcomes, evaluation of the fit with the sponsorship property or personality, and identification of the optimal properties with which to be associated. This requires measurement and profiling of the relationship equity that is resident in the properties and personalities with which the company is considering an association. This is achieved by developing relationship profiles of sponsorship properties and matching these with profiles of the company's corporate and brand relationship equity. Then, through the use of sophisticated measurement tools and analysis, as described in Chapter 8, a report card can be developed that will identify which sponsorship properties and personalities fit best with the brand. Only if the emotional loyalty that target segments have towards sponsorship properties and spokespersons, and the relationships they have with brands, is captured can an informed decision be made that allows for the optimal matching of sponsorship properties, events, and spokespersons with brands.

Developing the Fit

This approach to strategic sponsorship examines the fit between a sponsoring company and its brands and the range of options it has before it in terms of sponsorship properties. Most companies are regularly faced with sponsorship decisions. In small firms these involve whether to sponsor the local Little League team on its trip to the state championship and to support the graduation dance of the local high school. In major corporations, however, the decisions often involve millions of dollars. Should we sponsor the U.S. Open Tennis Championships, the America's Cup Race, the national tour of the Three Tenors? Should we select Kelsey Grammer, Bill Cosby, or Shania Twain as our spokesperson? Should we sponsor a Chair in Strategic Marketing at Ohio State University or take up the option to have a new stadium in Montreal bear our corporate name?

By reducing the likelihood of selecting properties where the fit is poor, a company or brand can maximize the payback from sponsorship decisions. By optimizing the fit between properties and a sponsoring company or brand, a company can maximize the payback from sponsorship decisions in terms of greater transference of equity from the property to the sponsor, a stronger sense of association and loyalty, and generally a more solid customer relationship. Ideally, the customer's response to a company's sponsorship of an event or property in which the customer is interested is one of sharing—"This is great; they're interested in the same things I'm interested in."

So that we can achieve the optimal selection of sponsorship opportunities, these should be viewed from one of four approaches, as outlined in Figure 11-2. The first approach includes all sponsorship with overt commercial motives, such as national tours by rock bands, Formula One racing, and Super Bowl telecasts. For major organizations, branding is the focus of these types of sponsorships.

The second approach includes sponsorships undertaken less for commercial reasons and more for community-minded reasons, such as symphony orchestras, art galleries, and food banks. The rationale for supporting these endeavors is to associate the corporation with events or organizations that society deems worthy. Through association occurs a transfer of meaning and emotional equity from the sponsored property to the sponsoring brand.

Figure 11-2 Sponsorship Decisions

The third type of sponsorship approach is categorized by corporate donations, such as to foundations and other charities. The purpose of this type of sponsorship is most often associated with philanthropy and social responsibility.

The fourth application of sponsorship involves the selection of spokespersons and endorsers: individuals and groups with which the brand might become associated. These may be selected through any of the three approaches discussed above. The spokespersons must also be strategically selected to ensure an optimal fit between them and the company or brand they will represent or be associated with. Nike, for example, places great emphasis on selecting spokespersons to ensure they fit the positioning and culture of the brand.

Transferring Meaning to the Brand

Figure 11-3 presents a conceptual framework for considering how the meaning transference process occurs. This is a model of the relationship between the customer's level of involvement with the event or sponsorship category, his or her association and relationship with specific properties within that category, the consumer's relationship or emotional involvement with the brand, and the expected payback to be received from associating the brand with the category and with specific properties.

For example, a major corporation such as Volvo may be considering an association with tennis, and particularly with the women's professional tour. Specifically, it has an opportunity to be the principal sponsor of a tournament held annually in Hilton Head. How should Volvo reach a decision to sponsor this tournament? In addition to weighing the obvious factors such as cost, attendance, and television viewership anticipated, the company must consider other aspects of the decision. These relate to the softer issue of what impact an association with women's tennis and with this particular tournament will have on the relationship between the Volvo brand and its target segment of customers. Will customers perceive a fit between Volvo and women's tennis? What is the nature of the relationship that the target customer has with tennis in general and with the Hilton Head tournament in particular? We might even extend our analysis to examining the fit between the target customers' relationship with Volvo and their relationship with other brands and companies that may also be sponsors of this tournament.

In a research project to determine the best use of sponsorship budgets and the most appropriate property or personality for the company to be associated with, data are collected at each level of the model to develop indices that can be analyzed to determine the extent and nature of the correlation and linkages between them. To continue with tennis as an example, a single index would be produced for research participants (target customers) to determine their behav-

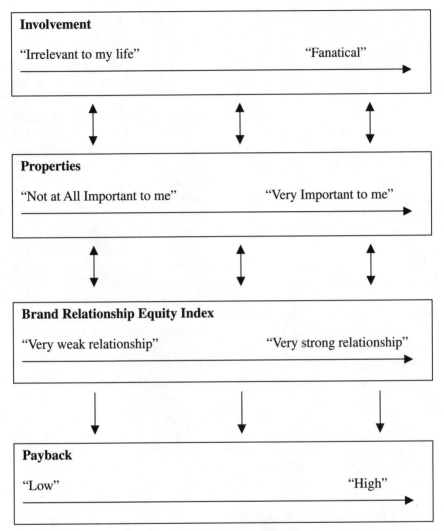

Figure 11-3 Conceptual Model of the Linkages between Involvement with the Category and the Consumer's Relationship with the Brand

ioral, attitudinal, and emotional involvement with tennis. This includes the importance of tennis to the individual, his or her behavior relating to tennis (viewer, player, coach, reading about, kids playing, etc.), and his or her emotional attachment to tennis (closeness, memories, centrality to his or her life, etc.).

A similar index can then be produced for each of the various tennis properties that are being considered for sponsorship. This index would include behavioral measures relating to respondents' contact with the property (visits, watching, reading about, etc.), as well as their attitude and emotional connection with the property or event. If the company is considering a number of possible sponsorships, for each property an overall index of customers' relationship with the property would be calculated. These properties might include the Hilton Head tournament, the NCAA Championships, the U.S. Open, the Olympic tennis team, and minor tennis programs.

Next, the consumer's relationship with the brand is measured, including the dimensions of the relationship as well as closeness, desired closeness, emotional tone of the relationship, frequency of buying, likelihood to recommend, and share of spend. These components of the relationship were described in detail in Chapter 8. From the brand relationship measures, a single index can be produced that includes all these various measures. This represents the customer's brand relationship equity index.

Detailed and sophisticated analysis of the data then permits the identification of segments of tennis-involved consumers, some of whom will be very involved in many aspects of tennis, others in certain aspects but not others, and some in only a few aspects. Then the nature of the relationship each segment has with the brand can be investigated. This enables the brand manager to understand the extent to which sponsorship involvement with tennis and with specific tennis properties is a predictor of a close, loyal relationship with the brand, which in turn drives payback variables such as intention to buy or repurchase, referral activity, and loyalty.

The net effect of this exercise is that Volvo executives are in a much better position to determine the payback that could be obtained from association with tennis in general and with the specific tennis property under consideration. This can then be compared with the benefits to be gained from associating with another sport or with the Metropolitan Opera or with a national program of college mathematics competitions.

The Company We Keep

We tend to be labeled by the associations we make, the people with whom we become friends, the groups with which we associate, and the clubs to which we belong. In this chapter we have extended that concept to include the brands of products we use and the companies that provide us with products and services. It should be obvious that as consumers we do establish genuine strong, close relationships with brands, as we do with other commercial entities. We become loyal to brands in much the same way that we become loyal to local retailers.

The principles underlying the establishment and management of brand relationships are identical to those governing relationships in any other context. The dimensions of relationships that are present in a brand context are precisely those that we have discussed earlier in the context of service companies. The difference is that customers of brands do not have the same kind of contact with the companies that own those brands that they do in other situations, although that is changing as interactive technology evolves. The objective in cultivating brand relationships is exactly what it is in other contexts: to create a bond with the customer that is satisfying to the point where that customer will come back and buy our products and services over and over again and will tell his or her friends about us.

Relationships with brands are grounded in emotion. The brands become like old friends, things that we can rely upon to perform and to help define who we are. There is no equity in a brand unless and until strong brand relationships exist. That is why new brands are devoid of long-term value until they develop a following of customers who feel an emotional attachment.

Sponsorship is a field that has been largely neglected or done very unstrategically in many firms. Yet it is an aspect of management that can be made very strategic through applying the principles of customer relationships. By mining the emotional equity in the relationships that consumers have with various sports, teams, arts organizations, events, and personalities, companies can establish associations with those properties that can enhance their own relationships with target customers by enhancing and reinforcing their connection to the sponsored properties. This area is ripe for expansion in the future as companies get far more strategic with their sponsorship budgets.

We will now extend the concept of customer relationships further, to other groups that are important to the success of any organization and to the strategic management of a relationship focus in the organization.

12

Achieving a Competitive Advantage through Relationships

It's All in How We View It

It should be obvious that the view of customer relationships that has been presented in this book represents a management philosophy rather than a set of tools to be applied. In that sense it differs markedly from what is currently practiced by many firms in the name of relationship marketing. In order to practice *relationship-based marketing*—or even better, relationship-based *management*—executives and leaders of organizations must be focused on the cultivation and enhancement of genuine relationships with customers and others. This is a long-term view of the world, one that is prepared to forgo short-term gains for long-term success. It is, then, not a marketing concept in the narrow definition of that term, but closer to concepts like corporate culture and leadership. Managers who gravitate naturally to a long-term, relationship-based view of corporate performance have an innate understanding of the value to be obtained from developing solid relationships and the contribution these make to the development of a competitive advantage for the firm.[1]

It is also a view that should extend, in those organizations that are truly relationship-focused, beyond their dealings with customers to include other groups that are critical to the success of the organization. In fact, it is a mutually reinforcing strategy to extend a relationships view to a firm's dealings with its employees, suppliers, and other groups that can influence its success.

The relationships view of organizations is a very rich one. The fundamental principle that a company will reap rewards from the cultivation of solid, genuine relationships with its customers applies equally well to other groups. While the

[1]W. Glenn Rowe and James G. Barnes, "Relationship Marketing and Sustained Competitive Advantage," *Journal of Market Focused Management* (1998): 281–97.

rewards are obviously different, companies that take a strategic approach to the cultivation of close relationships with employees, suppliers, dealers, media, shareholders, and the community will also achieve solid benefits as a result. As we move into this view of relationships in an organizational context, we are clearly moving farther away from a classic marketing view. This is entirely in keeping with our position expressed earlier, that our view of genuine customer relationships is more than a relationship marketing view of the world. As we expand the target publics to whom this strategic approach may apply, we offer insights that are of value for strategists and managers in human resources, public relations, media relations, and corporate affairs departments, among others.

This chapter also presents a strategic overview of how a company can make relationships with customers and others an essential component of its strategy for growth and long-term success. The chapter examines how a firm can position and differentiate itself on the basis of how it creates customer relationships. It also examines the concept of relationship segments; exploring the argument that all customers are not equal or the same and that therefore they demand different types of relationships. The chapter builds upon the concepts explored in detail in the previous chapters and addresses several key issues, including how to begin to implement a company-wide approach to managing customer relationships, how to get buy-in from internal stakeholders, and how to ensure that the customer remains at the center of any initiatives.

James Masciarelli of Archer Consulting says, "At the end of the day, a company's only sustainable competitive advantage is its relationships with customers, business partners and employees . . . A commitment to developing effective relationships strengthens the fabric of the organization in the long run."[2]

Employees are one obvious group that is critical to the success of a firm. Too many companies pay lip service to the importance of employees and fail to follow through by implementing human resources policies that enable them to develop strong relationships with their employees. Suppliers are also a critical element in the creation of products and services, but too often companies fail to put sufficient effort into developing supplier relationships. Only when the supplier fails to meet deadlines or goes out of business does the firm begin to think about the importance of having reliable suppliers.

Other stakeholders, such as channel members, shareholders, media, and the community in which the firm operates, are also critical to the long-term success of the firm. Indeed, solid relationships must exist with each of these publics. Otherwise a firm places itself in a delicate situation, especially now that the business rules of many industries are being rewritten by the emergence of the

---

[2] James P. Masciarelli, "Are You Managing Your Relationship?" *Management Review* (April 1998): 41.

Internet and e-commerce. Without strong relationships in place with the various stakeholders, it becomes easier for competitors to enter a market.

Applying Relationship Principles to the Value Chain

Companies do not operate in isolation. They rely on other stakeholders to fulfil their obligations to the customer. While strong customer relationships are obviously critical to the success of a firm, so are other relationships. For instance, suppliers are critical to ensuring that input products and services are available to get the output product or service to the customer. Employees give companies the mechanism for providing customers with a humanistic approach and are critical to the company's ability to create genuine relationships with its customers. Dealers may for some companies be the only interaction, albeit an indirect one, that they have with customers. Shareholders represent a critical stakeholder group for companies because they provide the capital necessary to maintain operations and allow the company to grow. And members of the community at large are of critical importance in towns where a firm may be a major employer. In any situation, the community should be viewed as the source of social support and future employees. Traditionally, these partners have been viewed as a linear chain, starting with suppliers and finishing with shareholders and community. The customer must be viewed as the centerpiece of a company's operations and the other stakeholders as there to support the company in the fulfillment of customer needs. This is illustrated in Figure 12-1.

Companies must recognize that it is critical that they work at strengthening relationships with each of these various stakeholder groups and that an integrated approach to developing these relationships is the only effective way to ensure that these relationships grow and flourish. However, with such varied stakeholders and varied needs, it may be difficult to solidify relationships with each stakeholder group. Considering the importance of a company's employees in allowing the delivery of an effective strategy for building customer relationships, let's begin by looking at employee relationships.

Employee Relationships

"Creating shareholder value" and "sustaining long-term corporate profitability" are two of the most frequently heard phrases in the management literature in recent years. But what do they mean exactly? And more importantly, how can they be achieved? It is useful to consider a comprehensive model of the factors

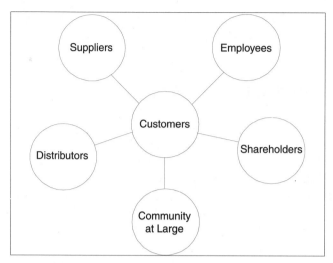

Figure 12-1 Stakeholder Relationships

that lead to shareholder value. Using various inputs from employees and customers, we can understand what drives market and financial performance.

The long-term success of any company depends on its ability to satisfy customers to the point that they will not only continue to do business with the company but be enthusiastic supporters of the company. The ability of a firm to achieve high levels of customer satisfaction rests largely in the hands of its employees. If employees do not deliver superior service and demonstrate a commitment to customers, then service levels will slip and customers will depart for the competition. The company's success in delivering superior service depends on its ability to satisfy its employees and encourage them to commit to long-term customer satisfaction. It is the employees who interact with customers on a daily basis and have the power to make or break the relationship through their contacts with customers.

A company that is able to create a positive working environment and a motivated and committed workforce is better positioned to deliver the kind of customer service that will keep customers coming back. Therefore, long-term customer satisfaction and shareholder value may be said to begin in the cultivation of genuine relationships with employees. Satisfied employees lead to satisfied customers and to the kind of corporate performance that produces satisfied investors.

Organizations should have a marketing view of the human resources function. In other words, there should be widespread acceptance within a company that it is the people who work there who have the potential to influence customer satisfaction and the likelihood of building long-term customer relationships. All tools and programs that are oriented toward creating employee satisfaction are indirectly related to customer satisfaction.

To create the desired customer relationships, employees must be prepared to go the extra mile to fulfill the needs of customers. This does not occur if employees are not motivated to perform to the best of their abilities. And the motivation may not have to be linked to financial rewards. Ijeoma Ross observes, "It's not the money thing. What you pay people, the benefits you give them might be important to get them in the job. But to get the best out of that investment is going to depend on how you treat them."[3] Employees have to know that their interventions make a difference and that their work is valued. But they will know this only if management makes it a priority to communicate it to them.

Integrating Marketing and Human Resources

A totally integrated program of research and communications can bring together the essential elements of corporate success. The results will identify for management the steps that should be taken to improve employee and customer satisfaction levels and relationships. Typically, these improvements will come through the development and implementation of communications programs, improved systems and processes, and forward-thinking human resources policies.

To achieve this, research on corporate climate, employee attitudes, relationships and satisfaction must be undertaken. Collecting this information from employees represents an opportunity for companies not only to benchmark the health of employee attitudes and relationships, but also to provide important data which will serve as predictors of customer service quality and satisfaction going forward. Secondly, research on customer satisfaction, service quality, and customer relationships must be undertaken. This would include the technical measures of service quality and the image of the company as well as information on customer relationships and perceptions of value. Once the data have been collected, linkages can be identified between the various sources of information. It will then be possible to consider how improvements in employee attitudes and satisfaction can translate into improved customer satisfaction and into more solid relationships with customers. This model is illustrated in Figure 12-2.

By tying together the marketing and human resources functions in a landmark project such as this, companies gain much greater insight into a broadened definition of what marketing is. It is more than the conventional marketing functions

---

[3] Ijeoma Ross, "It Takes More Than Money to Energize Employees," *Globe and Mail* (Toronto), (7 November 1997), B12.

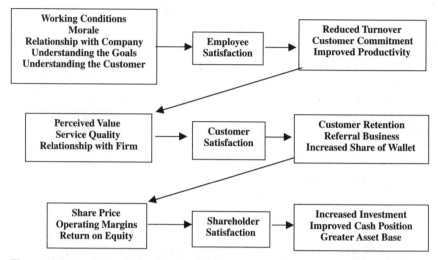

Figure 12-2 Shareholder Value Creation Model

of advertising, pricing, and product development. It extends to customer service, the addition of value to what we offer the customer, and other strategic aspects of what we do and how we operate. This integrated view adds to how companies can achieve employee commitment to customer satisfaction.

Senior management that is committed to the integration of the customer and the employee will receive considerable dividends in the future. It is essential to be able to measure on an ongoing basis the impact that employee relationships have on customer attitudes and retention and the resultant impact on corporate performance indicators. Once data have been collected from employees and customers, an integrated model can be constructed that links the employee into the payback model that we examined earlier. At this point, senior management will understand the factors that are most important in creating long-term shareholder value and can determine the payback to the company from improving customer satisfaction levels and strengthening customer relationships. That payback will be evident in the form of greater share of customer spending, increased loyalty and retention, and increased propensity to recommend the company to others. Incorporating employee satisfaction and relationships data into the analysis allows management to see the payback in enhanced customer relationships and shareholder value that can be derived from an investment in employee recruitment, training, motivation, recognition and reward programs—in short, in human resources.

Sears, Roebuck and Company have been one of the leading companies in developing and implementing nonfinancial measures to assess the impact of employee satisfaction on customer satisfaction and employee satisfaction on profitability. This groundbreaking piece of research, has been labeled the *employee-customer-profit model*,[4] has started an incredible amount of discussion about the impact employee satisfaction has on overall company profitability. For instance, Sears has been able to quantify the connection and to demonstrate that a 5-point improvement in employee attitudes leads to a 0.5% improvement in revenue growth. The relationship exists at the store level, and the company knows that if they can improve employee attitudes by 5 units, this will lead to a 1.3 unit increase in customer impressions and a 0.5% increase in store revenue growth.

Sears has such confidence in their model that they have implemented an incentive plan for senior management that is based on the three links in the chain. One-third of the compensation is based on employee measures, another one-third on customer measures, and the final one-third on financial measures.

Valuable lessons can be learned from the Sears model. For instance, if a linkage can be found at the satisfaction level, do linkages exist at the relationship level? Is it possible to measure employee relationships and link these to customer relationships and then further link these to traditional financial measures such as revenue and share price? This intuitively makes sense and argues for the development of an integrated model that links the three levels of the chain. If this existed, companies would be in a position to predict future profitability. For instance, a company could measure the strength of its relationships with employees and know that if the strength of the relationship had increased by a certain level because of strategies they had employed, they could within a certain time frame profitability would increase by, say, 5%. Imagine the competitive advantage the company would gain developing and implementing such an integrated model.

These linkages in the Sears model point to strategic directions relating to the management of the human resources function. For instance, every employee should be informed of the importance of customer satisfaction and of the factors that drive it. It is also clear that the results of such an integrated research program will have important implications for the development of training programs, the reward and motivation of employees, and internal communications.

In fact, taking such an approach to the linking of employee relationships to customer relationships and on to shareholder value argues for applying a very similar approach to the cultivation and management of employee relationships, as we have been discussing in this book with respect to customer relationships. I would suggest, in fact, that progressive companies consider establishing a parallel model that would operate side by side with the customer relationship program within an organization and would be devoted to the creation of strong,

---

[4] Anthony J. Rucci, Steven P. Kim, and Richard T. Quinn, "The Employee-Customer-Profit Chain at Sears," *Harvard Business Review* 76 (January-February 1998): 82–97.

close, genuine relationships with employees. This is of critical importance to the creation of customer relationships and suggests that precisely the same principles should be employed, including an emphasis on the creation of the right forms of value for employees and attention to a drivers of employee satisfaction model.[5]

Supplier Relationships

Suppliers are sometimes overlooked in the assessment of a firm and its relationships, likely because the selection of suppliers is all too often considered at an operations level rather than at a strategic level and is very often based on who can deliver the product we want at the lowest price. But without strong relationships with suppliers, a firm may be placing itself in a very precarious and undesirable situation. Suppliers are critical in allowing companies to meet their commitments to their customers.

If a firm's relationship with suppliers is weak, there is no certainty with regard to when product shipments will arrive and therefore no promises can be kept with customers. For instance, we may tell customers that a shipment will arrive on Wednesday but our weak supplier relationships mean that the shipment does not arrive until Saturday. If the customer arrives to pick up his or her order and it is not there, feelings of frustration and mistrust begin to develop. This situation need not happen often before the customer becomes dissatisfied and considers moving his or her business to the competition. Thus, reliability is a strong argument for developing supplier relationships.

But what is the payback from good supplier relationships? Certainly, counting on them to deliver is one issue. Undoubtedly, there will come a time when a firm will need a certain item delivered immediately. Without a strong relationship, it may be more difficult to get the items that are required. Consider the situation from the supplier's viewpoint. If they have more orders than they can process, to whom will they ship the goods? Will it be the company that is always trying to get a better deal by negotiating price on every order, or will it be the company with which they have been dealing for many years and that has always been prompt in paying their bills? The answer to this question is clear.

How does a firm develop strong relationships with its suppliers? By applying the same concepts and principles that we have been discussing throughout this book. It means that while price may be a very critical factor in sourcing supplies

---

[5] Peter A. Dunne and James G. Barnes, "Internal Marketing: A Relationships, Value-Creation View," in *Internal Marketing: Directions for Management,* ed. Barbara R. Lewis and Richard J. Varey (London: Routledge, 2000).

for many companies, it should not always be the focus of discussions. It means periodically telephoning to thank them for going out of their way to get a particular order to you when they were operating under a tight deadline. It means treating them like you would treat others whose relationship you value.

And how do you measure whether you have developed a relationship with your suppliers? At the very least, ask them. How to do this may depend on how large the company is and how many suppliers there are. A medium-sized firm with a small number of suppliers may wish to bring in a research firm to undertake depth interviews, while a much larger firm with a larger number of suppliers may undertake a full-scale quantitative research study. Regardless of the methodology employed, the focus of the exploration must be on the same dimensions of relationships—trust, commitment, empathy, and others—that we have been discussing throughout this book. The research must be undertaken periodically to determine whether relationships have been strengthened and where additional attention is required.

Channel Relationships

Some firms rarely if ever have any direct contact with their end customers. Instead, they rely on members of their distribution channel—retailers and dealers—to sell their products and services. In such a case, the distribution partner represents the company to the customer. For a company like Heinz, for example, having to work through retailers means they must have strong brand relationships with the end consumer, as discussed in Chapter 11. It is of considerable importance in industries where manufacturers rely on dealer networks to periodically assess the health of dealer relationships. This is also important in those distribution channels where agents and others may represent a number of competitors, as in the travel industry. Airlines, hotel chains, resorts and cruise lines are cognizant of the importance of relationships with travel agencies.

In this situation, great emphasis should be placed on dealer education and training to ensure that the needs of the end customer are addressed. The level of service must also be ensured to be consistent from dealer to dealer, regardless of location. Without a dealer training program, this level of consistency will never be achieved. Consistency can also be achieved by having in place a mechanism for dealer selection. Not every possible dealer should be utilized, as there are certain individuals and companies that would not adequately represent the firm. Selecting a less-than-desired dealer jeopardizes the long-term financial success of the firm by endangering its relationships with its end customers.

Relationships with dealers and retailers should be considered as important as relationships with employees. Like employees, retailers and dealers are often seen as representing the firm in the eyes of the customer. The same principles, therefore, must apply. Many large companies, including the automakers, have well-established dealer relationship programs focused on maintaining strong relationships with dealers. The reasons are obvious. In a sense, the company has delegated contact with its customers to these independent retailers. Even though, through technology, manufacturers can do a better job than in the past of dealing directly with end customers, dealers still play a very important role in the distribution of the product. These "gatekeepers" have the potential to make or break the brand relationship that companies like Ford, General Electric, and Maytag have with their customers.

Shareholder, Community, and Other Relationships

It is important to the long-term success of a firm that it maintain close, solid relationships with a number of other publics. For example, strong relationships with shareholders are critical. As shareholders, they have an ownership in the company and therefore are at financial risk should the company not grow as intended. Many companies operate an investor relations program to ensure that shareholders are kept informed of developments. Shareholders need to receive communications on a regular basis so that they are aware of the strategic direction of the company and are not surprised when unexpected circumstances arise.

Developing community relationships means demonstrating a commitment to the community to improve the quality of life of individuals. The Body Shop has shown over the years its concern for the environment through the in-store container recycling programs that they have implemented, as well as their refusal to sell products that have been tested on laboratory animals. Ben & Jerry's, since its inception, has donated a percentage of pre-tax profits to community-related causes, resulting in a corporate culture that values the environment and strives to make improvements.

Again, companies that are focused on developing and maintaining positive relationships with shareholders, community, and other groups must apply the same principles that we have been discussing throughout this book, with the same objectives in mind. Just as the cultivation of genuine customer relationships is grounded in the establishment of an emotional connection between the company and its customers, so too is the establishment of other forms of relationships. The same relationship dimensions and principles guide them: creation of value, engendering of trust and commitment, and regular two-way communications. Applying these principles to the development of shareholder relations, community relations and media relations programs should provide a valuable insight into how stronger relationships can be built with these important stakeholder groups.

The Failings of Relationship Marketing

I have observed before that the view of customer relationship building described in this book is not to be confused with "relationship marketing" as it is practiced in many firms, particularly larger companies, or with a technology-focused view of customer relationship management. The latter term, with its ubiquitous acronym CRM, has been associated very closely in recent years with the use of software and databases to direct marketing activities at consumers in the name of relationship building. I have avoided referring to the building of genuine customer relationships as *marketing* because I don't believe it bears a great deal of resemblance to marketing as it has been practiced for the past 50 years, nor do I believe that building such relationships should be the sole purview of the marketing department. If that responsibility is delegated to marketing, rather than being the responsibility of the entire firm, then it will surely fail.

Susan Fournier, Susan Dobscha, and David Glen Mick have best captured the current thinking in the relationship marketing field.[6] Their article discusses the issues that must be addressed if the concept of relationship marketing—one that is based on a genuine and true relationship—does not get mixed up with concepts that were never intended to be associated with the relationship marketing terminology. They observe that "relationship marketing is powerful in theory but troubled in practice."

Many companies have obviously approached the implementation of relationship marketing without having an understanding of or an appreciation for what constitutes a genuine relationship. For instance, Fournier, Dobscha, and Mick suggest that a genuine relationship is based on the sharing of personal information. This is often not the case for corporations that maintain detailed customer databases containing customers' personal information, purchase history, credit history, and the like. These companies place great emphasis on gathering the customer information but are not prepared to disclose similar information to the customer, which is what would occur if a genuine relationship existed.

The terms of a warranty on a particular product may not be fully disclosed until after the sale. The customer may experience problems with the product,

[6] Susan Fournier, Susan Dobscha, and David Glen Mick, "Preventing the Premature Death of Relationship Marketing," *Harvard Business Review* (January–February 1998): 42–51.

contact the manufacturer to receive a replacement, but be told that the warranty is no longer valid because an authorized representative of the manufacturer did not service the product. By this time it is too late for the customer to do anything, and feelings of frustration and mistrust are produced as a result. Fournier, Dobscha, and Mick suggest, "Perhaps we do not understand what creating a relationship really means; that is, how customers' trust and intimacy factor into the connections we are trying to make."[7]

Many companies, while they purport to be building relationships, are really trying to stimulate sales. Many so-called relationship programs are really designed to reward frequency of purchasing and increased spending rather than the building of genuine loyalty. Thus, customers who are members of frequent-flier or frequent-guest programs receive rewards because of the volume of business they give an airline or a hotel, although that volume of business may have nothing at all to do with genuine loyalty. Meanwhile, a customer who is genuinely loyal and gives the company 100% of his or her business, but whose volume is lower, does not qualify for the same treatment. Such programs have little to do with building relationships. Let's call them what they are—rewards programs—because they do a very effective job of rewarding those customers who spend the most money with a company.

These rewards programs also have the potential to stimulate the development of relationships. It is conceivable that by stimulating repeat buying in the name of receiving rewards, a company allows a customer to get to know them better, which may lead to the development of a genuine relationship. I joined Hilton HHonors, the frequent guest program of Hilton Hotels, more than 10 years ago. By staying principally at Hilton Hotels over the years, I have developed close relationships with staff at two hotels in particular, the Toronto Hilton and the Conrad International in Dublin. At both hotels I am made welcome by individual employees whom I have gotten to know over the years. I now go back to these properties more for the warm welcome than for the benefits associated with the rewards program.

If "relationship marketing" programs were really about relationships, companies would return calls and make it easy for customers to contact them. Genuine relationships are characterized by two-way communications. Far too often, relationship marketing programs are driven by databases that determine what "personalized" correspondence or communication is to be directed at what customers. But once a customer tries to contact the company, he or she is likely to encounter a maze of voice mail with instructions to press 1 for this and 2 for that. They often find themselves at a dead end where a recorded voice suggests

---

[7] Ibid., 44.

that they submit their questions via e-mail, presumably to receive faster service.[8] Such treatment certainly sends a message to customers that companies really don't want to deal with them—and this in a time when companies are supposedly clambering to establish relationships. If ever there was evidence of confusion about the terminology, this is it.

Finally, companies whose perspective on customer relationships is grounded in the use of databases to mine data with a view to initiating outbound contact with customers are often guilty of sharing the information provided by customers with others. They interrupt dinner with telemarketed sales offers and bombard prospective customers with e-mail deals. This is not what would happen in a genuine relationship. These companies do not respect the privacy of their customers, nor do they protect the information that has been entrusted to them.

In the name of developing relationships with customers, many companies have in fact delegated the responsibility for developing customer relationships, arguably among a company's most valuable assets and the key to its future, to software developers and IT specialists whose goal is preparing databases to be mined in search of patterns that will reveal some hidden need for the company's products or services. Such a view is not at all customer focused. The goal, quite simply, is to sell more stuff. Far too much emphasis is being placed on the use of technology to cultivate customer relationships. The current reliance on databases, predictive modeling, and data mining is in fact intended to promote efficiency in getting the right messages or offers into the hands of the right people, thereby optimizing the probability that the customer receiving the message will be in the market for or will find attractive the product or service on offer. But what does that have to do with developing a genuine customer relationship? The answer is "nothing."

The Perils of Short-Term Thinking

To implement a program aimed at the establishment of genuine relationships with customers demands a new management philosophy in most companies, one that is clearly focused on the long-term payback from such an approach to doing business. This will require many managers to change their view of how a business achieves success. Making the sale is no longer the goal. Keeping the customer coming back because we have succeeded in satisfying some higher-order need is what determines the long-term success of a company.

[8] Ross Laver, "Hello, Is Anyone Home?" *Maclean's Magazine,* 10 April 2000.

Yet many firms remain mired in short-term thinking. They are driven by meeting this month's sales goal or this quarter's earnings per share target. In fact, we persist in rewarding managers for the achievement of such short-term goals, *without giving a great deal of thought to whether, by doing so, we are contributing in any way to the cultivation of long-term customer relationships.* There is no equity in this short-term view. I completely understand why it is important for a firm to achieve such short-term targets, but I also believe that those targets should be established with one eye on what they contribute to the development of genuine customer relationships. I can think of a number of instances where achieving short-term goals is, in fact, counterproductive in terms of creating genuine relationships.

Some firms just don't seem to get it. They do not organize or operate in a way that encourages the cultivation of customer relationships. In fact, they seem entirely focused on generating sales. They strive to achieve short-term successes and reward employees and managers for doing so. They often appear single-mindedly focused on the use of price and other marketing tools to drive sales. They appear not to understand the potential that exists to increase gross margins and generate repeat and referral business by creating genuine relationships with customers. Theirs is a very narrow view of customers and of what marketing is all about.

The Danger of Lip Service

The danger is very real, if we are not careful, of saying one thing in the interest of developing relationships with customers and doing something quite different. Although very few firms seem to have gotten it right, being seen as interested in customer relationships is very much in vogue today. Many of the companies we come in contact with every day are encouraging us to come back by telling us just how important we are to them.

To return one last time to the issue of technology and the customer's interaction with it, consider a situation that we all find ourselves in practically every day. We are calling the customer service department (a little irony in the name) of XYZ company and we encounter their IVR system, which invites us to press a series of buttons to reach the right department or the group of agents in the call center who can best deal with our problem. Inevitably, we find ourselves put on hold because "all of our agents are currently helping other customers." We wait what seems an eternity while having to listen to music that we would never choose to listen to or, worse still, recorded advertisements for the company's products or services. Periodically, the music or advertising is interrupted by a pleasant voice advising us to stay on the line because "your call is important to us." Who are they kidding? If the call were important, they would have answered it by now. Companies should study how much business they lose by implementing technologies such as these incorrectly and thereby ending any hope of establishing relationships with customers.

In recent years, Air Canada and its connector airlines made a habit of thanking the passengers on each flight for their business, telling them how much Air Canada appreciates their flying with the airline "because we know you have a choice." Unfortunately, this announcement was made, apparently as a matter of company policy, even on those routes where the company had a virtual monopoly. On such routes the announcement was met with derision because it simply served to remind passengers that they had no choice but to fly with Air Canada. Therefore, what seemed like a nice gesture in theory sounded hollow and meaningless to passengers who actually felt captive. Now that Air Canada has taken over the operations of its failing rival Canadian Airlines International and literally has a monopoly on business travel within Canada, they no longer make the announcement.

Despite my loyalty to Hilton Hotels and my 10-year membership in Hilton HHonors, I was surprised recently to receive a joint promotion from Hilton and Air Canada that provided me with a Hilton HHonors gold VIP card. The problem was that I already had a Hilton VIP gold card, having worked my way up through the ranks to gold status several years ago. By rewarding me with "Instant Gold VIP status," Hilton was sending me rather mixed messages. Not only did they seem not to realize that I already had achieved that status and that I have been spending 30 to 40 room nights a year at their properties, they were sending the even more disturbing message that they were actually *giving away* gold cards to certain members of Air Canada's Aeroplan program.

By undertaking a marketing initiative that was database driven, predicated on wanting to migrate loyal Air Canada customers to Hilton hotels, Hilton had unwittingly offended a loyal customer. When I wrote to the President and COO of Hilton HHonors to seek an explanation, I received no reply, giving credence to the observation that communications is essentially one-way in programs such as this. While the companies involved bombard customers or prospective relationship partners with telephone calls, e-mail, and special offer mailings, they make it difficult for customers to contact them or don't respond to customer letters or messages.

Better Know the Customer

To implement relationship marketing so that genuine customer relationships result, Fournier, Dobscha, and Mick suggest that marketing managers and individuals responsible for overseeing customers' interactions must begin to think and act like the targeted customer. "Understanding the customer will above all require us to get out into the field. And that doesn't just mean the researchers. It means senior managers, middle-level managers, engineers. If the target customer that a Kraft Foods manager is pursuing is the so-called middle-American mom, that manager should rent a van, drive her team to DeSoto, Missouri, and 'live with the natives.' "[9] Indeed, this approach is a new, different view of marketing and of the customer. But it is consistent with everything that a program to stimulate relationships represents—it is of critical importance to really understand the customer. By this I do not mean the superficial understanding that comes from analyzing data collected from credit card applications or at the point of sale. This is not customer understanding; it is exactly what it is, data collection.

To gain a deeper understanding of customers and an appreciation for the fact that different groups of customers want different relationships with companies they deal with, companies that are committed to a relationships view of the world must engage in a relationship segmentation exercise. In my work with firms on both sides of the Atlantic, we have demonstrated the insights that can be gained from applying a customer relationship dimension to a standard segmentation analysis.[10]

To understand the nature of relationship segments, we must include in research with customers the kinds of relationship measures discussed in Chapter 8. By doing so, we can produce a very rich profile of customer segments that can then guide management strategy to strengthen relationships where they are weak and to identify where relationships are strongest. In addition to the standard demographic and psychographic/lifestyle bases for market segmentation, we can overlay the relationship profiles with detailed information on the state of the relationship that customers have with the client firm.

In my work with clients, we typically produce five or six distinct segments of the customer base. We then produce detailed profiles that prove to be extremely valuable for management in plotting relationship strategies. These profiles are illustrated in Figure 12-3. They contain detailed demographic data on the customers in each segment and on their patterns of interaction with the company, including spending, types of products and services bought, and frequency of purchasing or contact. Depending on how the data are collected and

---

[9] Fournier, Dobscha, and Mick, 50.

[10] For more information on the concept of relationship segmentation, see Judith A. Cumby and James G. Barnes, "Relationship Segmentation: the Enhancement of Databases to Support Relationship Marketing" (paper presented at the 1996 Research Conference on Relationship Marketing, Goizueta Business School, Emory University, Atlanta, Ga., June 14–26, 1996); John Forsyth et al., "A Segmentation You Can Act on," *The McKinsey Quarterly*, no. 3 (1999): 6–15; and Jos M. C. Schijns and Gaby J. Schröder, "Segment Selection by Relationship Strength," *Journal of Direct Marketing* 10(3) (Summer 1996): 69–79.

Demographics		Relationship Segments				
		Segment 1	Segment 2	Segment 3	Segment 4	Segment 5
Gender	Female	40%	50%	55%	60%	53%
	Male	60%	50%	45%	40%	47%
Education	Less than high school	4%	10%	15%	46%	20%
	Completed high school	38%	60%	50%	44%	60%
	Completed university/college	58%	30%	35%	10%	20%
Full-time Employment		85%	70%	60%	25%	53%
Marital Status	Married/Co-habitating	45%	70%	60%	50%	55%
	Single	53%	25%	35%	20%	35%
	Widowed/divorced/separated	2%	5%	5%	30%	10%
Average age		32	42	38	60	45
Average Household Income ($US)		$44,000	$60,000	$65,000	$38,000	$41,000
Average Household Size		2.9	4.0	3.5	2.2	3.3
Technology Index score		5.0	3.5	2.5	1.2	3.0
Relationship						
Satisfaction		4.2	8.5	7.3	8.0	6.5
Closeness		4.0	7.5	5.5	7.3	5.2
Closeness Gap		2.0	1.0	1.0	1.0	1.3
Emotional Tone		−2.3	5.0	2.3	4.9	3.3
Relationship Dimensions*	Trustworthiness	1	1	1	3	2
	Commitment to me	4	8	7	5	1
	Meaningfulness	3	3	5	4	9
	Affiliation	7	7	8	7	4
	Respect	5	4	6	6	7
	Vulnerability	9	10	9	10	8
	Reliance	8	5	3	2	5
	Connection	10	9	10	8	10
	Understanding	6	2	2	1	3
	Empathy	2	6	4	9	6
Relationship Index		29.7	72.0	55.3	82.0	65.0
Value						
Importance*	Price-based	4	4	3	2	5
	Access/convenience-based	2	3	2	4	1
	Service-based	1	1	1	1	3
	Community-based	6	6	6	6	4
	Enabling-based	3	5	5	5	7
	Surprise-based	7	7	7	7	6
	Relationship-based	5	2	4	3	2
Payback						
Average Annual Expenditures with company		$460	$500	$375	$300	350
Percentage of Total Expenditures with company		32%	75%	54%	83%	60%
Number of years as a customer		3.2	10.2	8.3	15.4	12.3
Very likely to be a customer in two years		20%	75%	50%	85%	65%
Very likely to recommend to family/friends		5%	65%	35%	70%	50%

* Demonstrates the relative importance of each dimension (rank ordered).

Figure 12-3 Relationship Segments

whether customer data are available from company databases, a great deal of information can be applied to this component of the profiles.

In addition, customer surveys that feed the segmentation exercise can yield valuable information about customers' patronage of other firms in the industry, their usage of the products and services they own, and their household lifestyle, including leisure-time activities, vacations, and media usage. All of this is extremely useful in developing the rich profiles of customer segments that begin to allow the company to say that they understand their customers. But the real value of relationship segmentation comes from the information obtained on the nature and health of customer relationships.

One of the most important pieces of information relates to our discussion in Chapter 4 of the value that firms create for their customers. We routinely now ask customers to indicate the importance they attach to companies with which they deal creating various forms of value. Then we ask them to rate the client company on the extent to which it is creating these forms of value for their customers. We then have a value component to add to the relationship profiles.

Finally, we include in our research for many of our larger clients a major component that measures the current health of customer relationships, as illustrated in Chapter 8. Armed with these data, we are in a position to prepare insightful profiles of each customer segment that not only indicate the overall health of the relationship as measured by customer satisfaction and the overall relationship equity index, but also to indicate the *nature* of the relationship. We can indicate for each customer segment the emotional tone of the relationship, where it is strong and where it is weak, which dimensions of the relationship are most important in influencing overall satisfaction, which relationships are at risk, and so on. Research such as this points management in a direction that will lead to strategies to address relationships that are vulnerable, those that are strong and require a minimum of intervention, and those that may not be salvageable.

An Integrated View—More Than Marketing

It should be obvious that I believe very strongly that the implementation of relationship marketing cannot be left to the marketing department. The components necessary to implement a relationship-based view are broad ranging and require input and a concerted effort from all departments. Much of what contributes to the success of a relationship-based approach has little or nothing to do with marketing as it has been managed in most firms. Rather, several different departments must be involved in developing and implementing relationship strategies. It's not about marketing; it's a philosophy dealing with how we treat customers, how we serve them, how we create value for them. Other departments are at least as important as marketing in accomplishing the goals of customer relationship building.

The tools of the marketing function are absolutely necessary if a solid footing is to be established upon which customer relationships can be built. We have to get the product, price, distribution, and communication right if we are to have a chance to build genuine relationships with customers. But these are not enough to ensure that relationships are built. In an age where marketing tools are becoming increasingly commoditized, we have to look to the other aspects of how we interact with customers and what we can offer them to create a competitive advantage. Increasingly, companies are turning to the building of relationships based upon the softer aspects of how we interact with customers.

For companies considering implementing a relationship-based strategy, one of the key points that I have learned from working with clients is that there must be a company-wide commitment to seeing the initiative through to the end. It most cases this can only occur if the senior management, in particular the president and CEO, have bought into the idea. Without their support, there may not be enough driving force to overcome any hurdles that are encountered during the implementation phase. In too many cases it is middle management that is delegated the task of pushing this initiative forward.

One of the issues in delegating the responsibility is that those charged with implementation tend to view the situation with the "silo outlook" and often have difficulty in seeing all the issues at hand. If it is the marketing department that is driving the initiative—which is often the case—they tend to see the world through marketing glasses and often fail to recognize the importance of involving the human resources, operations, and finance departments. With an appreciation for how the actions, programs and policies of other departments of the company make the customer feel, there is little hope for the successful implementation of a customer relationship program.

Earlier in this chapter I suggested a model that could be used to approach customers from the viewpoint of all stakeholders. The premise was that the customer must be at the center of all interactions, with all stakeholders being focused on satisfying the customer and all decisions being made with the customers' needs in mind. This model can also be applied to internal operations of the firm.

Emotional links can only be established in a services environment when there is an emotional linkage between employees and the customers. Without management and employee commitment to understanding and improving customer interactions with the firm, any initiatives are doomed to fail before they even begin. The human resources department must be intimately involved with implementing the new way of thinking right from the start. Training is needed, and compensation must be focused on the long-term success of the firm. When short-term success is the goal, commissions and the like may force employees to make decisions that are not in the best interests of creating long-lasting relationships with customers.

Those involved in the organization in implementing such a new approach to the customer must be educated. They must fully understand what a relationship-based view involves and does not involve.

The IT department must be intimately involved throughout the entire implementation process. However, it is critical that they be viewed as a supplier to the process—a supplier of information—and not be responsible for driving the implementation. I have seen examples where the IT department, for whatever reason, has been too involved in the implementation, with the end result that the relationship marketing strategy became an application of processes similar to the customer relationship marketing (CRM) model, where genuine relationship building is replaced with database-driven initiatives aimed at an unwitting and unappreciative customer.

The IT department must be able to design and implement an information system that meets the requirements of the corporate relationship building strategy. In some cases some of the necessary information may already be available; other times it may be available only in an unusable format. It is up to the IT department to identify what information is currently available and understand what changes must be made to put it into a format that will support the new relationship-based strategy.

The operations side of the business must be involved to ensure that optimal systems and processes are in place. This is critical because, unless there is a widespread understanding of what our telephone and billing systems and others are doing or have the potential to do to customer relationships, a new approach to creating genuine relationships with customers is likely to fail. The operations people need to work very closely with the IT department and with external consultants if they are brought in. External consultants who have been through similar experiences can be critical to the overall success of the implementation. Do not be afraid to spend the additional resources necessary to get these people; in the end the additional costs will be recovered.

Back to Basics

One of the key premises of a relationship-based strategy is that the way we treat people is the basis for differentiating ourselves from the competition. If we treat people right, the probability of their becoming repeat customers increases. But what does treating them right mean? It means that we must get the core product or service correct. As was observed in Chapter 3, where we first presented the drivers of customer satisfaction model, it means more than selling a good product at a good price. It means providing customers with peripheral offerings that add value for the customer as well as placing great emphasis on creating a positive experience for the customer every time he or she comes in contact with the firm. By taking this approach, it is possible to differentiate a firm from its competitors.

To develop a relationship-based strategy, the firm must make a commitment to creating value for the customer. However, the definition of value must be from the customers' perspective, not the firm's, as different customers may define value in completely different ways. The company must offer different segments of customers different forms of value.

It is possible to create value for customers through the relationships they have with the firm. This encompasses the positive emotions elicited from customers by having dealt with the firm in question; it is not the direct result of the firm's products or their prices. It results from treating customers with respect and making them feel special. When we are successful, we achieve a state of genuine customer loyalty, with all of the attendant payback that this implies. We also achieve the very desirable state where customers begin to refer to preferred service providers as "my broker" and "my hairdresser."

The fundamentally important point to be made is that a relationship-based view of dealing with customers and managing a company is both very simple and very difficult. It is simple because, reduced to its most basic elements, it involves treating customers well and making them feel good about dealing with us so that they will come back again and again. It is difficult because of the complexities of managing large companies, in particular the many components that collectively "touch" the customer, and coordinating activities so that all aspects of the interaction with a firm are consistently geared to creating customer satisfaction, leading to a genuine relationship.

Building the Process—Thinking Differently

As I have argued throughout this book, successfully implementing and managing this new way of thinking requires a change in corporate culture. But why can't we just make a few small changes, call it relationship marketing, and get on with it? Too many companies are doing this already, and it is these companies that are making it difficult for other firms to attempt to establish real relationships with customers.

As I discussed above, a relationship-based strategy requires a cross-firm thinking, much beyond the traditional marketing mix that many firms seem to believe is sufficient. A strategy aimed at creating genuine customer relationships cannot be implemented without an understanding of what the state of the current relationships is. Otherwise any strategies that are put in place are simply a shot on the dark.

Once we know where we stand in creating genuine relationships with our customers, it should be possible to plot a strategy that will strengthen relationships where they are weak and begin to build relationships where none exists at present. It means beginning to build a process that starts with the core product or service that we sell and ends with a focus on how everything that we do in dealing with customers makes those customers feel toward the firm. The relationship-based view is all-pervasive. It must dominate thinking throughout the company and must pervade all decisions, not just in marketing areas, which have traditionally been charged with responsibility for the customer, but in all departments.

Getting the Troops On-Side

Companies that choose to go down the road that I have been advocating in this book—the road toward genuine customer relationships—must first understand that the path will not always be easy to follow. They may be tempted to veer from the path they have set because difficulties will undoubtedly be encountered and resistance will likely be seen at many points along the way. Not everyone sees the value in this approach. Some remain focused solely on the sales-oriented view of the customer—sell them more stuff! However, as I have shown in this book, the payback from plotting this new direction, one that truly has the customers' needs at heart, can be expected to yield large dividends in both monetary and nonmonetary terms.

A question that is always asked is, "How do I get started?" It is imperative to recognize that this new approach requires a different way of thinking. Companies who choose to implement a system that is focused on building customer relationships must realize that they are headed down a road that will require much change within the company—change in corporate thinking, culture, and even values. It requires a commitment initially from the CEO and board of the company that must then permeate the organization so that all employees, including those who never get close to meeting or even talking to a customer, are committed to building close relationships. Such change cannot be driven from the middle of an organization. Delegating responsibility for a customer relationship building program to one department and then walking away is a recipe for disaster.

Also, companies must avoid taking a communications-based approach to relationship development. One of the least effective strategies is to announce that from now on we are committed to the development of close relationships with our customers. Once we start telling people that we value their business, we had better be prepared to live that commitment in everything that we do. As soon as it becomes clear to customers that we really do not value them or that we are anything but committed to building a relationship, they will abandon ship very quickly. The cynicism that will be generated in customers and employees alike will make it very difficult for the company to move on to build genuine relationships in the future. As a result, I advocate not announcing to customers that we are committed to service or to satisfying them or to relationship building. When we are, it will be obvious, but until then, we are just inviting criticism because it will be painfully obvious to customers that we are not. Nike had it right: "Just do it!"

In companies that are driven by a powerful finance department or by a board and CEO who are focused on financial results, it may be difficult for them to understand the payback from strengthening customer relationships. To some people, relationship building is a soft and fuzzy concept. They need to see the numbers on that payback.

The only way to overcome this narrow view may be to provide these individuals who are focused on financial results with forecasts of the long-term payback to be realized from having strong customer relationships. Such results would come in the form of future spend, share of wallet, probability of remaining a customer and referring others, and the like, which could be used in the development of an integrated model for predicting the long-term monetary value of a loyal customer. Only if we take this approach and speak in financial terms will the financial management team begin to understand the payback. This will ultimately assist in garnering management support for the implementation of a relationship-based approach to doing business.

I have had very positive results in convincing CEOs and CFOs of the value of implementing a relationship-based view of managing the organization when I show them the payback to be realized from the change in emphasis. They can usually appreciate the financial implications and the asset-creating benefits of such an approach and then understand the investment implications and the returns to be realized from that investment.

Lack of a senior management commitment can be a limiting factor in the ultimate success of any initiatives that are taken to strengthen customer relationships. Experience has shown that firms must have a champion, someone who is willing to go to extreme measures to ensure that the customer remains at the center of any organizational changes that must be undertaken. It is easier to drive this change in organizational thinking if that champion is the CEO and the board is on-side. There will undoubtedly be individuals who will need to be reassigned to other duties under the new, customer-focused organization. There will also be individuals who, for whatever reason, cannot or will not buy into the new philosophy. These people may have to be retrained or assigned to other duties where they cannot influence directly the implementation of the customer relationship view.

While lack of a senior management commitment will ultimately doom initiatives aimed at creating a relationship-based approach to dealing with customers, other issues may cause this to happen as well. For instance, I have found that in many cases it is not senior management that does not buy into the idea of being customer focused. Too many times, senior management has bought into the idea but delegated the responsibility to implement to a vice-president, who in turn delegates it to more middle management. By the time the dust settles, the people who are responsible for seeing the project to its completion were not involved in the initial discussions, are not fully aware of what their responsibilities are, and are really not interested in the project because it interferes with their already numerous tasks and duties, which they do not have time to complete. In such a case, they have no ownership of the project and do not wield sufficient power in the organization to make changes, even if they did agree with what is being proposed.

The bottom line is that taking a relationship-based approach to dealing with customers makes considerable sense. It represents a way for a company to set itself apart from its competition and develop links with customers that will see it reap the dividends for many years into the future. But it will likely not be easy to implement, particularly in a company that has been oriented toward optimizing sales and short-term profits. While the approach that has been presented in this book comes naturally to many small firms, turning around the thinking of a large organization will be a difficult task indeed. But the potential payback is so considerable that it is well worth the effort.

Index

About the Author

JAMES G. BARNES, PH.D., is professor of marketing and former Dean of Business Administration at Memorial University of Newfoundland. He founded Omnifacts Research, one of Canada's leading marketing research companies, and is executive vice president and former chairman of The Bristol Group, an integrated marketing communications and information consultancy with clients throughout North America and Europe. Dr. Barnes is the author of six books, including the bestselling textbook *Fundamentals of Marketing* (now in its ninth edition), and regularly delivers management courses and seminars in North America, Europe, Asia, and Australia. In 1997 he was named an inaugural winner of the *Financial Post* Leaders in Management Education Award, and in 1999 he was elected a Fellow of the Professional Marketing Research Society of Canada. His client list includes Molson, CIBC, Kraft Foods Canada, circom, An Post, North Limited, and Tesco.